The Countdown Cookbook

Also by
FLORENCE KERR
HIRSCHFELD

*Cooking
with Love*

THE

Countdown Cookbook

*An Array of
Quick and Delicious Meals
with Preparations Timed
Minute by Minute*

BY

FLORENCE KERR HIRSCHFELD

HOUGHTON MIFFLIN COMPANY BOSTON

WITH DECORATIONS BY
GUNN ASSOCIATES

Second printing w

Library of Congress Catalog Card Number: 68-31399
Printed in the United States of America

". . . the purpose of a cookery book is one and unmistakable. Its object can conceivably be no other than to increase the happiness of mankind."

JOSEPH CONRAD

This book is dedicated to the happiness of those who share the recipes and to a husband of perceptive and discriminating taste.

Acknowledgments

THE COOKING WORLD is a realm of comradeship, of give and take, offering sheer enjoyment in the exchange. Each encounter adds to the pyramid of recipe collections and the storehouse of fascinating addenda.

As the concept of this book developed many friends contributed solid assistance and suggestions, giving clues to a variety of cooking needs. I thoughtfully listened and as the book evolved, tried in turn to supply answers to a cross-section of the requests.

Aware that every recipe carries a responsibility to the prospective cook, I knew it was important to emphasize meticulous testing and careful recording. As the menus emerged, the recipes were again screened for balance in preparation, timing, eye appeal and compatible flavors.

A superb staff assisted in these endeavors. Josephine Changelian, home economist and capable housewife, reviewed each page. Her contact with adult gourmet classes proved a sounding board; exploring the constantly growing cooking world was true adventure. From the vantage point of the practicing hostess-cook, Mary Ann Soboroff contributed invaluable suggestions and precise effort in the compilation. Naomi Zemans added editorial clarity and counsel. My sincere thanks go to these capable people and my deep appreciation for the rewarding accomplishment of our concerted efforts.

I wish it were possible as well to extend my thanks here to the many other people whose interest has been constant stimulus and support. May you all share my happiness in cooking.

FLORENCE KERR HIRSCHFELD

Contents

Introduction

To THE CONSTERNATION of the genial traffic policeman on a corner
near my home I would rather cross the street on the diagonal than
negotiate the extra steps in crossing at right angles. This reflects my
early training in the shortest distance between two points, training I
now try to practice in my kitchen.

With cooking short-cuts today's kitchen can be geared to the
complex high-speed world around us, and time, that precious com-
modity, can be conserved through the use of convenience foods,
modern appliances, and careful planning. This book is designed for
people involved in an enlarging circle of activities, the busy housewife engaged in community affairs, the career girl, the man who
likes to cook — for all those who enjoy good food but for whom
time is at a premium.

The menus and recipes in *The Countdown Cookbook,* which vary
from hearty campfire stew to exotic dishes, are offered with time-
saving schedules for swift preparation. Each menu is accompanied by
its own carefully planned and timed Cooking Countdown, which
structures cooking time in 10-minute intervals from 60 minutes down
to zero. At the end of an hour, zero time, a delicious meal is coordi-
nated, each dish ready for serving. The total cooking time for any
one menu does not exceed an hour; many menus require only part of
the hour; just one recipe in each menu requires the maximum time.
Individual recipes in each menu have been chosen so that no more
than one dish is in the oven at the same time, unless the temperature
is the same for each, and you will never have three saucepans to stir
at one time.

The Countdown is a guide to organization. No two people do
things in exactly the same way or in exactly the same time. But the

schedule will help you evaluate your speed in the kitchen so that you may adjust your own rate of preparation. To make the most efficient use of the Countdown, there are a few things you should do:

1. Choose your menu.
2. Read each recipe carefully.
3. Organize your supplies, ingredients and utensils.
4. Check the starting time for each recipe with the Cooking Countdown and note cooking time.
5. Unless otherwise indicated, preheat your oven for at least 10 minutes before cooking time.

Time-saving suggestions for varying many of the recipes will be found under the headings *Another Way, Variations* and *Quick Alternates.* Under other headings will be found items (often desserts) which *must* be prepared in advance, and many which *may* be prepared a day or more ahead, to fit the cook's schedule and make mealtime more comfortable.

The menus have been left unadorned, in streamlined form, and can be adjusted for either simple or elaborate service. Each recipe is a complete unit and may be replaced or substituted in other menus. Feel free to make changes; use your imagination and please your individual taste. For convenience, menus are grouped according to entrée categories. The recipes for hors d'oeuvres, which appear in a separate section, offer many ideas for amplifying the menus when you are giving a party.

The last section of the book departs from the Countdown format with recipes for Dinner-in-a-Dish. This kind of recipe has many advantages. It may be prepared in advance (or on the spot with a minimum of effort), and it may be served from the casserole or other dish in which it is cooked. As it contains the elements of a two- or three-course meal, a choice of salad and dessert is all that is needed to complete the menu.

Informality is the keynote in this age of do-it-yourself activities. With limited time and lack of help, buffet service offers an attractive and carefree solution. It is equally effective for a large or small group. Select your serving pieces and set your table well in advance. Whether you serve at the dining table or from the buffet will depend on your facilities. For large numbers, small tables can easily be arranged in various rooms. Card tables, either the conventional or the extension type, and collapsible aluminum tables all work well together. For serving dessert and coffee a tea cart or auxiliary card table is handy.

Make use of the wonderful accessories available for buffet service. They are no longer just practical appurtenances but well-designed pieces that add interest and glamour to any table. The electric skillet provides efficient cooking in a minimum of time, and turned to low heat keeps food warm for serving. Many dishes, cooked separately, may be placed on an electric hot tray and kept at the right temperature. The chafing dish has returned to favor; some recipes may be cooked in it, others transferred to it later for piping hot service. The fondue dish promotes enjoyable conversation while your guests participate in preparing their meal. Casseroles are charming and a real boon to the hostess. Food prepared in casseroles well in advance can be brought easily from freezer to oven and from oven to table at short notice.

Remember to arrange your food in a decorative, eye-appealing way. Serve seafood over ice cubes, with colored toothpicks adding a festive look. Border entrée platters with accompanying vegetables, or mound pasta in the center for a lovely look, paying attention to contrasts in color. Serving a whole meal on one platter is a good time-saver. To make it colorful add a garnish of crisp parsley or watercress, a dash of paprika, lemon slices or red radishes. These are only a few of the many attractive, interesting embellishments that are available.

All of the recipes in *The Countdown Cookbook* are geared to time-saving cooking, for pleasurable and tasteful dining, whether with family or with guests. The book is meant to be a guide in the use of convenience foods and in efficient kitchen organization, and to provide ideas for attractive menus that can be prepared on a limited schedule. It is offered with best wishes to all those who are blessed with more taste for good food than time for cooking.

The Countdown Cookbook

Off to a Good Start—
Appetizers and Hors d'Oeuvres

THOUGH THE WORDS *hors d'oeuvre* and *canapé* are French, the appetizers themselves are popular around the world. In America, where they have been greatly elaborated, they offer a unique kind of dining. Originally designed to add a razor's edge to blunted appetites, the delectable "bits" were but a bite with an aperitif. Now, they contribute to entertaining in a major way. Along with heartier dishes, with appetizers as a nucleus, a veritable cult has developed; I call it the great Fork and Finger Society.

Americans have added charm to this important form of entertainment by borrowing freely from the comparable traditional foods of faraway nations — the Smorgasbord of Scandinavia, the Antipasto of Italy, the unornamented Zakuski of Russia, and other offerings from the Middle East, the Orient and elsewhere. Color, variety and ingenuity are characteristic of hors d'oeuvres regardless of origin. In this New World melting pot, we have boiled down the best and skimmed the dross, emerging with many prize-winning innovations.

Hors d'oeuvres are ideal for many occasions. The modish and informal cocktail party favors simply served foods of the fork and finger type, as does the closely allied Buffet Supper, with the addition of artfully arranged casseroles, chafing dishes, molds and other dishes of substantial nature. As an adjunct to the main course of a more formal meal, they fill gaps in service and time, not to mention appetites. They are perfect food for snacks, for refreshment after sports, for the "break" during a meeting and as an extra fillip for afternoon tea.

For first course service in the living room, the small appetizer still holds its own. A delicious, eye-appealing morsel, it challenges a cook's creativity. The extra time involved in its assembling is offset by present-day appliances and readily available convenience foods. Happily, advance preparation and freezing of the more involved hors d'oeuvres make it possible to have this opening scene of a meal well under control ahead of time. Prepared in quantity, hors d'oeuvres are available at a moment's notice on the other side of your freezer door.

Appetizers were in use as early as 3000 B.C., and as might be expected, the assortment is limitless. Those that follow have been culled with an eye to convenience and minimum preparation time. (With a few exceptions hors d'oeuvres have not been included in the menus of later sections.) When making your selection choose compatible recipes to achieve contrast in food content, color and texture. Check to make sure that your oven will be free if it's needed; compare the preparation time with the Cooking Countdown so that making the appetizer won't interfere with plans for your meal. Spreads, dips and salads may seem simple and uncomplicated in comparison to the detailed tinier tidbits, but they can be delicious and seldom require cooking. The tidbits are easily eaten with only cocktail picks, forks or fingers. For other appetizers, have plates and napkins at hand.

With a few well-chosen hors d'oeuvres your guests will be off to a rollicking, relishing start.

Hot Hors d'Oeuvres

ARTICHOKE PUFFS

Luscious is the word for these.

1 15-ounce can artichoke hearts, drained and halved	2 egg whites
30 toast rounds (approximately)	⅔ cup mayonnaise or salad dressing
2 tablespoons melted butter	¼ teaspoon Worcestershire
⅛ teaspoon salt	⅓ cup grated cheese

Set artichokes aside to drain well. Spread toast rounds with butter. Add salt to egg whites and beat until stiff; fold in mayonnaise, Worcestershire and cheese. Place artichoke half on toast round, cover thickly with egg white mixture and place on cooky sheet. Broil under moderate heat about one minute or until puffed and lightly browned. Makes about 30.

Artichoke Puffs may be assembled an hour in advance with no concern about the egg whites. Broil and serve.

VARIATIONS

1. Use 1 cup mayonnaise and omit cheese.

2. Instead of artichoke halves, substitute shrimp, other seafood, cherry tomatoes, chopped scallions, onion slices or chopped chutney.

BUBBLING MUSHROOMS

This deliciously simple recipe proved so popular in *Cooking with Love* that it seems worthwhile to list it again.

16 medium large mushrooms
¼ cup melted butter or margarine
½ teaspoon salt
¼ teaspoon savory
1 3-ounce package cream cheese, softened

1 tablespoon sour cream
2 tablespoons minced chives, dried or fresh

Rinse mushrooms and remove stems; drain on paper toweling, dip in melted butter coating evenly, then dust with salt and savory. Combine cream cheese, sour cream and chives; blend well until creamy and smooth. Fill caps liberally with cheese mixture in smooth high mounds, about 1 teaspoonful in each. Place on well-buttered baking pan and broil 7 to 8 minutes, 6 inches from heat. They will be brown and bubbly. Serves 4 to 5.

Spear these with pick or cocktail forks.

MUSHROOMS VERNON

1 pound large mushrooms
6 tablespoons butter or margarine, melted
¼ cup cracker crumbs
2 tablespoons minced parsley

3 tablespoons chopped shallots or green onions
½ teaspoon salt
⅛ teaspoon paprika
1 teaspoon lemon juice

Wash mushrooms quickly, remove stems, chop finely and set aside. Heat 2 tablespoons butter in skillet; add mushroom caps and sauté 3 minutes, then remove from skillet. To same skillet, add remaining butter, chopped stems and other ingredients, mixing well. Fill mushroom caps with crumb mixture; place under broiler, 3 inches from heat, and broil about 5 minutes until bubbly and hot. Serve at once. Makes about 16.

For convenience fill the mushroom caps well in advance. Broil and serve when needed.

ANOTHER WAY

Add ½ pound ground beef to the 2 tablespoons butter in skillet; sauté until pink disappears, then add mushrooms and proceed with method. Makes an excellent entrée and will serve 4.

HOT MUSHROOM SPREAD

Mushrooms have an incomparable flavor.

2 tablespoons butter
1 cup finely chopped mushrooms
½ teaspoon salt
¼ teaspoon pepper
¼ teaspoon garlic powder

2 egg yolks, slightly beaten
¼ cup cream
Melba toast and/or onion-flavored crackers

Heat butter in skillet; add mushrooms and sauté 5 minutes. Add seasonings. Combine egg yolks with cream; stir into mushroom mixture gradually and heat thoroughly. Serve on Melba toast or crackers. Makes about 2 dozen appetizers.

A chafing dish is a charming server. Have your spread heating over a low flame and spoon onto toast or crackers.

RUMAKI

These succulent appetizers are well worth the time involved in their preparation. They can be assembled as long as twenty-four hours before you serve them; they will be steeped in delicious flavor, and will need to be put into the oven for only a half hour while you do the final check on your table or hairdo before the guests arrive.

½ cup soy sauce
½ cup light brown sugar
2 tablespoons minced onion or 1 tablespoon minced dried onion

12 chicken livers, halved
12 water chestnuts, halved
12 bacon slices, halved

Combine soy sauce, sugar and onion in a 1-quart bowl. To assemble Rumaki, place ½ liver and ½ water chestnut together on bacon slice; roll up bacon around the two pieces and fasten securely by spearing with a toothpick. Place in bowl of marinade. Cover and refrigerate a minimum of 4 hours, stirring gently 2 or 3 times to marinate evenly. Drain well. Place a cake rack on a foil-lined cooky sheet and place prepared Rumaki on rack. Bake in preheated 400°

oven 20 to 30 minutes, turning once, until evenly browned and crisp. Quickly arrange on platter and serve at once. Makes 24.

Rumaki freeze very well. Simply remove from freezer and unwrap. Place in 400° oven and bake 10 minutes or until sizzling hot. Serve at once.

They may be marinated overnight.

OTHER WAYS

1. Center your platter of Rumaki with a small bowl of dipping sauce. Prepared Cantonese sweet and sour sauce is very good, as is a tangy sauce made with ½ cup of catsup and 2 tablespoons of prepared horseradish.

2. Rumaki make an excellent luncheon or supper dish. Serve 5 or 6 pieces of Rumaki on 2 toast points for each person, garnish with a sprig of crisp watercress, and pass a platter of assorted raw vegetable fingers.

SPARERIBS KYOTO

2 pounds spareribs	1 cup soy sauce
1 cup honey	¼ cup gin or sake

Allow at least ½ pound lean spareribs for each person. Have your butcher separate ribs and cut in halves. Combine remaining ingredients and pour over ribs. For additional flavor, marinate overnight, if possible. Drain and reserve marinade. Place on rack in shallow pan and bake at 350° for 1 hour, or until tender, basting frequently with marinade. Serves 4 for entrée, 6 to 8 for appetizer.

BEEF POCKETS

A wonderful hors d'oeuvre to have in the freezer.

Beef Filling

1 tablespoon vegetable oil	¼ cup chili sauce
¼ cup chopped onion, fresh or frozen	¼ pound ground beef
	1 teaspoon Worcestershire
¼ cup chopped green pepper or 1½ tablespoons flakes	½ teaspoon salt
	2 tablespoons cracker crumbs

Heat oil in skillet; add onions and green pepper and sauté 5 minutes. Add beef and simmer about 10 minutes until all pink in beef has disappeared. Add remaining ingredients, blending well. Will fill about 4 dozen pockets.

Dough

2 10-ounce packages refrigerated flaky biscuits
(8 biscuits)

Separate biscuits and divide each one in thirds; press each third with palm to a 3-inch circle. Makes 4 dozen 3-inch circles.

To assemble Beef Pockets

Place a well-rounded ½ teaspoon of beef filling on each circle of dough; fold in half; moisten edges and press together with tines of fork to seal. Bake on greased cooky sheet about 13 minutes, according to package directions, or until lightly browned. Makes 4 dozen.

For a shiny brown crust, before baking, brush each pocket with milk or egg yolk beaten with 1 teaspoon milk.

To freeze: wrap pockets securely in foil. To serve frozen pockets, place in 400° preheated oven for about 15 minutes until thoroughly heated.

COCKTAIL FRANKFURTERS TAHITIAN

These little franks are always popular and happily there is never a leftover.

1 pound cocktail frankfurters
Grape Chili Sauce

Separate frankfurters, if necessary. Prepare Grape Chili Sauce and add frankfurters. Reduce heat and simmer 15 to 20 minutes until hot and "shiny" glazed. A bowl with a warmer or a chafing dish is attractive service. Serves 6 to 8.

For the convenience of having the dish out of the way, it may be prepared early in the day; the flavor will improve and reheating is simple.

Grape Chili Sauce

1 12-ounce bottle chili sauce   1 10-ounce jar grape jelly
3 tablespoons lemon juice

Combine ingredients, blending well. Bring to boiling and add specified accompaniments; delicious as a sauce for livers or fish. Makes about 2 ½ cups.

LEMON CHILI MEATBALLS

Meatballs

3 slices white bread, crusts removed	1 teaspoon salt
	⅛ teaspoon pepper
1 cup water	¼ teaspoon paprika
2 pounds ground beef	1 egg
1 small onion, grated	½ cup ice water
Lemon-Chili Sauce	

Soak bread in water for a few minutes; squeeze dry. Combine with all remaining ingredients except Lemon-Chili Sauce, mixing very well. Form into walnut-sized balls; drop into simmering Lemon-Chili Sauce and cook 20 minutes. Allow to stand, for flavor improves.

Make the recipe at least an hour in advance if possible. Serves 8 as an appetizer.

Lemon Chili Sauce

1 12-ounce bottle chili sauce
1 6-ounce can frozen lemonade

Combine ingredients and heat to boiling, stirring occasionally. Makes 2½ cups delicious sauce.

It may be conveniently prepared the previous day or early the same day.

ANOTHER WAY

Simmer the meatballs in Grape Chili Sauce (page 8).

SESAME BEEF CUBES

Tender beef with an exotic flavor.

¼ cup soy sauce
3 tablespoons sliced fresh ginger
4 cloves garlic, halved (about 1 tablespoon)
1½ teaspoons sugar
1 tablespoon sesame seed, toasted
tops of 3 green onions, sliced
1½ pounds beef tenderloin, cut in ¾-inch cubes
2 tablespoons salad oil
1½ tablespoons soy sauce

To make the marinade for the beef, combine the ¼ cup soy sauce, ginger, garlic, sugar and onions. Stir beef cubes into the marinade; let stand for ½ hour, stirring once or twice. To serve, heat oil in an electric frying pan. Add the drained meat cubes and cook, stirring to brown all sides, for about 2 minutes, or until done to your liking. Turn out on a warm plate; sprinkle with soy sauce, then with sesame seed. Makes about 4 dozen.

A slice of bread in the bottom of the pan will prevent spattering during the cooking.

To toast sesame seeds, place in shallow pan in 350° oven for 10 minutes, stirring as they brown.

WING DIPPERS

These morsels stimulate conversation and taste.

12 chicken wings	3 tablespoons salad oil
½ cup seasoned flour	1 cup prepared barbecue sauce

Separate chicken wings into 3 pieces, discarding third tip section. Place in paper bag with seasoned flour and shake until pieces are well coated. Heat oil in skillet and sauté over moderately high heat until evenly browned, about 20 minutes. Place on a platter in spokelike fashion, center with a bowl of barbecue sauce and use the wings as dippers. Makes 2 dozen dippers. Serve hot or cold.

Wing Dippers may be prepared early in the day.

Seasoned Flour

1 cup flour	½ teaspoon white pepper
1 tablespoon paprika	1 tablespoon salt

Combine all ingredients and blend well. This is a convenient combination to have on hand. A good rule is to use ¼ cup for each pound of poultry or fish.

ANOTHER WAY

Glazed Wing Dippers. Add ½ cup orange marmalade when wings have browned and sauté an additional 10 minutes, turning and coating until glazed.

ANGELS ON HORSEBACK

These tidbits serve a double purpose. In the United States they are a favorite appetizer, while in England they are often served as a savory for the final course.

2 dozen raw oysters, drained	¼ cup dried bread crumbs
1 tablespoon lemon juice	8 strips bacon, cut in thirds
4 drops Tabasco	2 tablespoons snipped parsley

Toss oysters with lemon juice and Tabasco. Roll each in bread crumbs and place on bacon strip; roll and fasten with a toothpick, then sprinkle with parsley. Place on shallow baking dish and bake in preheated 450° oven about 12 minutes or until bacon is crisp. Makes 24.

Pieces may be broiled for about 10 minutes; turn often and shake pan gently to prevent sticking.

OTHER WAYS

1. Substitute smoked oysters for raw and omit seasonings.

2. Substitute plump pitted prunes for oysters.

OLIVES IN BLANKETS

If you enjoy the sharp saltiness of an appetizer, try these.

24 large pimiento-stuffed olives
12 slices bacon, halved

Place an olive on each bacon slice and roll up, enclosing olive. Secure with toothpick. Arrange on baking pan and place under broiler 4 inches from heat for about 3 to 4 minutes on each side or until rolls are brown and crisp. Serve piping hot. Makes 24 appetizers.

PRUNES IN BLANKETS

A wonderful combination.

24 pitted prunes
1 3-ounce package cream cheese

24 pecans or walnut halves
12 slices bacon, halved

Stuff each prune with a generous ½ teaspoon cream cheese and a half pecan or walnut. Roll in bacon slice and fasten with toothpick. Broil 4 inches from heat about 3 or 4 minutes on each side or until rolls are brown and crisp. Serve piping hot. Makes 24 appetizers.

ANOTHER WAY

The prunes may be stuffed with liver pâté, cocktail onions or anchovy fillets.

CHAFING DISH CLAMS DIAVOLO

This zesty living room starter was sent to me in Chicago, by a lovely lady from Toledo, Ohio, whom I met while visiting in Stevensville, Michigan. Such well-traveled recipes help to answer the frequent question, "Where do you get all your recipes?"

3 tablespoons butter
½ green pepper, finely chopped
1 small onion, finely chopped
1 10½-ounce can minced clams, drained
¼ pound sharp English Cheddar cheese

¼ cup catsup
1 tablespoon Worcestershire
1 tablespoon sherry
¼ teaspoon cayenne pepper
Melba toast rounds

Heat butter in skillet or chafing dish; add green pepper and onion, then sauté until tender but not browned. Add remaining ingredients and heat, stirring until cheese is melted and mixture blended. Serve on Melba toast rounds from chafing dish or other dish with flame or candle warmer. Serves 4 to 6.

CRABMEAT PUFFS

2 egg whites, beaten stiff
1 cup mayonnaise
1 7-ounce can crabmeat, flaked

¼ teaspoon seasoned salt
¼ teaspoon onion salt
36 1½-inch toast rounds
paprika

Combine egg whites, mayonnaise, crabmeat and seasonings; blend gently. Pile on toast rounds, about 1 tablespoon crabmeat mixture on each. Sprinkle with paprika and broil 3 minutes until puffy and lightly browned. Makes 36 puffs.

SCALLOPS IN GARLIC BUTTER

A bonanza for garlic addicts; subtly delicious.

1 12-ounce package frozen scallops
3 tablespoons butter or margarine
1 clove garlic, halved
1 tablespoon chopped chives or
green onions

¼ teaspoon dried tarragon (optional)
¼ teaspoon salt
dash freshly ground pepper

Accompaniment: parsley sprigs

Defrost and dry scallops. (Use fresh if you prefer.) Melt butter in ovenware skillet; add garlic and sauté until brown; discard garlic. Add remaining ingredients and mix well. Remove from heat and add scallops; allow to stand in sauce for about ½ hour or until ready to broil. Place 4 or 5 inches from broiler heat and broil for about 3 minutes on each side, or until golden brown and bubbly, basting once or twice while broiling. Serve from skillet, if you wish, or on individual plates; garnish with parsley sprigs. Serves 4.

CANTON SHRIMP

1 pound shrimp, frozen or fresh
5 slices bacon

China Town Sauce
2 tablespoons sesame seed

Garnish: 2 cups crisp shredded lettuce, sliced in ¼-inch strips

Defrost frozen shrimp, if used; clean and devein (do not remove tails when peeling fresh shrimp, as they add a gay touch). Slit shrimp along vein line; do not cut through and spread two halves, opening shrimp to form "butterflies." Cook for 3 minutes in 1 inch of salted water (using ½ teaspoon salt to 1 cup of water) until quite pink. Sauté bacon partially on each side; remove to paper toweling, then cut each slice in thirds. Place shrimp in one layer in skillet and cover evenly with China Town Sauce. Sprinkle with sesame seeds and top with bacon pieces. Place in broiler 6 inches from heat and broil 5 minutes or until well heated. Spread shredded lettuce over platter and cover with hot shrimps and sauce. The hot shrimp and cold lettuce are an exotic combination. Serves 6 to 8 as an appetizer. This is a lovely dish for a luncheon or a light supper and will serve 4.

China Town Sauce

½ cup catsup	2 tablespoons brown sugar
2 tablespoons soy sauce	¼ teaspoon powdered ginger
2 tablespoons peanut oil	¼ teaspoon powdered garlic
2 tablespoons honey	3 green onions, finely sliced
3 tablespoons white vinegar	¼ cup apricot preserves

Combine all ingredients, blending well. Makes about 1 cup sauce.

SHRIMPS DE JONGHE

A quick and delicious version of the classic dish.

1 pound cooked, cleaned and de-veined medium-size shrimp or 3 4½-ounce cans shrimp	1 teaspoon salt
	1 teaspoon parsley flakes
	1 teaspoon instant green onion flakes
2 garlic cloves, minced, or 1 teaspoon garlic powder	½ teaspoon crushed tarragon (optional)
¾ cup dry bread crumbs	¼ cup dry sherry
½ cup softened butter or margarine	

Garnish: watercress sprigs

If using canned shrimp, drain and rinse in cold water. Combine remaining ingredients, blending very well. Toss shrimp with ½ of crumb mixture and place in 6 individual ramekins or shells; top with remaining crumb mixture. Bake in preheated 400° oven about 15 minutes or until lightly browned. Serves 6.

The shrimp mixture may be arranged in shells or ramekins early in the day and baked just before serving. Or bake in a single casserole and spoon onto serving plates.

TUNA PUFFS

A breeze to prepare; featherweight in texture and light on the budget,

2 6½-ounce cans or 1 13-ounce can tuna
¾ cup fine cracker crumbs
1 egg, slightly beaten
2 teaspoons onion flakes
1 tablespoon Worcestershire
1 tablespoon finely snipped parsley
¼ teaspoon coarsely ground pepper
1 teaspoon prepared horseradish

Coating

1 egg, well beaten
½ cup dry cracker crumbs, approximately
shortening for frying

Flake the tuna and combine with remaining ingredients, blending very well. Roll with palms into balls about 1 inch in diameter (a heaping teaspoonful is about right). Dip in well-beaten eggs, then roll in cracker crumbs. Heat vegetable shortening or salad oil to a depth of ¼ inch in skillet; add tuna balls and fry quickly, turning once. Do not let the shortening come to the smoking stage, as puffs will burn. Serve piping hot. Makes about 3 dozen.

To broil Tuna Puffs

Melt 3 tablespoons butter or other shortening on baking pan. Roll puffs in shortening and place pan on broiler rack, 5 to 7 inches from heat. Broil 5 minutes on each side or until golden brown.

A great convenience is to freeze the puffs on a foil baking pan. Remove from freezer; drizzle with 3 tablespoons melted shortening and proceed as directed.

MINI BLINI

Intriguing bits of finger size.

Mini Blini Crêpes

1 egg, slightly beaten
¾ cup milk
½ cup sifted flour
1 teaspoon baking powder
¼ teaspoon salt
1 tablespoon sugar
2 tablespoons butter, melted
Cossack Caviar (page 20) or
Cream Cheese Filling

Combine egg and milk, beating until well blended. Sift flour, baking powder, salt and sugar together; add to egg mixture and stir in butter.

Toss cheese with flour; rub chafing dish or electric skillet with cut side of garlic clove. Add wine, heating over low heat just until bubbles begin to form on surface. Add about ¼ cup cheese at a time, stirring constantly with wooden spoon or wire whisk until mixture is completely blended. Add salt, pepper and kirsch; heat slowly. Serve bubbling hot. Each guest spears a bread cube, dunks it deep in the fondue, and turns to coat bread. Serves 4. Serve with coffee or tea with the accompaniment of small glasses of kirsch, or if you prefer, serve with the same type of dry white wine used in the fondue.

If possible, cut bread so each cube has crust on it. You are less likely to lose it in the fondue.

OLIVE NUGGETS

Freeze these to have on hand. They are real gems.

¼ cup butter, softened (whipped butter is preferred)
1 cup sharp Cheddar cheese, grated
¼ teaspoon salt
¼ teaspoon paprika
½ cup sifted flour
3 dozen small pimiento-stuffed olives, thoroughly drained and dried

Cream butter and cheese until well blended. Add salt, paprika and flour; mix well. Place in refrigerator and chill a minimum of 20 minutes. Roll dough into ¾-inch balls. Make an indentation with finger in each ball. Place olive in indentation and wrap dough around to enclose it completely. Place on cooky sheet and bake in pre-heated 400° oven 15 to 20 minutes or until brown. Serve hot or cold. Makes 3 dozen.

To have on hand, place prepared unbaked Nuggets on cooky sheet and put into freezer. When firm, place gently in plastic bag; seal tightly and return to freezer. Bake as needed. They will keep for several weeks.

QUICK CHEESE STRAWS

1 package pie crust mix, for	¾ cup grated cheese
1-crust pie	2 tablespoons boiling water
	paprika

Combine pie crust mix and cheese, blending well; add water and mix until dough forms a ball. Roll out on floured board or pastry cloth to ¼-inch thickness. Cut in strips 5 x ½ inches. Twist into spirals; sprinkle with paprika. Place on cooky sheet and bake in preheated 425° oven 8 to 10 minutes or until golden brown. Serve hot or cold. Makes about 3 dozen.

Baked Cheese Straws freeze very well. Store in plastic wrap.

SALTY PUFFED CRACKERS

Delicacies!

| 24 salted crackers | ¼ cup grated Parmesan cheese |
| ice water | 2 tablespoons sesame seeds |

Place crackers in ice water in one layer for 10 minutes; remove carefully with pancake turner and arrange on well-buttered cooky sheet. Sprinkle generously with cheese and sesame seeds, using more if needed to coat well. Bake in preheated 450° oven 12 to 15 minutes until puffy and brown. Serve immediately while piping hot. Makes 24 and will serve 8 or more.

Cold Hors d'Oeuvres

With only a few exceptions, cold appetizers may be made in advance and arranged on a serving dish in readiness to be presented. They provide a twofold blessing to the hostess. Served as the guests arrive, they set the conversational ball rolling, and meanwhile allow time for final preparation of the hot morsels which will shortly appear. With this hors d'oeuvre relay under way, gaiety can begin at once and continue without pause.

ARTICHOKE PETALS

A very pretty plateful.

1 large cooked artichoke (see page 250)
1 1-ounce jar tiny Danish shrimp
¼ cup mayonnaise
¼ teaspoon dill weed
1 teaspoon lemon juice
⅛ teaspoon coarsely ground pepper

Cook artichoke early in the day; refrigerate. Remove leaves of artichoke and arrange in circular rows covering a round platter. Drain and rinse shrimp; drain again and mix with remaining ingredients. Place a shrimp on the fleshy end of each petal. Makes about 20 morsels.

COSSACK CAVIAR

A dish with a ritual.

1 4-ounce can caviar, imported or domestic, red or black
2 hard-cooked egg yolks, sieved
2 hard-cooked egg whites, sieved
½ cup finely chopped onion
1 cup sour cream
Mini Blini Crêpes (page 15) or cocktail rye bread

Place caviar in a bowl; then, if you wish, set it in a bed of ice. Around this arrange four small bowls of sieved egg yolks, sieved egg whites, onion and sour cream. Place the warm blini on a separate plate. Each guest takes a blini, tops it with caviar, then with the other accompaniments of his choice; the usual routine is sour cream, then onion, egg yolk and egg white. Serves 6 to 8.

Delicious! But if your guests are caviar fans, it will only serve 4.

LIVER PÂTÉ BUDGETEER

Continental flavor with a light (on the budget) touch.

½ pound baby beef or calf liver
2 tablespoons butter
1 cup sliced onions
2 hard-cooked eggs
¼ cup water

¼ cup chicken fat or butter
1 tablespoon Worcestershire
¾ teaspoon salt
⅛ teaspoon seasoned or freshly ground pepper
2 tablespoons dry cracker crumbs

Remove tendons and membranes from liver; heat butter in skillet; add liver and onions. Sauté, tossing to brown evenly, about 10 minutes or until liver is lightly browned and just pink inside. Do not cook longer than necessary, or liver will toughen. Mash through a food mill, grinder or coarse sieve with the hard-cooked eggs to make a fine paste. (If you wish, you may chop the mixture in a wooden bowl.) Heat water in skillet in which liver was cooked and add ¼ cup butter, mixing until melted. Strain into liver mixture and blend with remaining ingredients. Press firmly into 2-cup mold; remove to serve. May be served warm, or refrigerate and serve cold. Turn out on platter and border with cocktail rye or rye crackers. Makes almost 2 cups.

May be prepared 3 to 4 days in advance.

GARBANZOS CONFETTI

The basis for this unusual appetizer is becoming a commonplace market item — canned garbanzos or chick-peas. The mixture is good alone, and is a perfect addition to meat or fish hors d'oeuvres. If there are leftovers, try sprinkling the flavorful garbanzos and their marinade over a crisp green salad. Good to have on hand.

2 1-pound cans chick-peas
1 2-ounce jar pimientos, finely sliced

Confetti Marinade

1½ cups white vinegar
¾ cup sugar
2 or 3 cloves garlic, crushed

1½ teaspoons salt
2 teaspoons grated lemon peel
2 tablespoons dry parsley flakes

Combine rinsed and drained chick-peas with sliced pimientos; spoon into four 8-ounce jars. Combine vinegar, sugar, garlic, salt, lemon peel and parsley in a saucepan. Bring mixture to a boil; pour over chick-peas and set aside to cool. Place in refrigerator and let stand 2 to 3 days to absorb flavor. Makes about 4 cups.

Keeps indefinitely.

The Confetti also makes welcome "bread and butter" gifts. Double the quantity; pour into hot sterilized jars and seal tightly. Wrap in gay colored paper.

MARINATED MUSHROOMS

1 4-ounce jar button mushrooms
Italian style dressing

Drain liquid from mushrooms and replace with sufficient Italian or French dressing to cover. Let stand overnight. Serves 4, with other appetizers.

SHERRY MUSHROOMS

Follow procedure for Marinated Mushrooms, substituting dry sherry for Italian dressing. Let stand several hours or overnight. Increase quantity as needed.

Serve with tray of assorted vegetables or toss with any combination of vegetables such as green beans, artichoke hearts, tiny carrots, sliced water chestnuts or diced raw green pepper, fresh or pickled.

Marinate the mushrooms a week in advance; then you'll be ready for "sudden" cocktail company.

STUFFED ARTICHOKE HEARTS

1 1-ounce jar red caviar
1 15-ounce can artichoke hearts, drained

1 3-ounce package cream cheese, softened
1 tablespoon cream
⅛ teaspoon salt

Combine cheese, cream and salt, mixing until well blended. Spread artichoke hearts apart, leaving opening in center. Stuff with cream cheese and top with caviar. Stand upright on serving platter, giving a festive look to any assortment. Makes about 15.

ANTIPASTO SALAD

According to Homer, salad was the food of the gods, and when properly presented, it still is. Through the years, its scope has broadened; the ingredients and variety of combinations have multiplied and it has become an increasingly important course.

On the West Coast, which emphasizes color and drama in dining, eye-appealing salad is characteristically served as a first course. This custom has been adapted to dining styles in other regions of the country, and salad is now finding its way into the living room as an hors d'oeuvre.

The Italian antipasto has a similar mien, and the combination of the two ideas has brought the Antipasto Salad to a top-rung position in modern dining. It has the advantage that it can be prepared with "on hand" pantry staples which, in their plentiful variety, offer pleasing choices to each individual. As a do-it-yourself living room course, Antipasto Salad is a conversational joy.

Do-It-Yourself Antipasto Salad

Start with an attractive bed of lettuce or curly endive. Then in the center of the platter place one of the following:

> seafood (mounds of crabmeat, shrimp, lobster or chunks of cold fish)
>
> tuna (drain and turn out in its cylinder form)
>
> tomatoes (sliced or quartered)
>
> mixed cooked vegetables (the cooked frozen ones, great when chilled)
>
> cooked sausages (such as pepperoni, salami, bologna or cocktail franks)

Border the platter with alternating clusters of a selection of the following:

sardines	anchovies, rolled and/or fillets
salami, thinly sliced	hard-cooked eggs, quartered
celery hearts	prosciutto or ham
radish roses	assorted cheeses
olives	green pepper, fresh or pickled

A good addition to this list are the Marinated or Sherry Mushrooms (page 22).

The ingredients in both categories can be modified; use your imagination and have some fun creating colorful patterns with your preferred delicacies.

For individual service in the living room or as a first course at the table, arrange your selection on salad plates. Serve with Oil and Vinegar dressing (page 409), your own or prepared, or pass cruets, each containing oil or vinegar so that your guests may dress their salads as they prefer.

OTHER WAYS

1. Appetizer Salad Bolognese

2 heads romaine lettuce	1 cup French Blend Dressing
8 slices salami, sliced in strips	1 4-ounce can mushrooms, drained
5 slices cheese, Cheddar or Muenster, cut in strips	1 2-ounce can anchovy fillets

Tear lettuce into bite-sized pieces and arrange on platter. Place salami strips through center and border with cheese strips. Crisscross anchovy fillets over cheese. Combine French Blend Dressing (page 267) with mushrooms and pour over completed salad arrangement. May be tossed or served with a portion of each ingredient. Serves 6.

2. Antipasto Salad Parmesan

2 6-ounce cans artichoke hearts, drained or 2 9-ounce packages frozen artichoke hearts	1 head lettuce
	Salad Dressing Parmesan
	1 2-ounce can rolled anchovy fillets

Garnish: parsley sprig bouquet

If using frozen artichoke hearts, cook according to package directions. Drain either variety and chill. Tear lettuce in bite-size pieces into salad bowl. Pour Salad Dressing Parmesan over lettuce and toss lightly. Arrange artichoke hearts on top and garnish with rolled anchovy fillets; center with a parsley sprig bouquet. May be arranged on platter. Serves 6. When arranging on platter, sliced salami and sliced tomatoes are a generous addition.

Salad Dressing Parmesan

1 ⅝-ounce envelope Parmesan cheese salad dressing mix	salad oil
vinegar	1 hard-cooked egg, chopped
water	1 teaspoon snipped parsley
	1 teaspoon chopped onion

1 tablespoon anchovy paste

Prepare Parmesan cheese salad dressing mix according to package directions, with added vinegar, water and salad oil. To it add egg, parsley, onion and anchovy paste. Shake very well to blend thoroughly.

Parsley Bouquet

Tie fresh luxuriant parsley into a solid spray. When tied, it gives a slightly different effect.

STEAK TARTARE

1 pound top sirloin or boneless beef chuck	½ teaspoon freshly ground pepper
1 tablespoon grated onion, or ½ teaspoon onion powder	2 tablespoons capers
	1 egg yolk
1 teaspoon salt	1 teaspoon Worcestershire
	1 tablespoon cognac (optional)

Accompaniments

lettuce	anchovy fillets, halved
chopped onion	capers

cocktail rye bread or pumpernickel

Grind the beef as close to preparation as possible; it must be freshly ground. Combine all ingredients, mixing to blend smoothly and well. Mound on a bed of lettuce and serve with accompanying bowl of chopped onion, anchovy fillets and capers. Pass a tray of cocktail rye bread or pumpernickel slices. Serves 6 to 8.

ANOTHER WAY

Stuff celery stalks with Steak Tartare; eliminate bread and the maneuver of spreading.

ANCHOVY STUFFED EGGS

6 hard-cooked eggs	2 tablespoons mayonnaise
1½ tablespoons snipped fresh or frozen chives	4 teaspoons anchovy paste
2 teaspoons lemon juice	2 tablespoons red caviar and/or sliced pimiento olives

Slice eggs in half, lengthwise, and remove yolks to a small bowl. Add remaining ingredients except caviar, blending well until smooth and creamy. Mound anchovy mixture in hollow of egg white and top with caviar or slice of pimiento olive. Place on platter with slices of cocktail rye or make an assortment with a center of cheese mold or dip (page 35). As the stuffing is rich, the eggs may be quartered after filling. Also, in smaller pieces, they make better finger food. Makes 12 halves or 24 quarters.

DEVILED SARDINE EGGS

6 hard-cooked eggs, halved
Sardine Spread (page 36)

Remove yolks of eggs, retaining whites for shells. Add yolks to Sardine Spread; add 2 teaspoons lemon juice. Mix very well. Fill whites of eggs, mounding high.

Deviled Eggs may be prepared early in the day; refrigerate.

CARDINAL EGGS

8 hard-cooked eggs
½ pound cooked lobster meat, canned, fresh or frozen
½ teaspoon grated onion
1 teaspoon finely snipped parsley
1 teaspoon chopped pimiento
1 tablespoon chili sauce

⅓ cup mayonnaise or salad dressing
¼ teaspoon celery salt
parsley sprigs
leaf lettuce
lemon wedges, paprika

Shell eggs and cut in half lengthwise; remove yolks and reserve for filling. Chop lobster meat coarsely and combine with yolks, onion, parsley, pimiento, chili sauce, dressing and celery salt. Fill egg halves with lobster mixture and top with tiny sprigs of parsley. Line platter with leaf lettuce and arrange eggs; garnish with lemon wedges, piped with paprika. Serves 8.

Cardinal Eggs may be prepared early in the day; cover with plastic wrap and refrigerate.

FRUIT SALAD HERRING

Lovely to look at, delicious to eat.

2 8-ounce jars herring fillets in wine sauce
1 cup sour cream
1 large red onion, thinly sliced
1 orange with rind, thinly sliced and quartered

1 lemon with rind, thinly sliced and quartered
1 lime with rind, thinly sliced and quartered
1 apple with skin, diced in ½-inch pieces

Topping: paprika and/or snipped parsley

Remove herring from wine sauce, drain; discard onions. Combine with remaining ingredients and marinate for at least one hour in the refrigerator. Improves as it stands, and is a good keeper. Serve in a bowl and dust with paprika.

Herring may be prepared 2 to 3 days in advance. Serves 8 to 10.

NOVA SCOTIA SALMON VINAIGRETTE

½ pound smoked, sliced Nova Sco-
tia salmon
1 tablespoon capers, drained
2 green onions or scallions, finely
sliced
½ cup sliced pitted ripe olives

3 tablespoons wine vinegar
¼ cup salad oil
2 teaspoons prepared mustard
⅛ teaspoon coarsely ground pepper

Cut the salmon slices into squares, approximately one inch; place in
shallow dish. Distribute capers, onions and olives evenly over salmon
pieces. Combine vinegar, oil, mustard and pepper and pour over
salmon, tossing lightly, being careful not to shred the pieces. Cover
and place in refrigerator several hours or overnight to marinate.
Serve on a bed of leaf lettuce with buttered pumpernickel bread.
Serves 6 to 8 as an appetizer.

This is another fine preparation to have on hand and will keep
several days.

RED CAVIAR POLKA DOTS

1 8-ounce package cream cheese,
softened
2 tablespoons mayonnaise
2 tablespoons sour cream
½ teaspoon lemon juice
¼ teaspoon onion powder or
juice

¼ teaspoon dill weed
¼ teaspoon salt
1½ teaspoons unflavored gelatin
½ cup milk
¼ teaspoon Maggi or Worcestershire
1 4-ounce jar red caviar

Accompaniments: lemon wedges, caraway rye bread and/or crackers

Blend cream cheese, mayonnaise, sour cream, lemon juice, onion
powder, dill and salt. Combine gelatin with milk in a small saucepan
and let stand five minutes, then place over low heat and stir until
dissolved. Combine with cream cheese mixture; add Maggi or
Worcestershire. Fold in caviar gently so as not to break any of the
delicate globules. Pour into oiled 2-cup mold; chill. Unmold on
platter and rim with lemon wedges, caraway rye bread and/or
crackers. Makes 2 cups; serves 6 to 8.

This is best when prepared a day in advance.

GOURMET TOUCHES

1. Parsley Crackers

Spread in advance to have ready for that extra fillip.

> 2 tablespoons softened butter
> 2 tablespoons snipped parsley
> 24 butter crackers (approximately)

Combine parsley and butter, blending until smooth; spread on crackers. To serve, place under broiler for about 2 minutes or until bubbly. Serve at once. Makes 2 dozen.

2. Rolled Buttered Toast

Good with salads, with hors d'oeuvres or a cocktail.

> 1 thinly sliced loaf of bread, crusts removed
> softened butter or margarine

Roll each bread slice with rolling pin until very flat. Spread with softened butter, roll slices into cylinders, and place seam side down at one end of a damp towel, folding towel over to cover bread rolls. To serve, spread tops lightly with additional melted or softened butter. Place on baking sheet and under preheated broiler for about 2 to 3 minutes to brown evenly. Make the number needed, allowing about 3 per person. Serve at once.

3. Watercress Sandwiches

Roll slices of bread and spread with butter as for Buttered Toast. Place a sprig of watercress to extend over bread at one end. Roll and place seam side down on one half of damp towel and cover with other half. Serve within 2 hours.

4. Asparagus Sandwiches

Roll bread around spears of canned, drained asparagus.

5. Cheese Sandwiches

Spread flattened bread slices with one 8-ounce package cream cheese softened with 2 tablespoons cream. Tuck a sprig of watercress at edge so leaves protrude when rolled. Roll lightly and place seam side down on damp towel. Cover with damp towel. To serve, arrange on platter with needed number. There will be 1 cup of cheese spread, which will make 16 to 18 sandwiches. Allow 3 per serving.

6. Mushroom Filled Rolled Toast

A wonderful salad accompaniment and an hors d'oeuvre. Instead of butter, spread bread with Mushroom Filling.

Mushroom Filling

½ pound mushrooms, finely chopped or ground
2 tablespoons butter or margarine

¼ teaspoon onion powder
½ teaspoon salt
1 teaspoon lemon juice

12 slices bread (crusts removed), rolled thin

Add mushrooms to heated butter in skillet and sauté about 5 minutes. Add remaining ingredients except bread, blending well. Spread about 1 tablespoon of mixture on each slice of bread, roll and prepare as for Buttered Toast. Bake in preheated oven 425° for 15 minutes or toast under broiler, watching carefully. Makes about 1 dozen rolls.

7. Sardine Filled Sandwiches

1 3½-ounce can sardines, drained
1 hard-cooked egg, mashed
1 teaspoon onion juice
1 teaspoon Worcestershire

1 teaspoon lemon juice
12 slices white bread, crusts removed, rolled thin

Combine first 5 ingredients, blending until smooth and creamy. Spread sardine mixture on bread and proceed as for Mushroom Filled Rolled Toast. Makes about 12 sandwiches.

Double the recipe to make 1 cup.

8. Melba Crisps

Cut slices as thinly as possible from an unsliced loaf of white bread, remove crusts. Place slices in one layer on a cooky sheet and into a preheated 350° oven; bake 10 to 15 minutes, turning once, until crisp and lightly browned. They are delectable and make an all-purpose accompaniment.

If you need the toast in a hurry or cannot procure sandwich bread, use thinly sliced white bread; trim crusts and roll as thin as possible with a rolling pin. Bake as for above recipe, in preheated 350° oven for 10 to 15 minutes.

9. Toast Points

Toast white bread slices; cut in halves or quarters. Remove crusts if desired.

SHRIMP RÉMOULADE

There are innumerable recipes for the sauce. They all agree in sharpness and flavor. The mustard should be a creole or a more pungent type.

Rémoulade Sauce

1 cup mayonnaise
½ cup Dijon type mustard
1 green onion minced or 1 teaspoon dried, green onion
2 tablespoons catsup

1 tablespoon parsley flakes
1 teaspoon Worcestershire
2 tablespoons prepared horseradish

Accompaniment

1½ pounds medium-size shrimp, cleaned, cooked, deveined

1 large head iceberg lettuce, shredded

tomato wedges

Combine all sauce ingredients, blending well. Arrange shrimp on shredded lettuce on individual salad plates and dress with Rémoulade Sauce. Garnish with tomato wedges. Have ingredients well chilled. Serves 6 to 8.

The Rémoulade Sauce is fine to have on hand. Good over fish and cold vegetables.

BLOCK OF CHEESE AND CHUTNEY

This appetizer can be prepared in "nothing flat," and is attractive and toothsome.

1 8-ounce package (block) cream   ¾ cup mango chutney, chopped
cheese   Melba toast rounds

Center cream cheese block on serving plate; prick with tines of fork or make small gashes with a knife; pour chopped chutney over cheese. Surround with Melba toast rounds. Have bread and butter knives at hand for self-service and let everyone help himself. Serves 6.

BLOCK OF CHEESE AND CAVIAR

This version was given to me by a bachelor colleague-cook who favors the cheese and caviar combination. Before leaving for his office in the morning, he pricks the cheese with vigor and covers it with caviar, allowing the combination to stand at room temperature until his return in the evening, conveniently ready to serve.

For your choice, prepare the appetizers in advance or as a quick last-minute preparation.

1 8-ounce package cream cheese
1 1¾-ounce jar caviar, red or black, domestic or imported
cocktail rye

Center cream cheese on serving plate; prick with tines of fork to make indentations and cover with caviar. Allow to stand at room temperature and serve with cocktail rye. Serves 6.

BLOCK OF CHEESE AND WORCESTERSHIRE

Gash cheese block as in preceding recipes and top with 2 tablespoons Worcestershire. Serves 6.

CARAWAY CREAM CHEESE SPREAD

1 8-ounce package cream cheese, softened
1 medium onion, grated
1 teaspoon light prepared mustard

1½ teaspoons anchovy paste
2 tablespoons caraway seed

Accompaniment: assorted crackers and/or cocktail rye

Combine all ingredients, mixing well. Turn into small bowl and cover with plastic wrap. Refrigerate several hours or overnight. Place bowl on tray and border with crackers and/or cocktail rye. Makes 1¼ cups.

BRANDIED CHEESE

½ cup processed Cheddar cheese spread
1 3-ounce package cream cheese
1 teaspoon anchovy paste

2 tablespoons unflavored gelatin
3 tablespoons half-and-half cream
¼ cup sour cream
1 tablespoon brandy

Accompaniments: crackers, sliced apples and celery hearts

Blend cheese spread, cream cheese and anchovy paste together. Sprinkle gelatin on cream, then dissolve over moderate heat, stirring constantly. Add to cheese mixture, blending thoroughly; gradually add sour cream and brandy. Pour into greased 2-cup mold and refrigerate until firm. To serve, turn out on small flat plate; border with crackers, sliced apples and celery hearts. Almond-stuffed green olives are a good color contrast. Serves 6.

OLIVE CHEESE ROLL

½ pound blue cheese, softened
1 8-ounce package cream cheese, softened
¼ cup butter, softened
1 cup chopped ripe olives

1 tablespoon lemon juice
2 tablespoons finely chopped green onions
¼ cup chopped parsley
Melba Crisps (page 30)

Cream cheeses and butter together; mix with olives, lemon juice and onions. Shape into single roll 1½ inches in diameter; roll in parsley, coat evenly. Place in refrigerator; chill until firm, about 3 hours. Place on tray, bordered with Melba Crisps. A wonderful freezer luxury at hand for any emergency. Serves 12 to 15.

ONION CHEESE LOGS

Make three, freeze two

2 8-ounce packages cream cheese, softened

2 6-ounce jars Old English Cheddar cheese spread

½ pound blue or Roquefort cheese

1 clove garlic, minced

1 large onion, grated

Coating: ½ cup snipped parsley, ½ cup chopped nuts

Combine all ingredients for cheese log and blend well. Place mixture on waxed paper and form into 3 equal logs. Chill logs until firm; roll in the coating, prepared by combining parsley and nuts. Chill in refrigerator until ready to serve. Each roll serves 6 to 8.

May be made 2 or 3 weeks in advance, and frozen. Defrost as needed.

DIPS FOR CHIPS

The ease with which dips are made, their keeping qualities and popularity with young and old make them a star attraction. Serve them with a variety of crackers with crisped fresh vegetables, sliced or in strips or in chunky flowerets, and with the traditional potato chips.

A distinct advantage in serving dips is the fact that they must be prepared in advance. They are best when chilled, and a little time gives the flavors a chance to "marry."

The following dips, with the exception of Guacamole and the Avocado Dip, may be prepared a day in advance and some may be frozen as indicated in the recipe.

1. Anchovy Dip

1 cup sour cream
3 tablespoons anchovy paste

¼ teaspoon garlic powder
1 teaspoon Worcestershire

Combine all ingredients and blend well; chill. Makes about 1 cup.

2. Avocado Dip

2 ripe avocados, peeled, pitted and mashed
2 tablespoons lemon juice
2 tablespoons mayonnaise or salad dressing

1 tablespoon grated onion
1 teaspoon Worcestershire
2 drops Tabasco
½ teaspoon salt

Combine all ingredients and blend well. Cover and chill thoroughly. Makes about 2 cups.

As suggested in the Guacamole recipe, if the lovely green of the avocado fades, give it a boost with the help of a drop or two of green vegetable coloring.

3. Cream Cheese Clam Dip

1 8-ounce package cream cheese
2 teaspoons lemon juice
2 teaspoons Worcestershire
½ teaspoon salt
¼ cup sour cream

1 7½-ounce can minced clams, drained
⅛ teaspoon garlic powder (optional)

Cream cheese until smooth and blend in remaining ingredients; mound in bowl and serve with an assortment of crackers, and/or potato chips. If the dip seems too heavy, thin with a small amount of half-and-half cream. Makes about 2½ cups.

Another good refrigerator "keeper."

4. Crab Dip

2 7-ounce cans crabmeat
1 8-ounce package cream cheese, softened
⅛ teaspoon salt
⅛ teaspoon curry

1 tablespoon lemon juice
¼ teaspoon onion powder
1 teaspoon Worcestershire
¾ cup sour cream

Accompaniment: Melba toast rounds

Drain crabmeat; remove cartilage and separate into small pieces. Mash cheese until creamy and combine with remaining ingredients blending thoroughly. Fold in crabmeat until evenly distributed. Place in refrigerator to chill. Serve with Melba toast rounds. Makes 3 cups.

If you prefer, make the Crab Dip early in the day. The flavor is delicate and may be lost with an earlier preparation.

5. Guacamole

Traditional recipes do not include tomatoes; adding them gives unique flavor and contrasting color.

3 avocados, finely chopped or mashed	1 teaspoon salt
	½ teaspoon pepper
2 tomatoes, finely chopped	1 tablespoon lemon juice
1 small onion, grated	¼ teaspoon chili powder

dash of Tabasco

Combine all ingredients and blend well. Serve as a dip for corn chips. Guacamole should be tightly covered until ready to serve in order to preserve its delicate green color. Makes 1½ to 2 cups.

In spite of precaution, the color may dull; to restore brightness, I add 1 or 2 drops of green vegetable coloring. The flavor will not be impaired.

Do not prepare the Guacamole more than an hour or two in advance.

6. Sardine Spread

1 4-ounce can sardines in oil	½ teaspoon Worcestershire
2 hard-cooked eggs, chopped	¼ cup mayonnaise
1 tablespoon lemon juice	36 Melba toast rounds
1 teaspoon prepared horseradish	sliced pimiento olives

Accompaniment: cherry tomatoes

Drain sardines and mash with eggs, lemon juice, horseradish, Worcestershire and mayonnaise; blend until very smooth. Spread on Melba toast rounds just before serving and top with a slice of pimiento olive. Place bowl of cherry tomatoes in center of platter and surround with "sardined" disks. Makes about 3 dozen.

Sardine Spread may be prepared 2 to 3 days in advance. Refrigerate until needed.

OTHER WAYS

1. Double the recipe; place in bowl and serve as a dip with corn chips.

2. Cardinal Eggs (page 27) on lettuce make a pretty border around the bowl of Sardine Spread.

7. *Southern Spread*

1 8-ounce package cream cheese, softened	¼ teaspoon monosodium glutamate
1 4½-ounce can deviled ham	½ teaspoon onion juice
1 tablespoon dry white wine	1 teaspoon prepared horseradish
⅛ teaspoon seasoned salt	⅛ teaspoon dry mustard

Accompaniment: rye toast rounds

Combine all ingredients and blend well. Turn into 2-cup jar or mold. Chill thoroughly (the freezer is always a "hurry-up" method for chilling). Turn out on platter; border with rye toast rounds. Makes 1¾ cups.

This will keep in the refrigerator for several days.

8. *Smoked Oyster Dip*

½ pint sour cream	2 teaspoons lemon juice
1 4-ounce can smoked oysters, drained and mashed	2 drops Tabasco

Combine all ingredients and blend well. Chill. Makes about ¾ cup. The definite flavor of the oysters makes this a good "keeper."

9. *Tangy Dip*

½ cup mayonnaise or salad dressing	2 tablespoons horseradish
½ cup sour cream	1 small onion, chopped fine
½ cup chili sauce	1 teaspoon celery seed
	dash Tabasco

Combine all ingredients and blend well; chill. Makes about 2 cups.

This dip refrigerates well for several days.

Prize Beef

In America, no food rivals the popularity of meat, and in a contest beef would emerge the undisputed winner. From hamburger to the chopped steak of a deluxe menu, from frankfurters to tenderloin, from pot roast to rib roast, there is a cut for every taste and every pocketbook. When properly and tenderly prepared, even the least expensive cuts of beef are delicious. A well-seasoned pot roast slowly cooked produces a succulent all-time favorite, invariably greeted with cheers.

The beef recipes presented here are a cross section for varying budgets. Some cook quickly, others more slowly, but all are simple to prepare and will fill the air with inviting kitchen aromas. Unadorned or embellished, beef is consistently dependable and satisfying main course fare.

▶ Piedmont Beef and Peppers

Piedmont Beef and Peppers   Brown Rice
Caesar Salad   Caramel Peaches

COOKING COUNTDOWN

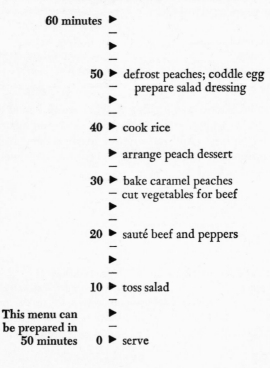

60 minutes ▶
—
▶
—
50 ▶ defrost peaches; coddle egg
— prepare salad dressing
▶
—
40 ▶ cook rice
—
▶ arrange peach dessert
—
30 ▶ bake caramel peaches
— cut vegetables for beef
▶
—
20 ▶ sauté beef and peppers
—
▶
—
10 ▶ toss salad
—
This menu can ▶
be prepared in —
50 minutes 0 ▶ serve

PIEDMONT BEEF AND PEPPERS

The man of the house once cooked this meal for us in Piedmont, California.

2 tablespoons butter or margarine
2 pounds beef tenderloin (or flank steak), thinly sliced
1 large onion, thinly sliced
1 large green pepper, cut in 1-inch dice
1 pound fresh mushrooms
1 cup diced celery
2 tomatoes, cut in sixths
2 tablespoons soy sauce

¼ teaspoon seasoned pepper
¼ cup domestic sweet Concord grape wine
1 teaspoon seasoned salt
1 teaspoon Worcestershire
3 bouillon cubes
2 cups boiling water
1 tablespoon instantized flour
3 cups brown rice (cooked according to package directions)

Heat butter in large skillet and add beef slices; sauté 5 minutes. Add onion slices, green pepper, mushrooms and celery and again sauté 5 minutes, tossing lightly. Add remaining ingredients and blend well. Simmer an additional 5 minutes and serve at once over rice or fine noodles. Serves 6 to 8.

CAESAR SALAD

2 quarts romaine lettuce, torn in bite-sized pieces

1 egg, coddled
½ cup grated Parmesan cheese

2 cups packaged croutons

Caesar Dressing

1 teaspoon salt
1 clove garlic, minced
black pepper, freshly grated
½ cup salad or olive oil

½ teaspoon dry mustard
2 tablespoons Worcestershire
¼ cup wine vinegar
¼ cup fresh lemon juice

Wash and refrigerate drained lettuce; tear into bite-sized pieces in salad bowl. Coddle egg and set aside. Combine Caesar Dressing ingredients in covered jar; shake to blend well. Arrange greens in bowl; toss with Caesar Dressing. Break egg into salad; toss again. Sprinkle with cheese and top with croutons. Serves 8.

To coddle an egg

Cover egg with cold water and bring to boiling. Remove egg and drop into cold water.

CARAMEL PEACHES

SHE made the dessert!

8 slices white bread	3 teaspoons cinnamon
½ cup melted butter	whipped cream or whipped topping
6 tablespoons brown sugar	mix
3 10-ounce packages frozen peaches, defrosted	

Remove bread crusts and cut bread in quarters. Pour butter into a shallow dish and dip one side of each bread square lightly in butter. Layer 4 slices of bread in bottom of baking dish, buttered side down. Sprinkle with 2 tablespoons of the brown sugar, cover with peaches and spread evenly. Sprinkle with 2 more tablespoons of brown sugar and 1 teaspoon cinnamon. Layer with remaining 4 slices bread, buttered side up, and sprinkle with remaining sugar and cinnamon. If any butter remains, pour it over the top. Bake in preheated 350° oven 30 minutes until bubbling and hot. Serve hot, topped with a dollop of whipped cream. Serves 6 to 8.

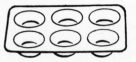

► Genghis Khan

Genghis Khan   Fluffy Rice   Sauces
Fresh Fruit and Cheeses   Wine

COOKING COUNTDOWN

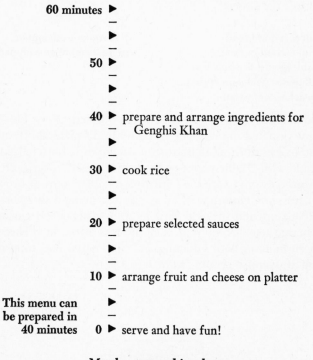

60 minutes ►
—
►
—
50 ►
—
►
—
40 ► prepare and arrange ingredients for
—   Genghis Khan
►
—
30 ► cook rice
—
►
—
20 ► prepare selected sauces
—
►
—
10 ► arrange fruit and cheese on platter
—
This menu can ►
be prepared in —
40 minutes   **0** ► serve and have fun!

May be prepared in advance:
     Sauces for Genghis Khan

GENGHIS KHAN

Here is a new member of the fondue family, and like the others, it provides the fun of communal preparation. The broth for cooking bubbles invitingly in the electric frying pan, centered on the table; the individual ingredients to be selected are arranged about it in attractive fashion. Each guest makes his choice and then proceeds as described in the recipe.

Broth for cooking

3 10-ounce cans chicken broth
3 chicken bouillon cubes

1 tablespoon monosodium glutamate

1 teaspoon ground ginger

Ingredients to be cooked

1½ pounds raw shrimp, cleaned and deveined
1 pound beef tenderloin, or boneless sirloin of beef, cut in ¼-inch slices
½ pound whole medium-size mushrooms

1 4-ounce can water chestnuts, sliced
1 pound spinach, green and crisp
2 zucchini, cut in ¾-inch slices
3 raw chicken breasts, boned and cut in ¼-inch slices
6 cups cooked rice (2 cups raw)

Heat broth ingredients to boiling in electric frying pan; reduce heat so mixture just bubbles. Arrange the raw "to be cooked" ingredients around the frying pan, each in its separate bowl. The guests make a selection of raw food and sauce on individual serving plates, then, with chopsticks or forks, place raw food in the boiling broth until cooked to desired doneness. The cooked morsel is then dipped in the sauces and eaten with rice. The dripping juices moisten the rice succulently. Serves 10 to 12.

Make a choice of the following sauces:

Plum Sauce (Duk Sauce)

¾ cup plum jelly
½ cup chopped chutney

1 tablespoon sugar
1 tablespoon tarragon vinegar

Combine ingredients and blend well.

Sweet Sauce

¾ cup apricot preserves
¼ cup frozen orange juice, defrosted

Combine and blend well.

Sherry Mustard Sauce

¼ cup dry mustard
¼ cup dry sherry or hot water

1 tablespoon salad oil
1 teaspoon sugar

Combine and blend well.

Hot Sauce

½ cup prepared barbecue sauce   3 tablespoons catsup
4 drops Tabasco

Combine and blend well.

Sauces may be made in advance.

Fresh Fruit and Cheeses

A platter of cheeses and fruit can be attractively composed. Place a ball of Edam with its red color in the center of a doily-lined platter. Arrange an assortment of 3 cheeses in cubes or slices around the platter and alternate them with your selection of fruits. Sliced apples, pears and bunches of grapes contrast well with Edam.

Serve with crackers and a bottle of wine at hand.

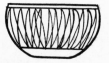

▶ Beef Teriyaki

Beef Teriyaki   Chinese Bean Sprouts
Rice Formosa   Peas
Kumquat Compote
Date Tart Hong Kong or *Fortune Cookies*

COOKING COUNTDOWN

60 minutes ▶ bake date tart

▶

—

50 ▶

—

▶

—

40 ▶ marinate steaks

▶

—

30 ▶ heat kumquat compote

▶

—

20 ▶ cook bean sprouts

▶ broil steaks

—

This menu can be   **10** ▶ cook rice
prepared in 40 minutes   —
if you use Quick   ▶ heat peas
Alternate for Date   —
Tart Hong Kong   **0** ▶ serve

May be prepared in advance:
Date Tart Hong Kong

BEEF TERIYAKI

2 T-bone steaks, 1 inch thick
½ cup soy sauce
¼ cup dry white wine

2 tablespoons sugar
1 teaspoon grated fresh ginger or powdered ginger

1 clove garlic, minced (optional)

Slash fat at edges of steaks one inch apart to prevent curling; dry with paper toweling and place in shallow pan. Combine remaining ingredients for marinade and pour over steak; let stand 15 minutes or longer in refrigerator, turning to marinate evenly. Place under preheated broiler, 3 inches from heat; turn when brown and of desired doneness. For a 1-inch beefsteak, broil 10 minutes for rare, 12 minutes for medium, 14 minutes for well done. Serves 4.

CHINESE BEAN SPROUTS

2 tablespoons peanut oil
1 1-pound can bean sprouts
1 stalk celery, sliced into ½-inch strips
1 teaspoon onion flakes

2 tablespoons soy sauce
1 teaspoon sugar
1 teaspoon salt
½ teaspoon monosodium glutamate

Heat oil in saucepan, stir in bean sprouts, celery and onion flakes, cooking for one minute. Combine soy sauce, sugar, salt and monosodium glutamate and add to bean sprout mixture. Cook 5 minutes until thoroughly heated. Serves 4.

RICE FORMOSA

1 package instant onion soup mix
2 cups water

2 cups precooked rice
1 1-pound can peas

Combine soup mix and water. Bring to boil. Add rice and stir well. Cover and remove from heat and let stand 10 minutes. Toss again lightly with a fork just before serving. Turn out on platter; make hollow in the center with a spoon and fill with heated, drained peas. Serves 4.

KUMQUAT COMPOTE

**1 6-ounce jar preserved kumquats
1 orange, thinly sliced and quartered**

Combine kumquats in their own syrup with orange sections. Simmer over moderate heat for 10 minutes and serve in individual compote dishes. Serve hot or cold. Serves 4.

May be prepared in advance, but only if it suits your convenience.

DATE TART HONG KONG

**1 cup dates, pitted and finely chopped
1 cup chopped walnuts
1 cup sugar
2 tablespoons flour**

**2 eggs, well beaten
1 teaspoon vanilla or ½ teaspoon rum extract
whipped cream or prepared dessert topping mix**

Combine all ingredients, except whipped cream, blending well. Pour into well-greased 8 x 8-inch baking pan. Place in 350° preheated oven; bake 45 minutes. Cool, then crumble in large pieces. Arrange in sherbet glasses or low bowls and serve with whipped cream or one 4-ounce package dessert topping mix, prepared according to package directions. Serves 6 to 8. May be prepared in advance.

QUICK ALTERNATE

Fortune cookies, available in many markets, would end this menu on a high note.

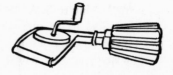

► Sukiyaki

Sukiyaki   Cellophane Noodles
Wined Cherries
Tropical Ginger Cookies or *Sugar Nut Rolls*

COOKING COUNTDOWN

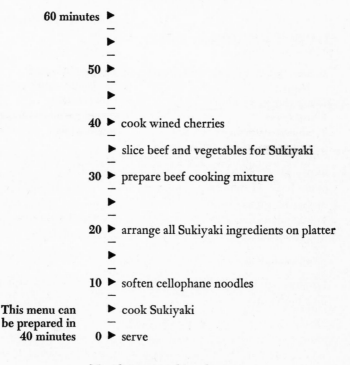

60 minutes ►
              —
            ►
              —
       50 ►
              —
            ►
              —
       40 ► cook wined cherries
              —
            ► slice beef and vegetables for Sukiyaki
              —
       30 ► prepare beef cooking mixture
              —
            ►
              —
       20 ► arrange all Sukiyaki ingredients on platter
              —
            ►
              —
       10 ► soften cellophane noodles
              —
This menu can   ► cook Sukiyaki
be prepared in —
40 minutes   0 ► serve

Must be prepared in advance:
Tropical Ginger Cookies

SUKIYAKI

A delicious, quick, fun dish, beautiful to see. The many variations are equally simple and, though the preparation may be a dramatic performance, the production is inexpensive. To set the stage have the raw beef and vegetables attractively arranged on a platter, a pitcher of the cooking mixture nearby, the electric skillet at moderate heat.

Cooking Mixture — "Warishita"

½ cup soy sauce
½ cup sherry or sake
½ cup consommé

½ teaspoon monosodium glutamate
1 teaspoon sugar

Combine all ingredients in serving pitcher. Set aside.

Beef and vegetables for Sukiyaki

½ cup raw cellophane noodles
2 pounds top sirloin or tenderloin, sliced in paper-thin 1 x 2-inch strips
2 large onions, halved and sliced thin, crosswise
1 4-ounce can water chestnuts, drained and sliced

1 8-ounce can bamboo shoots, sliced
2 cups celery, sliced
¼ pound mushrooms sliced, or 1 4-ounce can mushroom pieces
½ pound spinach, stemmed
2 tablespoons peanut oil, suet or other shortening

Cover cellophane noodles with boiling water; let stand 5 minutes to soften. Drain and heat with cooked Sukiyaki.

Prepare about a quarter of the mixture at a time unless your skillet is unusually large. Heat shortening in skillet; add beef and stir-fry quickly. Put meat to one side in skillet and add vegetables in separate mounds. Pour a proportionate amount of cooking mixture over skillet contents and cook over moderate heat about 10 minutes, until heated and bubbly, tossing while heating. Add noodles. Serve from skillet. Serves 6.

Vegetables may be cut up in advance. Refrigerate in plastic bags.

As the meat is sliced very thin, it needs little cooking. If you prefer less cooking of the beef, add it last.

Cellophane noodles (Shirataki) are available in Japanese stores or in some supermarkets. 3 cups fluffy rice is a good substitute.

OTHER WAYS

Omit beef — substitute 2 cups diced cooked shrimp, fresh or frozen. 1 thinly sliced green pepper may be added or substituted for another vegetable. Stemmed watercress, sliced Chinese cabbage and snow-peas are other alternates.

WINED CHERRIES

¾ cup sweet cherry or grape wine
3 tablespoons currant jelly
1 2-inch stick cinnamon
1 1-pound can bing cherries,
   drained

¼ cup slivered almonds or coarsely
   chopped pecans

Combine wine, jelly and cinnamon; cook rapidly for 5 minutes. Place cherries in bowl, cover with wine mixture. Sprinkle with nuts; serve hot or cold. Serves 4.

ANOTHER WAY

Add one 6-ounce can sliced peaches, drained.

TROPICAL GINGER COOKIES

1¼ cups butter
⅓ cup brown sugar
1½ cups molasses
1 egg
2 teaspoons ginger

1½ teaspoons cinnamon
1½ teaspoons allspice
5 cups sifted flour
½ cup boiling water
4 teaspoons baking soda

½ teaspoon salt

Cream butter and sugar together until light and fluffy. Add molasses and egg. Mix until very well blended. Sift spices and 2 cups flour together. Add to creamed mixture alternately with boiling water. Add another cup flour and mix well. Sift remaining 2 cups flour with baking soda and salt. Stir thoroughly into batter. Drop by tablespoonfuls on baking sheet, several inches apart. Bake in pre-heated 375° oven for 10 minutes. Cool thoroughly before storing in cooky jar. Makes about 4 dozen.

QUICK ALTERNATE

Sugar Nut Rolls

Theory has it that a cook's formula should be secretly involved. This time-saving simplicity offers deliciousness proving there are exceptions to every rule.

8 brown and serve butterflake rolls	2 tablespoons butter
¼ cup brown sugar	⅓ cup chopped pecans or walnuts
	¼ cup raisins

Spread leaves of rolls apart to about ½-inch depth. Combine sugar and butter in small saucepan and heat until sugar dissolves. Tuck nuts and raisins proportionately between separated sections of rolls; place on greased baking sheet and pour syrup over each. Bake in preheated 375° oven 15 minutes or until lightly browned. Serve immediately, while very hot. Makes 8 rolls.

Prepare the rolls ahead of time and bake and reheat or arrange them and heat before serving.

▶ Lemon Baked Sirloin Steak

Lemon Baked Sirloin Steak
Savory Mashed Potatoes   Italian Asparagus
Chocolate Fondue

COOKING COUNTDOWN

60 minutes ▶ bake sirloin steak

—

▶ chill salad greens; chill asparagus

—

50 ▶ make dressing

—

▶

—

40 ▶ cook potatoes

—

▶

—

30 ▶ prepare chocolate fondue and dippers

—

▶

—

20 ▶ assemble salad

—

▶ beat potatoes

—

10 ▶ heat chocolate fondue

—

▶

—

0 ▶ serve

LEMON BAKED SIRLOIN STEAK

This recipe for the ultra-tender sirloin steak has been fashioned in many formats, all similar. This one is a delicious combination resulting in well-sauced beef.

3 pounds sirloin steak, about ½ inch thick	1 cup chili sauce
1 tablespoon butter	2 tablespoons Worcestershire
1 medium onion, thinly sliced	¼ cup water
1 medium lemon, thinly sliced	½ teaspoon salt
	dash cayenne (optional)

Place steak in shallow pan; dot with butter; cover with onion and lemon slices. Combine remaining ingredients; pour over steak. Bake in preheated 400° oven 45 minutes for rare, 55 for medium and 65 minutes for well done, basting 2 or 3 times. If steak becomes too brown, cover lightly with foil. Cut a tiny slice to determine doneness. Serves 4 to 6.

As always, the oven thermometer is invaluable; place in fleshy part of steak. Do not touch bone and keep clear of bottom of pan.

ANOTHER WAY

The same recipe may be deliciously applied to the budget-wise chuck steak.

Place a 3½-pound chuck or blade-cut pot roast on large sheet of foil. Season and top as for sirloin steak; seal foil tightly, allowing air space in package. Place in roasting pan and bake in preheated 350° oven 2½ hours. Open foil or remove cover and allow to cook an additional 30 minutes or until tender and browned. Serves 6.

SAVORY MASHED POTATOES

4 medium white potatoes, peeled and quartered	1 teaspoon salt
	¼ cup milk
1 small onion, quartered	2 tablespoons butter
	paprika

Place potatoes, onion and salt in saucepan. Add sufficient water to cover. Boil gently until fork tender, about 20 minutes. Drain well and discard onion. Beat well with electric mixer, adding milk and butter gradually until potatoes are light and fluffy. Taste to see if more salt is needed. Place pot over hot water until ready to serve. Pile in bowl and dust with paprika. Serves 4.

ANOTHER WAY

Instant Savory Mashed Potatoes

Prepare 4 servings instant mashed potatoes according to package directions. Mix in ½ teaspoon onion powder and 1 teaspoon frozen chives. Place saucepan over hot water until serving time. Heap in bowl, sprinkle with additional chives, if desired. Serves 4.

ITALIAN ASPARAGUS

1 1-pound can green or white as-   1 head curly endive
   paragus spears, drained   Italian Dressing

Chill asparagus; wash endive, removing all discolored leaves. Wrap in paper toweling and chill. To serve, arrange endive on 4 individual salad plates. Top with 3 asparagus spears; pour 2 tablespoons Italian Dressing over each. Serves 4.

Italian Dressing

   ½ cup prepared Italian dressing   1 teaspoon snipped fresh dill or
   1 tablespoon sweet pickle relish   dill weed
   2 tablespoons chopped pimiento

Combine all ingredients and shake until well blended. Shake again just before serving.

CHOCOLATE FONDUE

12 ounces milk chocolate or semi-
sweet chocolate pieces
¾ cup heavy cream

¼ cup kirsch, Cointreau or other
liqueur
dippers: fruits and cakes

Combine chocolate and cream in top of double boiler; place over hot, but not boiling water, stirring until chocolate melts. Stir in liqueur and pour into small chafing dish or saucepan and place over candle warmer or other low heat to keep warm. Arrange dippers attractively on tray and serve with skewers of bamboo or with fondue forks. Let each guest choose his preference to dip into the chocolate. It's fun and will serve 6. If it seems to be running short a quick dash to the kitchen can supply more in a jiffy.

Select three or more of the following dippers, which should be chilled before serving. When the heated chocolate meets the cold dippers it "freezes."

1 pint strawberries, hulled
2 medium bananas, cut in ½-inch
slices

2 cups cubed pineapple
1 cake layer, cut in 1-inch cubes
tiny cream puffs

Use others of your choice which you may find interesting and appetizing.

► Steak Dinner U.S.A.

Broiled Porterhouse or *Sirloin Steak*   *Bercy Butter*
Julienne Potatoes   Stewed Crouton Tomatoes
Green Salad Trio, Italian Dressing
Whipped Pumpkin Pie or *Double Orange Sherbet*

COOKING COUNTDOWN

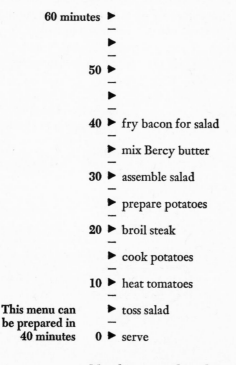

60 minutes ►
—
►
—
50 ►
—
►
—
40 ► fry bacon for salad
—
► mix Bercy butter
—
30 ► assemble salad
—
► prepare potatoes
—
20 ► broil steak
—
► cook potatoes
—
10 ► heat tomatoes
—
This menu can   ► toss salad
be prepared in   —
40 minutes   0 ► serve

Must be prepared in advance:
Whipped Pumpkin Pie

BROILED STEAK

"Please, Mrs. H., how do you really broil a steak?" The question was once asked of me by a charming and sophisticated young man who delights in cooking and serving simple, elegant dinners. A glance at his woebegone expression assured me he was in earnest and that the procedure was a matter of apprehension.

So here are some condensed rules for all of you who say a small prayer as you close the oven door on your sirloin or porterhouse steak.

1. If steak has a thick rim of fat, slash the rim at 2-inch intervals to avoid "curling."

2. Preheat the broiler.

3. Place the steak on the broiler rack.
    a. Do not season until later.
    b. Place a 1-inch steak 3 inches from heat.
    c. Place a thicker steak 5 inches from heat.

4. Broil one side to your taste according to chart below; steak should be brown. Season, turn on other side; broil same length of time.

5. For seasoning, sprinkle with seasoned salt or powdered beef seasoning, about one teaspoon per pound. A dusting of garlic or onion powder is flavorful, too, if it is to your liking. I dust on a sprinkling, and pop it back under the broiler for a few seconds to absorb the flavor, and turn it over. For a crusty steak, coat heavily with paprika before placing in broiler.

6. After steak has broiled total time, season second side.

7. Remove to a hot platter; add a lump or two of butter, letting it melt over surface; serve at once.

8. For a completely frozen steak, allow ⅓ to ½ again as much time.

9. Broiling thermometers are available in specialty departments.

But a roasting thermometer may be used effectively for broiling; when your clock says time is up, slide broiler rack away from heat and insert thermometer in thick part of steak, being certain not to touch the bone. It will respond immediately.

Time Chart for Broiled Steaks

Approximate time for each side:

size	rare	medium	well done	thermometer
1 inch	5 min.	7 min.	8 to 9 min.	130°
1½ inches	9 min.	10 min.	13 min.	140°
2 inches	15 min.	18 min.	20 min.	160°

The amount of steak to be served always poses a problem. Are you hale and hearty eaters, or will a smaller amount prove sufficient? With a large steak one can visualize the portions and judge their adequacy. As a rule, *8 ounces is a serving*, but when buying individual steaks, such as strip, club, or tenderloin, allow one steak per person. Depend on your market attendant to cut the correct amount. When carving a large steak, cut it with the grain, contrary to the usual rule.

Bercy Butter for Steak

⅓ cup white wine	1 tablespoon meat extract paste
1 tablespoon minced shallots	⅓ cup butter
1 tablespoon minced parsley	dash pepper

Boil wine with shallots and meat extract until reduced to about one half. Cool. Cream with butter, parsley and pepper. Adjust salt and refrigerate. Slice thinly onto broiled meat.

May be prepared early in the day.

Garlic Butter

Combine ½ cup softened butter with 1 clove minced garlic or ½ teaspoon garlic powder. Form into a roll and refrigerate. Slice a ¼-inch piece over steak as you place it on the platter.

BUTTER SAUCE ALTERNATIVES

Parsley Butter is made by adding 1 tablespoon snipped parsley to softened butter. Chive Butter is made by adding 1 tablespoon snipped chives to softened butter. Add other herbs, such as oregano, thyme, or basil to taste.

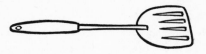

JULIENNE FRIED POTATOES

> Pray for peace and grace and spiritual food
> For wisdom and guidance, for all these are good,
> But don't forget the potatoes.
>
> JOHN TYLER PETTEE

For me, the lowly potato often soars to heights of superb culinary compositions and I am certain many others share this enjoyment. Here's a recipe, German in its basic plan, with a number of variations.

1. Basic Recipe

¼ cup butter	¾ teaspoon salt
4 medium potatoes, cut in ¼-inch strips	⅛ teaspoon pepper

Heat butter in skillet (the non-stick skillet makes for easy removal); add potatoes in one layer, pressing down to make them stick together. Dust with salt and pepper and cook covered, over moderate heat about 15 minutes until tender and browned on bottom. Turn over onto platter. Serves 4.

2. Julienne Fried Onions and Potatoes

To the basic recipe add 1 medium onion, coarsely chopped; if you wish, 1 teaspoon caraway seeds. My very favorite combination.

3. Quick Fried Julienne Potatoes

Instead of the raw potatoes, use cooked, sliced potatoes and proceed as above, cooking about 5 minutes, uncovered, until browned. You may use higher heat with cooked potatoes. Again, don't forget to press down with a wooden spoon or spatula occasionally to form a pancake-like result. Use this recipe for leftover potatoes.

4. Julienne Fried Potato Dinner

To any of the recipes, add 1 cup ham or 4 slices diced bacon, partially cooked. Toss with potatoes before placing in skillet.

QUICK ALTERNATE

Heat a can of prepared shoestring potatoes or drain a 1-pound can of small whole potatoes and brown them quickly in 2 tablespoons of butter.

STEWED CROUTON TOMATOES

Another simple selection.

2 1-pound cans stewed tomatoes   1 teaspoon butter
                       1 cup prepared croutons

Heat tomatoes and butter in saucepan; check for additional salt. Serve in small side dishes and top each with croutons. Serves 4 to 5.

GREEN SALAD TRIO

The bacon may be omitted. The crisp greens suffice.

1 head Boston lettuce   ½ cup Italian dressing, prepared
1 pound crisp fresh spinach   or from a dry mix
1 cucumber, sliced
4 slices crisp bacon, crumbled
   (optional)

Wash lettuce and spinach; remove coarse stems from spinach and tear both greens into bite-sized pieces. Add cucumber; refrigerate until serving. Toss with dressing, your own or prepared, and sprinkle with bacon if desired. Serves 4 to 6.

WHIPPED PUMPKIN PIE

Really modern but with old-time flavor.

1 3¾-ounce package vanilla whipped dessert mix
1 teaspoon pumpkin pie spice
½ cup cold milk
1¼ cups canned pumpkin, chilled
2 egg whites
dash salt

¼ cup sugar
1 prepared graham cracker crust or your preparation of baked or crumb crusts (recipes below)
whipped cream or whipped dessert topping mix

Place dessert mix and spice in bowl of electric mixer; add milk and blend at low speed. Increase speed to high and whip 3 minutes, scraping down sides of bowl often with rubber spatula. Blend in pumpkin, then beat at high speed 3 minutes and set aside. Beat egg whites until foamy; add salt and sugar gradually, about 1 tablespoon at a time, beating well after each addition until soft peaks form when beaters are raised. Fold into pumpkin mixture, blending well and push into pie crust, spreading evenly. Refrigerate a minimum of 3 hours. Serve with a rim of whipped cream or topping. Serves 6. Substitute ¼ teaspoon each of ginger, cinnamon, nutmeg and cloves, for pumpkin pie spice.

Unbaked Crumb Crust for 9-inch Pie

1⅓ cups fine crumbs (see note below)
¼ cup sugar

¼ cup softened butter or margarine
dash salt

Combine all ingredients and mix very well. Press firmly into sides and bottom of pie pan with fingers or back of spoon. Chill well before filling.

Baked Crumb Crust

Line pie pan with crumb mixture and bake in preheated 375° oven for 8 minutes. Cool.

Note: use vanilla wafers, graham crackers, zwieback, chocolate wafers, shortbread cookies, crackers, gingersnaps or others of your selection. A wide variety may be used.

Coconut Crust

> 2 cups flaked or shredded coconut
> ¼ cup melted butter

Combine coconut and butter; press evenly into 8 or 9-inch pie pan. Bake 20 to 30 minutes in 300° oven until golden in color.

QUICK ALTERNATE

Scooped orange sherbet, sauced with Cointreau or orange liqueur.

▶ V.I.P. Beef Tenderloin

Caviar Garni
V.I.P. Beef Tenderloin   Whipped Horseradish Cream
Parslied Potatoes   Carrots Glacé   Green Goddess Salad
Pear Custard Royale

COOKING COUNTDOWN

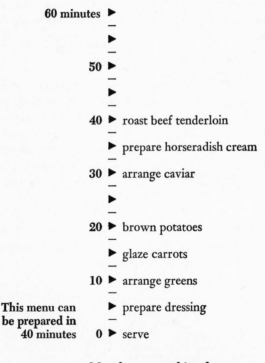

60 minutes ▶

▶

50 ▶

▶

40 ▶ roast beef tenderloin

▶ prepare horseradish cream

30 ▶ arrange caviar

▶

20 ▶ brown potatoes

▶ glaze carrots

10 ▶ arrange greens

This menu can
be prepared in   ▶ prepare dressing
40 minutes   0 ▶ serve

Must be prepared in advance:
Pear Custard Royale

CAVIAR GARNI

Caviar is a classic appetizer of ancient origin that may be served in various ways and with various condiments. The following assortment is one of the most popular.

3 2-ounce jars black caviar, domestic or imported
1 onion, finely chopped
1 cup sour cream

1 lemon, cut in 6 wedges
2 hard-cooked eggs, whites and yolks sieved separately
cocktail rye bread

Place bowl of caviar in center of a doily-lined tray. Arrange 2 or more of the accompaniments of your choice in small bowls around it. Circle with cocktail rye. For our taste, the onion and lemon are essentials and the others a matter of choice. Serves 6 to 8.

OTHER WAYS

Ice Ring for Caviar — This simple "cooler" is always a conversation piece. Use a 4-cup ring mold with center opening large enough to hold a small bowl. Try one for size. Fill mold with water and freeze. To serve, dip mold quickly in hot water and turn ice out on small platter with a rim, to catch water as ice ring melts slightly. Place bowl in center and fill with caviar. Place small platter on lazy Susan or larger platter and arrange accompaniments around the ice ring.

ANOTHER WAY

Ice Ring for Shrimp or Other Seafood — Fill center bowl with dressing and place shrimp on platter around ice ring; appetizing and practical as shrimp remain at chilled temperature.

V. I. P. BEEF TENDERLOIN

Beef tenderloin is an ultimate selection for a dinner party menu. Few dishes can boast such elegance of service combined with simplicity of preparation, both joys to a hostess's heart.

1 4-pound beef tenderloin	½ teaspoon freshly ground pepper
1 teaspoon celery salt	1 cup chili sauce
1 teaspoon salt	1 small onion, grated

3 tablespoons butter

Tuck ends of tenderloin underneath to make an even roll. Sprinkle with celery salt, salt and pepper. Spread evenly with chili sauce which has been combined with the onion; dot with butter. Place in preheated 425° oven and bake 35 to 40 minutes. It must not be cooked longer than 40 minutes; it is at its best when it is rare. Remove to platter and cut in 1-inch-thick slices. Pour pan juices over all and border with alternate arrangement of Parslied Potatoes and Carrots Glacé. Serves 8 to 10.

WHIPPED HORSERADISH CREAM

1 5-ounce jar horseradish, drained well	2 tablespoons sour cream
	1 tablespoon sugar
1 tablespoon tarragon vinegar	½ teaspoon salt

1 cup whipping cream, whipped

Drain horseradish thoroughly, through strainer; mix with vinegar, sour cream, sugar and salt, blending well. Fold into whipped cream. Makes about 3 cups.

Delicious with meat or fish.

PARSLIED POTATOES

¼ cup butter
1 teaspoon salt
1 teaspoon parsley flakes

2 1-pound cans new potatoes, drained

Heat butter in frying pan. Mix with salt and parsley flakes. Add potatoes and toss over moderate heat until evenly browned. Serves 8.

CARROTS GLACÉ

2 1-pound jars medium-sized whole carrots, drained
2 tablespoons butter or margarine

3 tablespoons brown sugar
2 tablespoons lemon juice

Combine carrots with remaining ingredients in a skillet. Mix well so carrots are coated. Cook over high heat until shiny and glazed, turning frequently, for about 5 minutes. Serves 8.

GREEN GODDESS SALAD

2 quarts assorted salad greens
Green Goddess Dressing

Have your greens thoroughly chilled and crisp; toss with dressing just before serving. Serves 8.

Green Goddess Dressing

½ cup mayonnaise
¼ cup dried parsley flakes
¼ cup sour cream
2 tablespoons tarragon vinegar

2 teaspoons lemon juice
4 heaping teaspoons anchovy paste
½ teaspoon garlic powder

Mix all ingredients together and let stand in refrigerator before serving.

May be prepared a maximum of 4 days in advance.

PEAR CUSTARD ROYALE

¼ teaspoon cinnamon
½ teaspoon rum extract
 1 2¾-ounce package egg custard
    mix

dash salt
 8 canned pear halves, drained
 2 tablespoons candied ginger,
    finely chopped

shaved semi-sweet chocolate

Combine cinnamon, rum extract, custard mix and salt. Prepare custard according to package directions. (This may be done early in the day or on the previous day.) Pour into 1-quart ovenware serving casserole; cover and chill. Just before serving, arrange pears, spoke-like, on custard, hollow side up, and fill each hollow with 1 teaspoon ginger. Shave chocolate with vegetable peeler directly onto pears. Serves 6.

This dish is most attractive when the custard comes to the rim of the dish and the pattern of the pears is visible. If you do not have a shallow ovenware serving dish, use a 9-inch cake or pie pan and cover completely with aluminum foil. To serve, place it on a compatible tray.

▶ Chafing Dish Dinner for Two

Steak Diana   Duchess Potatoes
Green Beans Almondine   Endive Salad
Cognac Cream

COOKING COUNTDOWN

60 minutes ▶
—
▶
—
50 ▶ prepare dessert fruit

▶ prepare potatoes
—
40 ▶
—
▶ arrange salad; chill
—
30 ▶ cook beans with almonds

▶
—
20 ▶ bake potatoes and keep warm
—
▶
—
10 ▶ cook steak Diana

This menu can   ▶
be prepared in   —
50 minutes   0 ▶ serve

Must be prepared in advance:
Cognac Cream

STEAK DIANA

Traditionally, the comparable recipe is Steak Diane, each performer usually modifying the preparation in his own fashion. By any name, it is party fare.

2 boneless 8-ounce sirloin or rib steaks, ¾ inch thick
2 tablespoons butter
2 tablespoons salad oil
1 teaspoon seasoned salt

¼ teaspoon coarsely ground pepper
2 tablespoons steak sauce
2 tablespoons cognac, warmed
2 tablespoons Chablis or sherry

1 tablespoon chopped chives, fresh or frozen

Trim steaks of all fat and pound with mallet or edge of saucer until very thin. Heat butter and oil in chafing dish or skillet; add steaks and sauté quickly over high heat until of desired doneness. Allow about 2 minutes on each side for rare, 3 minutes for medium. Dust with seasoned salt and pepper before turning steak, then dust reverse side. When browned on both sides, add steak sauce, turning steaks to blend well; pour in the warmed cognac and ignite — keep your face away from the pan as the flame is quite spectacular. When the flame dies down, remove steaks to hot platter; add Chablis to chafing dish stirring, scraping bits from bottom of pan; add chives; heat and pour over steaks. The dish deserves service with flourish. Serves 2.

For a large quantity, use a larger skillet, or two if necessary. You can best judge the proper utensil. It is a fine gourmet skillet dish.

DUCHESS POTATOES

2 servings instant mashed potatoes (1 cup)
1 tablespoon butter

1 egg yolk, beaten
½ teaspoon parsley flakes
1 tablespoon melted butter

Prepare mashed potatoes according to package directions, allowing ½ cup per serving. Combine with butter, egg yolk and parsley, blending well. Drop from tablespoon in mounds about 2 inches high onto greased baking sheet. Drizzle melted butter over potatoes and bake in preheated 450° oven for 10 to 12 minutes. The puffs may be prepared first, ready to be popped into the oven just before serving. For a very pretty look, pipe the potatoes from a pastry bag with a #9 star tip. Serves 2.

ANOTHER WAY

Use leftover mashed potatoes and proceed as above. Double the recipe without hesitation.

GREEN BEANS ALMONDINE

Prepare one 10-ounce package frozen beans with almonds according to package directions. Drain and toss with 2 tablespoons butter. Arrange on platter and border with Duchess Potatoes; dust with freshly ground pepper.

ENDIVE SALAD

1 head Bibb lettuce
1 stalk Belgian endive, cut in ½-inch slices
1 ¾-ounce jar sliced pimientos, drained

oil and vinegar dressing, prepared or your favorite recipe

Separate the lettuce leaves; wash, drain and place in plastic bag or paper toweling; refrigerate. To serve, arrange lettuce on 2 individual salad plates; spread endive over lettuce and sprinkle with pimiento. Moisten with oil and vinegar dressing. Serves 2.

COGNAC CREAM

½ pound ricotta or cream cheese
dash salt
¼ cup sugar
2 egg yolks, beaten
1 tablespoon brandy (cognac)

1 tablespoon sour cream or heavy cream
fresh or canned peach halves, raspberries or strawberries, fresh or frozen, defrosted

Combine cheese and salt in blender or bowl of mixer, preferably electric, mixing until very smooth and creamy; add sugar, eggs, cognac and cream and beat until thick and very smooth. Pour into low serving bowl and refrigerate until completely chilled, several hours or overnight. Center on platter and surround bowl with halved peaches, cut side up and filled with berries. Sauce each with Cognac Cream. Serves 4.

The cream is delicious on almost any fruit or combination; take your choice so it may best suit your menu.

For 4, use one 1-pound, 13-ounce can peaches or 7 to 8 halves drained and one 10-ounce package frozen berries, defrosted, or 1 pint fresh berries.

May be prepared the previous day.

QUICK ALTERNATE

Top fruit with one 8-ounce jar junior orange pudding (baby food). Add 1 teaspoon orange liqueur.

▶ Tournedos with Port

Tournedos with Port   Stuffed Tomatoes
Avocado and Onion Salad   Flaky Biscuits
Golden Broiled Oranges or *Poached Oranges*

COOKING COUNTDOWN

60 minutes ▶
    —
    ▶
    —
50 ▶
    —
    ▶
    —
40 ▶ prepare tomatoes
    —
    ▶ defrost vegetable; fill tomatoes
    —
30 ▶ bake tomatoes
    —
    ▶
    —
20 ▶ bake biscuits
    —
    ▶ arrange salad and dressing; refrigerate
    —
10 ▶ sauté steaks
    —
    ▶ broil oranges
This menu can be   —
prepared in 40 minutes   0 ▶ serve

Must be prepared in advance:
Golden Broiled Oranges

TOURNEDOS WITH PORT

This delicious menu is easily adaptable for 2, with beef tenderloin, the main course, prepared in the French manner.

4 filets of beef tenderloin, 1-inch thick, about 1½ pounds
2 tablespoons butter
1 teaspoon salt
¼ teaspoon coarsely ground pepper

4 slices toast
¼ cup port or other red dinner wine
1 4-ounce can mushroom stems and pieces, drained
½ cup sour or heavy cream
curly endive

Place filets in skillet in well-heated butter and sauté quickly at high heat for 3 minutes; sprinkle with ½ the salt and pepper and turn to sauté reverse side for 3 minutes; sprinkle with remaining salt and pepper. (At 3 minutes on each side, the filets will be rare; for medium, sauté them 4 minutes on each side.) Arrange toast on platter. Stack sautéed filets on one side of pan and add wine and mushrooms, stirring quickly; reduce heat and place a filet on each slice of toast. Add cream to wine mixture in pan and heat well over moderate heat, but do not boil. Pour immediately over filets and serve at once. The platter may be bordered with Stuffed Tomatoes, and a fringe of curly endive. Serves 4.

STUFFED TOMATOES

Modern convenience makes this glamorous-looking vegetable a simplicity of preparation.

4 firm medium-sized tomatoes
1 10-ounce package green beans in mushroom sauce

onion or garlic salt
1 tablespoon grated Parmesan cheese
1 teaspoon butter

Cut out the tops of tomatoes, removing stem end; carefully scoop out pulp and seeds and turn upside down to drain. Place plastic bag of vegetables in boiling water just long enough to defrost slightly.

Dust inside of tomatoes with preferred salt and fill with defrosted vegetables. Top with cheese and a dot of butter; bake in preheated 350° oven 30 minutes. Serves 4.

It is difficult to ascertain the number of tomatoes one package fills, as sizes of tomatoes vary. If any sauced vegetable remains, save it for the next day's lunch.

ANOTHER WAY

Any variety of frozen sauced vegetables may be used; there are spinach in cream sauce, peas in cheese sauce and sauced onions among others.

AVOCADO AND ONION SALAD

1 head Boston or small iceberg lettuce	1 avocado, peeled, cubed
	1 sweet red onion, thinly sliced

Oil and Vinegar Dressing (prepared, if desired)

Wash and drain lettuce; tear into bite-sized pieces and pile in small salad bowl. Add avocado and onion slices; dress with Oil and Vinegar Dressing and toss lightly. Serves 4.

Oil and Vinegar Dressing

6 tablespoons salad or olive oil	⅛ teaspoon freshly ground pepper
2 tablespoons wine vinegar	¾ teaspoon salt
	½ teaspoon paprika

Combine and mix until well blended. Makes ½ cup.

FLAKY BISCUITS

1 10-ounce package flaky biscuits

Select one 10-ounce package flaky biscuits from the refrigerator case in your market. Bake according to directions on package and serve piping hot with butter and jam.

GOLDEN BROILED ORANGES

An elegant dessert, simply prepared.

6 large oranges

1½ cups orange juice, fresh or frozen

¼ cup water

¼ cup bourbon or apple cider

1 cup sugar

¼ cup butter or margarine, softened

2 tablespoons Cointreau (optional)

Peel rind of 3 oranges very thin without cutting into white membrane; cut peelings with scissors into 1-inch slivers; place peel in saucepan with orange juice, water, bourbon and ½ cup sugar. Bring to boiling, stirring until sugar is dissolved, then simmer 20 to 30 minutes until peel is tender; set aside. Meanwhile, peel all oranges down to pulp, removing all traces of white membrane, and place oranges upright in a shallow baking dish. Combine remaining ½ cup sugar with butter and blend until creamy. Top each orange with mixture and place in broiler, about 6 inches from heat. Broil 10 minutes, basting with butter mixture as it melts, until oranges are glazed. Remove to serving dish or individual dessert plates or low bowls; pour over each the reserved warm orange peel sauce and a teaspoon of Cointreau. Serves 6.

OTHER WAYS

The sauce is sufficient for 8 oranges if you wish to increase the servings. The oranges may be served hot or cold. Make them in advance, place in serving dishes, dress with sauce and refrigerate — all set for service. Or they may be made in advance, reheated under the broiler and served with the reheated sauce.

QUICK ALTERNATE

Poached Oranges

A similar recipe with fewer ingredients.

Combine 1½ cups orange juice, ¼ cup water, ¼ cup bourbon, and ½ cup sugar in saucepan; bring to boiling and add 6 large peeled oranges. Simmer very slowly for 10 minutes, basting continually. Remove from heat to shallow dish; add 2 tablespoons Cointreau to orange syrup in pan, then pour over oranges. Cool; refrigerate until thoroughly chilled, or serve at room temperature.

▶ Steak au Poivre

Steak au Poivre   Potato Soufflé
Épinards et Ail (Spinach with Garlic)
Mock Marrons Glacés

COOKING COUNTDOWN

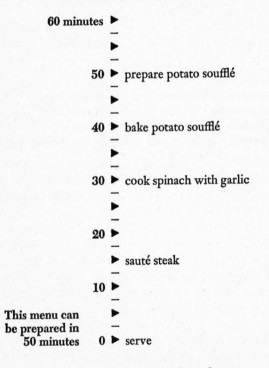

60 minutes ▶
— ▶

50 ▶ prepare potato soufflé
— ▶

40 ▶ bake potato soufflé
— ▶

30 ▶ cook spinach with garlic
— ▶

20 ▶
— ▶ sauté steak
—
10 ▶

This menu can — ▶
be prepared in —
50 minutes   0 ▶ serve

Must be prepared in advance:
Mock Marrons Glacés

STEAK AU POIVRE
(Peppered Steak)

Don't let the elaborate name deter you, for this recipe is simplicity itself. In discussing its preparation with the maître d'hôtel of one of our fine restaurants, I was interested to learn that it is a modern recipe and hence not found in most classic French cookbooks. That may account for the large number of people who claim proprietary rights to this succulent dish, one that requires a minimum of effort and affords a maximum of taste. The secret of the flavor is in the crushed peppercorns. Use either a mortar and pestle or a pepper mill. Coarsely ground pepper from the supermarket is good although the flavor is not as distinctive. This recipe is for one steak which will serve one person.

1 6-ounce tenderloin, Delmonico or New York cut steak	2 tablespoons butter
1 teaspoon crushed peppercorns or coarsely ground pepper	¼ cup dry red wine
	¼ cup cream
	1 tablespoon brandy (optional)

Press ½ teaspoon crushed pepper into each side of steak with heel of hand. Heat butter, add steak and sear quickly on both sides. Reduce heat and sauté about 5 minutes on each side; it will be rare. Cook longer depending on the degree of doneness you prefer. (Make a tiny gash to test.) Remove to warm platter; add wine to skillet mixing well blending with brown bits in pan. Add cream and stir until well heated. Pour immediately over steak and serve at once. For flair, pour warmed brandy over the steak, before adding sauce. Ignite the brandy and the spooned sauce will be an extinguisher. Prepare as many steaks as needed, using two skillets, if necessary. Serves 1.

Note: The various names of cuts of steaks are a matter of geography, so we have offered a choice, even though they may be duplicates.

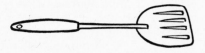

POTATO SOUFFLÉ

1 package instant mashed potatoes	1 teaspoon salt
	¼ teaspoon paprika
6 tablespoons grated Herkimer cheese or Cheddar cheese	4 egg yolks
	⅔ cup heavy cream
2 tablespoons grated onion	4 egg whites, stiffly beaten

Prepare potatoes according to package directions. Add cheese, onion, salt, paprika, egg yolks and cream. Beat thoroughly until smooth and thick. Egg whites must be stiff but not dry; fold into potato mixture until blended and smooth. Turn into 6-cup well-buttered soufflé dish or casserole. Place in preheated 350° oven and bake 35 to 40 minutes or until evenly browned and set. Serve at once to 6.

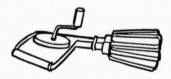

ÉPINARDS ET AIL
(Spinach with Garlic)

Spinach and garlic are wonderful teammates. Garlic being a matter of taste, we suggest that you use the minimum amount first and add more as your palate dictates.

2 10-ounce packages chopped frozen spinach	½ teaspoon salt
	½ to 1 teaspoon garlic powder
1 10-ounce can cream of mushroom soup	

Cook spinach according to package directions; drain, pressing out all excess moisture. Blend with mushroom soup, salt and garlic powder. Heat thoroughly. Serves 6.

MOCK MARRONS GLACÉS

The combination of ice cream and nutty cereal is delicately deceiving; it is a suave finale. Have it on hand for that unexpected dinner.

1 pint vanilla ice cream, softened
¼ cup grape nuts cereal
2 tablespoons light rum (optional) or ½ teaspoon almond flavoring

6 2-inch foil baking cups
2 tablespoons slivered almonds
whipped cream, from a pressurized can
candied cherries, for decoration

Blend ice cream, cereal and rum together. Spoon into foil baking cups; place filled cups in muffin pans to hold shape until frozen. Sprinkle with almonds; freeze until serving. A topping of cream and candied cherry gives a festive look. Serves 6.

ANOTHER WAY

Double the quantity; freeze in a 3-cup mold. Turn out and decorate with cherries and whipped cream.

Must be prepared 4 to 5 hours in advance. May be on hand in freezer for several weeks; store in plastic wrap.

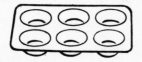

▶ Deviled Flank Steak

Deviled Flank Steak   *Noodles Romanoff*
Rosy Fruit Compote   *Brandy Custard*

COOKING COUNTDOWN

60 minutes ▶ combine barbecue sauce ingredients;
  —   marinate steak
        ▶
  —
50 ▶ cook custard; refrigerate
  —
        ▶
  —
40 ▶ bake compote
  —
        ▶
  —
30 ▶ combine Romanoff sauce
  —
        ▶ cook noodles; drain
  —
20 ▶
  —
        ▶ broil steak
  —
10 ▶
  —
        ▶ toss and heat noodles
  —
 0 ▶ serve

May be prepared in advance:
  Rosy Fruit Compote

DEVILED FLANK STEAK

A perennial favorite, continually growing in popularity.

1 ¾-inch flank steak, about 2   1 teaspoon seasoned meat tender-
  pounds   izer
                    Broiler Barbecue Sauce

Moisten steak and prepare with tenderizer as directed on label. Score steak lightly with a sharp knife in crisscross lines, forming 1-inch diamonds on both sides. Place in shallow baking pan. Spread Broiler Barbecue Sauce evenly over steak, marinating both sides. If you have time, let stand 1 hour or more in refrigerator. Place under preheated broiler 3 inches from heat and broil 4 to 5 minutes; turn steak and broil for 5 minutes longer. Do not cook too long as it should be rare. To serve, cut in thin diagonal slices across the grain and use pan drippings as sauce. Serves 4.

Broiler Barbecue Sauce

¾ cup barbecue sauce, prepared   ¼ teaspoon freshly ground pepper
  or your favorite recipe   1 tablespoon lemon juice
3 tablespoons steak sauce   1 tablespoon grated onion

Combine all ingredients, blending well. Makes 1¼ cups.

ANOTHER WAY

Two Alternate Marinades (also good for lamb or veal)

1. Orange Marinade

¼ cup soy sauce   1 teaspoon grated orange peel
1 garlic clove, minced, or ¼ tea- juice of orange, about ⅓ cup
  spoon garlic powder

Combine all ingredients, blending well. Makes about ½ cup.

2. French Dressing Marinade

To ½ cup French dressing add ½ teaspoon onion flakes and ½ teaspoon Worcestershire, blending well. Makes about ½ cup.

If possible, allow marinated meat to stand in refrigerator, for a length of time. It is simple to prepare it the previous night so it will stand for several hours; if it suits your convenience.

NOODLES ROMANOFF

1 8-ounce package medium noodles, cooked
Sauce à la Romanoff

Cook noodles according to package directions and rinse in hot water; drain and place in saucepan. Toss with Sauce à la Romanoff and heat slowly but well. Do not boil. Serves 4.

Sauce à la Romanoff

This simple sauce could have been detailed with the noodle recipe, but it is separated so you may use it over fish or salads. Served hot or cold, it is excellent.

1 cup sour cream   ¼ teaspoon garlic powder
1 teaspoon Worcestershire

Combine all ingredients, blending well. To serve hot, heat slowly and do not boil. Makes 1 cup.

ROSY FRUIT COMPOTE

The effort does not warrant the raves this compote receives; it is a hostess's delight.

1 1-pound 13-ounce can peach halves, drained	1 10-ounce can pineapple chunks, drained
1 1-pound can apricot halves, drained	1 10-ounce can Mandarin oranges, drained

1 1-pound can cherry pie filling

Combine well-drained fruits with cherry pie filling. Place in 1½ quart casserole and bake in preheated 350° oven for 30 minutes or until hot and bubbly. Serve hot in individual compotes. Serves 6 to 8.

May be prepared a day or two in advance, refrigerate. Reheat if desired.

The leftover compote keeps well a week or more.

BRANDY CUSTARD

1 4-ounce package vanilla pudding or pie filling mix   2 cups milk less 1 tablespoon
1 tablespoon brandy or cognac
nutmeg or whipped cream

Prepare pudding with milk according to package directions; allow to cool 5 minutes, then stir in brandy. Pour into 4 dessert cups or one 3-cup bowl. To serve, dust with nutmeg or top with a ribbon of cream from a pressurized can. Serves 4.

▶ Cheesed Cube Steaks

Cheesed Cube Steaks   Dilled Beans and Water Chestnuts
Accordion Cucumbers
Cherry Cobbler

COOKING COUNTDOWN

60 minutes ▶ bake cherry cobbler
—
▶
—
50 ▶
—
▶
—
40 ▶ marinate steaks
—
▶
—
30 ▶ slice and arrange cucumbers
—
▶
—
20 ▶ cook beans; combine with water chestnuts
—
▶
—
10 ▶ broil steaks

This menu can be   —
prepared in 40 minutes   ▶
if dessert is prepared   —
in advance   0 ▶ serve

May be prepared in advance:
Cherry Cobbler

CHEESED CUBE STEAKS

Economy with taste. The night I tested this recipe, we had unexpected guests. The result was approved by a show of cleaned plates, and I give you their recommendation.

4 cube steaks
½ cup prepared Italian dressing
1 tablespoon Worcestershire
½ teaspoon onion powder

4 slices processed American cheese
(optional)
parsley

Place the steaks in a shallow container. Combine dressing, Worcestershire and onion powder; pour over the steaks, turning them to coat completely with the mixture. Allow to stand 30 minutes, though they may marinate several hours if you wish to prepare them in advance. Place the steaks on a foil-covered cooky sheet and set 3 inches from preheated broiler. Broil 2 minutes and turn on other side; baste with pan drippings and broil 1 minute. Cover with sliced cheese and broil another minute until cheese is heated. If you prefer steaks rare, reduce broiling time to 1 minute on each side; baste as they are turned. Serves 4.

Individual service for the steaks is my preference. Place on heated dinner plate, adding a small amount of pan juices. Add a helping of Green Beans and Chestnuts and garnish with parsley and the Accordion Cucumbers.

Please observe the "optional" after the American cheese in the ingredients. It is a heartier dish with the cheese but very good without it.

If the occasion indicates a more choice selection of entrée, use the Cube Steak recipe but substitute another cut, such as New York cut, sirloin strips, porterhouse or sirloin steak. See chart for broiling time (page 59).

DILLED BEANS AND WATER CHESTNUTS

1 10-ounce package frozen green beans or 1 pound fresh green beans
1 4-ounce can water chestnuts, sliced and drained
1 teaspoon fresh dill or ½ teaspoon dill weed
2 tablespoons butter
freshly ground pepper

Cook beans according to package directions (if frozen) and drain; add chestnuts, dill and butter and shake over heat until butter is melted and vegetables are thoroughly heated. Turn into serving dish and sprinkle with ground pepper. Serves 4.

To cook fresh green beans, wash and cut into 1-inch lengths or "French cut" by slitting length of bean. Drop into boiling salted water, to a depth of 1 inch; use ½ teaspoon salt per cup of water. Simmer about 15 to 20 minutes or until done to your taste. For crisp vegetables, do a little testing on your own and find your preferred time.

Incidentally, 1 pound of fresh green beans will yield about 3 cups cooked. Though a recommended serving for a 10-ounce package of frozen vegetables is for 4, these are not generous. Here, too, you will learn best by simple experimentation.

ACCORDION CUCUMBERS

2 medium cucumbers
6 to 8 red radishes, thinly sliced

Peel cucumbers and cut into 2-inch lengths, then cut slits ¼ inch apart, about ½ inch deep through the length. Into each slit slip a slice of red radish, opening the cucumber sections, accordion-like. Makes about 8 sections.

Use them as a garnish. They may be marinated with an oil and vinegar dressing and used as a relish, if you wish, or as a salad on a bed of lettuce. The "accordion" makes a simple attractive arrangement. Serves 4.

CHERRY COBBLER

2 1-pound 5-ounce cans cherry   ¼ cup red cinnamon candies
  pie filling   1 10-ounce package pie crust mix
         ½ cup brown sugar, firmly packed

Combine pie filling with candies in a saucepan and simmer 5 minutes, stirring frequently. Measure ⅓ cup of the pie crust mix, firmly packed, then mix with cherry filling. Spread over bottom of 9-inch square baking pan. Blend remaining pie crust mix with brown sugar and sprinkle evenly over filling. Bake in preheated 400° oven 35 to 40 minutes or until filling is bubbly. If crumbs become too brown, cover lightly with foil. Serves 6.

May be prepared in advance; reheat and serve.

▶ B and B Pot Roast

B and B Pot Roast   Lazy Susan Baked Potatoes
Broccoli Bonanza   Tossed Salad with Roquefort Dressing
Haig's Strawberry Pie

COOKING COUNTDOWN

60 minutes ▶ bake potatoes
—
▶ prepare pie
—
50 ▶
—
▶ barbecue or broil beef
—
40 ▶ prepare dressing
—
▶
—
30 ▶ cook broccoli
—
▶ assemble casserole
—
20 ▶ bake broccoli
—
▶ arrange salad
—
10 ▶ arrange lazy Susan for potatoes
—
▶
—
0 ▶ serve

May be prepared in advance:
Roquefort Dressing
Haig's Strawberry Pie

B AND B POT ROAST

Bourbon gives unusual flavor to this bountiful barbecue roast.

1 4- to 5-pound pot roast, 1½-inch-thick blade cut or round bone
2 teaspoons meat tenderizer
¼ cup bourbon
1¼ cups water
¼ cup dark brown sugar
½ teaspoon seasoned pepper
2 teaspoons salt

For barbecue, grill or oven broiling, have the meat cut about 1½ inches thick. Wipe with paper toweling and remove excess fat to prevent unnecessary sputtering. Sprinkle with tenderizer, used according to directions on container. Combine remaining ingredients in large bowl; add beef; moisten completely and refrigerate from 5 to 24 hours, turning occasionally.

To barbecue

When coals are ready, place drained beef on grill and roast 20 minutes on each side; it will be rare, but very tender. Make a slit in meat with a sharp pointed knife to test for doneness and grill additional time, if you prefer well-done roast. Serves 6 to 8.

For crust with flavor, spread with thick paste of prepared mustard and coarse salt, on one side. Place on grill with mustard side down and roast as above, spreading second side after 20 minutes. Turn and roast additional 20 minutes or longer.

Either cut of pot roast has good flavor but the round bone may be sliced more evenly.

To broil

Prepare meat with tenderizer and marinade as for barbecue. Move broiler rack to lowest position; to preheat turn broiler heat unit to highest control. Drain roast and wipe with paper toweling; place on broiler pan and put in oven on rack. Broil 20 minutes on each side for rare roast; check by making a slit in meat with sharp pointed knife as for barbecued roast; if a more well-done roast is desired, continue to broil until done as you prefer it; check again with the knife. Serves 6 to 8.

BROCCOLI BONANZA

3 10-ounce packages frozen
chopped broccoli
1½ cups sour cream
2 tablespoons light cream
½ 1¼-ounce package onion soup
mix

½ teaspoon salt
1 3½-ounce can French fried
onion rings

Cook broccoli according to package directions, but several minutes less than time allowed; drain. Mix sour cream, cream, soup and salt. Combine with broccoli and place in 1½-quart casserole. Top with onion rings. Bake in preheated 325° oven 20 minutes. Serves 6 to 8.

LAZY SUSAN BAKED POTATOES

Bake potatoes your usual way, either in the oven or on the grill. Place a large bowl of sour cream in the center of a lazy Susan or large round platter and surround with an assortment of do-it-yourself toppings. Following is a list of suggestions — use any or all, or any others you may prefer.

shredded Cheddar cheese
crumbled blue cheese
chopped bacon
chives
chopped stuffed green olives
chopped nuts (peanuts are good)

QUICK ALTERNATE

Drain three 1-pound cans small, whole potatoes; sauté in 2 tablespoons butter and ½ teaspoon dry mustard, tossing until crusty brown. Serves 6 to 8.

ROQUEFORT DRESSING

For the salad, make your selection of favorite greens.

1 4-ounce package Roquefort cheese
¼ teaspoon garlic salt
¼ teaspoon onion salt

¼ teaspoon Worcestershire
¼ cup mayonnaise
1 teaspoon lemon juice
1 cup sour cream

Mash half of cheese with fork. Mix remaining ingredients into mashed cheese. Crumble remaining cheese into mixture. Makes 1½ cups.

Serve over 6 cups torn greens; assorted for your preference.

HAIG'S STRAWBERRY PIE

3 tablespoons cornstarch
1 cup sugar
2 tablespoons lemon juice
1 pint strawberries, crushed
red food coloring
1 pint strawberries
1 3-ounce package cream cheese, softened

½ cup sour cream
1 prepared 9-inch graham cracker crust
1 cup whipping cream, whipped
1 3-ounce package cream cheese, softened

Mix cornstarch and sugar; stir in lemon juice and crushed berries. Cook over medium flame, stirring constantly, until thickened. Reduce flame; cook 10 minutes. Add food coloring to make color bright red. Cool; then fold in remaining berries. If they are extra large, halve them. Combine cream cheese and sour cream; spread over bottom of crust. Pour in berry mixture. Chill. Fold cream cheese into whipped cream and spread over pie. Serve to 6.

If you wish, reserve several whole berries to use as garnish. Add several sprigs of fresh mint if you have it.

To speed the chilling, place in freezer.

▶ Belgian Beef in Beer

Belgian Beef in Beer
Tomato Rice   Sauerkraut Slaw
Blueberry Cheese Cake

COOKING COUNTDOWN

60 minutes ▶ make sauerkraut slaw
—
▶
—
50 ▶ cook beef
▶
—
40 ▶ prepare cheese cake
—
▶
—
30 ▶
—
▶
—
20 ▶
—
▶
—
10 ▶ prepare tomato rice

This menu can be   —
prepared in 50 minutes   ▶
if Sauerkraut Slaw is   —
prepared in advance   **0** ▶ serve

May be prepared in advance:
Sauerkraut Slaw
Blueberry Cheese Cake

BELGIAN BEEF IN BEER

1½ pounds boneless beef, chuck or round, cut 1 inch thick
½ teaspoon meat tenderizer
2 tablespoons butter or margarine
1 12-ounce can beer
½ teaspoon thyme
½ teaspoon salt
⅛ teaspoon white pepper
1 bay leaf
1 1½-ounce package onion gravy mix
1 1-pound jar onions, drained
1 tablespoon snipped parsley

Moisten meat and sprinkle with tenderizer; prick with fork as directed. Cut beef in ½-inch slices, 2 inches long. Heat butter in saucepan and add beef, sautéing until browned. Blend in beer, thyme, salt and pepper. Bring to boiling; cover and reduce heat. Simmer 30 to 40 minutes or until tender. Stir in gravy mix and onions; cook 5 additional minutes until heated. Place on platter and sprinkle with snipped parsley. Serves 4.

TOMATO RICE

1⅓ cups tomato juice
1 teaspoon caraway seeds
1 teaspoon sugar
½ teaspoon salt
1⅓ cups precooked rice
1 tablespoon butter or margarine (optional)

Combine tomato juice, caraway seeds, sugar and salt in saucepan. Bring to boiling and stir in rice. Remove from heat; cover and let stand 5 minutes. Add butter and fluff with fork. Serves 4.

QUICK ALTERNATE

Omit Tomato Rice and substitute one 1-pound can whole potatoes, drained.

SAUERKRAUT SLAW

1 1-pound 13-ounce can sauerkraut
¾ cup sugar
⅓ cup tarragon vinegar

1 cup finely chopped onion
1 cup finely chopped green pepper
1 cup finely chopped celery
lettuce

Wash the sauerkraut in cold water, tossing to separate strands; drain
and squeeze with hands to eliminate as much moisture as possible;
place in large bowl. Combine sugar and vinegar in saucepan and
heat until sugar dissolves; add to kraut with onion, green pepper
and celery; toss until thoroughly mixed. Place in refrigerator until
well chilled. Serve from a lettuce-lined bowl or on individual lettuce
cups arranged on salad plates. Serves 6 to 8.

Vegetables may be chopped in advance; refrigerate in plastic bags.

BLUEBERRY CHEESE CAKE

Old recipes improve with age and change; here is proof.

1 recipe graham cracker pie crust
(page 62)
1 8-ounce package cream cheese
⅓ cup lemon juice

1 15-ounce can sweetened condensed milk
1 1-pound can blueberry pie filling, chilled

Prepare the crust in an 8-inch round or square baking pan, 2 inches
high. Place in refrigerator. Combine cheese, lemon juice and milk
in blender or bowl, beating until very well blended. Pour cheese
mixture into prepared crust; refrigerate for 30 minutes; spread with
blueberry filling and chill until served. Serves 8.

► Paprikash and Pasta

Beef Paprikash   Parsley Macaroni
Pearberry Salad
Mincemeat Cream Pie

COOKING COUNTDOWN

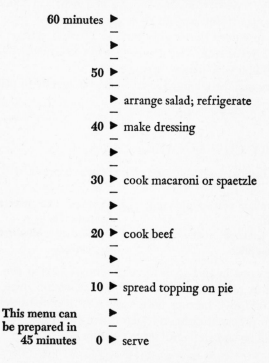

60 minutes ►
—
►
—
50 ►
—
► arrange salad; refrigerate
—
40 ► make dressing
—
►
—
30 ► cook macaroni or spaetzle
—
►
—
20 ► cook beef
—
►
—
10 ► spread topping on pie
This menu can ►
be prepared in —
45 minutes   0 ► serve

Must be prepared in advance:
Mincemeat Cream Pie

BEEF PAPRIKASH

One can't believe such a delicious dish can be prepared so quickly.

1½ pounds beef cube steaks
4 tablespoons vegetable shortening
1 clove garlic, minced, or ½ teaspoon garlic powder
1½ cups sliced onions (about 2
medium onions)

2 tablespoons paprika
1 teaspoon salt
½ teaspoon marjoram
1 10½-ounce can cream of tomato soup
1 cup sour cream

Accompaniment

1 8-ounce package elbow macaroni, cooked

3 tablespoons melted butter
2 tablespoons snipped parsley

Dry steaks with paper toweling and cut into 1-inch squares. Heat shortening in large skillet; stir in garlic and onions, then add beef. Cook over moderate heat about 10 minutes or until lightly browned and pink has disappeared from meat. Stir in paprika, salt, marjoram, tomato soup and sour cream. Simmer 5 minutes; do not boil. Toss macaroni with butter and mound on platter; cover with the goulash and garnish with parsley. Serves 4 to 5.

ANOTHER WAY

Perhaps you may like to serve this with Spaetzle which go very well with Beef Paprikash.

Spaetzle

1 egg, well beaten
⅓ cup water

¾ cup flour
½ teaspoon salt
1 tablespoon butter

Blend all ingredients well, stirring to a smooth, firm batter. Drop from a ½-teaspoon measure into boiling salted water (½ teaspoon salt to 1 cup water) and boil 10 minutes or until Spaetzle (dumplings) rise to surface and are firm. Drain and toss with butter. Makes about 2 cups.

If you like a larger dumpling, drop from a teaspoon measure.

PEARBERRY SALAD

A spicy and tart partner; try it with roast chicken or turkey, too. An attractive platter, simply prepared.

1 head Boston lettuce, washed
  and crisped
1 2-pound 10-ounce jar green

minted pear halves
1 package frozen cranberry-
  orange relish, thawed

Spicy Dressing

Separate lettuce into cups and place on platter; chill. Drain pear halves, reserving ⅓ cup of liquid. Place pear half in each lettuce cup, hollow side up; spoon cranberry relish into pear halves. Serve Spicy Dressing separately to those who wish it. Serves 6.

Spicy Dressing

¾ cup mayonnaise
⅓ cup liquid syrup from minted pears

Combine mayonnaise and pear syrup, blending well. Drizzle over salad. Makes about 1 cup.

MINCEMEAT CREAM PIE

A new twist to the traditional mincemeat pie, and a good one, too!

1 unbaked 9-inch pie shell
1 cup sour cream
3 eggs, beaten
⅓ cup light brown sugar
1 1-pound jar prepared mincemeat

2 cups diced, pared apples
3 tablespoons dark rum (optional)
Cream Topping

Make pie shell from your favorite recipe, frozen pie shell or pie crust mix. Combine all filling ingredients; pour into pie shell and place in preheated 425° oven; bake 15 minutes. Lower oven temperature to 350° and bake an additional 40 minutes, until filling is set. Cool thoroughly; spread with Cream Topping.

Prepare pie early in the day. Top before serving.

Cream Topping

1 cup sour cream
¼ cup confectioners' sugar

Combine cream and sugar and spread over cooled pie. Serves 8.

QUICK ALTERNATE

Mincemeat-Apricot Sauce on Pound Cake

4 ½-inch slices pound cake, your own or from the bakery	¾ cup apricot nectar
	1 tablespoon brown sugar
½ cup ready-to-use mincemeat	1½ teaspoons lemon juice
¼ cup chopped walnuts	

Combine all ingredients except cake in saucepan; bring to boiling and cook 5 minutes, stirring constantly. Serve warm over pound cake slices on individual dessert plates, if desired. Makes 1¼ cups. Serves 4.

The ingredients for the sauce may be doubled if more is desired.

▶ Beef and Mushrooms

Beef and Mushrooms   Quick Rice
Olive Cabbage Salad
Third Hole Chocolate Cake

COOKING COUNTDOWN

60 minutes ▶ bake cake
—
▶
—
50 ▶
—
▶
—
40 ▶ prepare salad; refrigerate
—
▶
—
30 ▶ slice vegetables for beef
—
▶
—
20 ▶
—
▶ stir-fry beef
—
10 ▶
—
**This menu can be
prepared in 40 minutes
if Quick Alternate is
used for dessert** ▶ cook rice
—
0 ▶ serve

May be prepared in advance:
Olive Cabbage Salad

BEEF AND MUSHROOMS

3 tablespoons peanut or vegetable oil
1 cup diced onions
1½ pounds tenderloin or flank steak, sliced ¼-inch thick
¼ cup soy sauce
¼ teaspoon garlic powder
½ pound mushrooms, halved
1 green pepper, cut in ¼-inch strips
2 tablespoons sherry
1 teaspoon Chinese bead molasses (optional)
2 cups rice or 1 3-ounce can Chinese noodles

Heat oil, add onions and sauté 5 minutes until tender but not brown. Add tenderloin and sauté for 5 minutes. Pour in soy sauce and dust with garlic powder; mix lightly. Add mushrooms, green pepper, sherry and molasses; cook 3 minutes until heated. Serve over 2 cups cooked rice or Chinese noodles. Serves 4.

ANOTHER WAY

Add 1 cup sliced green onions and/or one 4-ounce can water chestnuts, drained and sliced. Add with the mushrooms. I have made the bead molasses an optional ingredient. As with olives, there is always a definite "yes" or "no," and this is one instance where a matter of taste determines the choice. It is a good dish either way.

OLIVE CABBAGE SALAD

3 cups shredded cabbage
½ cup sliced celery
½ cup pimiento salad olives, coarsely chopped
½ cup mayonnaise
1 tablespoon tarragon vinegar
1 teaspoon onion salt

Toss all ingredients together lightly and refrigerate. Mix lightly before serving; pile into lettuce cups and top with pimiento olives. Serves 4.

The salad olives are available in jars; they are broken olives and some are in small enough pieces to use right from the container.

Time can be saved by purchasing the cabbage already shredded.

May be prepared early in the day.

THIRD HOLE CHOCOLATE CAKE

1½ cups sifted flour
 1 cup sugar
 3 tablespoons cocoa
 ½ teaspoon salt
 ½ teaspoon soda
 1 teaspoon vanilla

1 tablespoon white vinegar
6 tablespoons vegetable oil
1 cup water
2 1-ounce chocolate candy bars
  or 2 tablespoons sifted confectioners' sugar

Sift flour, sugar, cocoa, salt and soda in ungreased 8-inch square pan. Make three holes in dry ingredients. Put vanilla in one hole; vinegar in another and oil in another. Pour water over all and stir with a fork until smooth. Bake 40 minutes in preheated 350° oven. While cake is hot, place two candy bars on top and, as they melt, spread evenly, or dust with confectioners' sugar. Makes 9 small squares.

QUICK ALTERNATE

Though this is the quickest cake recipe imaginable, the alternate could be a can of sliced pineapple or spears of fresh pineapple, chilled — a good balance with this menu.

▶ Beef and Oyster Stew

Beef and Oyster Stew
Potato Pudding   Relish Finger Strips
Broiled Peach Cake

COOKING COUNTDOWN

60 minutes ▶ cook beef stew
▶
50 ▶ prepare and bake potato pudding
▶
40 ▶ crisp vegetable strips
▶
30 ▶
▶ arrange peach cake
20 ▶
▶
10 ▶
▶
0 ▶ serve

BEEF AND OYSTER STEW

2 pounds lean chuck cut in 1-inch cubes
1 teaspoon instant meat tenderizer
3 tablespoons flour
¼ teaspoon seasoned pepper
3 tablespoons butter or margarine
2 cups chopped onions, fresh or frozen
2 cloves garlic, minced, or ½ teaspoon garlic powder

1 cup water
1 bay leaf
1 ¾-ounce package mushroom gravy mix
1 cup water
2 4-ounce cans button mushrooms
1 1-pound can sliced carrots, drained
1 8-ounce can oysters or 12 fresh oysters
2 tablespoons chopped parsley (optional)

Brush meat with water; sprinkle with tenderizer and pierce thoroughly with sharp fork. Toss beef in flour, coating well; dust with pepper. Heat butter in skillet; add beef, onions and garlic and sauté until lightly browned, about 10 minutes. Add 1 cup water and bay leaf; cover and bring to boiling, then reduce heat and simmer 45 minutes or until tender. Check occasionally as there is tendency to stick; add water as needed. Stir gravy mix with 1 cup water and add to beef; add mushrooms, carrots and oysters; cook about 5 minutes or until oysters curl. Pour onto platter, arranging carrots attractively for color and garnish with sprinkled chopped parsley. Serves 4 to 6.

POTATO PUDDING

4 medium potatoes, peeled and grated (about 3 cups grated and drained)
3 eggs, well beaten
1 large onion, grated
1½ teaspoons salt

¼ teaspoon pepper
¼ cup melted butter or chicken fat
½ cup flour
½ teaspoon baking powder
2 tablespoons parsley flakes

Grate potatoes or cube them and place in blender with cold water to cover. Blend until coarsely chopped but not mushy; whether grated or blended, place in sieve and drain well (the blender is a mighty helper). Mix with eggs and then beat thoroughly with remaining ingredients; turn into well-greased 6-cup shallow casserole; bake in preheated 375° oven about 30 minutes, raise heat to 450° and bake an additional 10 minutes or until crisply browned. Cut in squares and serve piping hot. Serves 6.

To prepare potatoes in advance, grate into cold water and refrigerate.

RELISH FINGER STRIPS

Serve an assortment of crisp fresh vegetables cut in 3- or 4-inch strips:

Zucchini
> Peel and cut in ¼-inch wedges lengthwise.
> Before serving, dust with seasoned salt.

Carrots
> Cut in 3-inch lengths, slice in wedges, ¼-inch thick.

Hearts of Celery
> Crisp in ice water and drain.

Allow about 2 strips of each per serving.

BROILED PEACH CAKE

A hurry-up goodness.

4 sponge cake shells	2 tablespoons brown sugar
1 6-ounce can sliced peaches, drained	1 tablespoon butter
2 tablespoons chopped walnuts or sliced almonds	¼ cup sour cream (optional)
	4 maraschino cherries (optional)

The cake shells are those purchased at the market. Place them on baking sheet and fill centers with sliced peaches; sprinkle with nuts and sugar. Pour butter over each and place on broiler rack about 3 inches from preheated broiling unit; allow to broil until bubbly and lightly browned. If desired, top with sour cream and/or a cherry and serve at once. Serves 4.

Broil just before serving for about 3 minutes.

ANOTHER WAY

Pineapple tidbits or drained crushed pineapple make good fillings, or use other fruits of your choice.

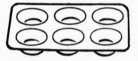

▶ Red Barn Stew

Red Barn Stew   Parslied Noodles   Bohemian Salad
Vermont Maple Mousse   Date Nut Cookies

COOKING COUNTDOWN

60 minutes ▶ prepare beef; cook
—
▶
—
50 ▶ prepare salad, mix dressing; refrigerate
—
▶
—
40 ▶ bake cookies
—
▶
—
30 ▶ cook noodles
—
▶
—
20 ▶ hard-cook eggs for salad
—
▶
—
10 ▶ toss salad
—
▶
—
0 ▶ serve

May be prepared in advance:
Date Nut Cookies
Must be prepared in advance:
Vermont Maple Mousse

RED BARN STEW

2½ pounds boneless beef, cut in 1-inch slices or 2 pounds beef and ½ pound veal
instant meat tenderizer
2 tablespoons shortening
2 onions, thinly sliced
2 teaspoons salt
¼ teaspoon pepper (freshly ground preferred)
2 teaspoons paprika
2 1-pound cans whole tomatoes
¼ cup sour cream (optional)
Parslied Noodles or mashed potatoes

Prepare beef with instant meat tenderizer according to directions; cut into 1-inch cubes. Heat shortening in skillet with tightly fitting cover and add meat and onions. Brown evenly over moderate heat, turning frequently. Sprinkle with salt, pepper and paprika; pour in tomatoes. Bring to boiling; reduce heat to simmer and cover. Cook 1 hour or until tender. Stir in sour cream; heat, but do not boil. Serve with noodles or mashed potatoes. Serves 4 to 6.

PARSLIED NOODLES

Toss 8 ounces cooked, drained noodles with 2 tablespoons butter and 1 tablespoon snipped parsley.

OTHER WAYS

Canned Vegetables

Add vegetables as a "stretcher" for a fuller meal. If you do not have time for the fresh vegetables, add one 1-pound jar drained, cooked onions and one 1-pound jar or can carrots, drained. Cook 10 minutes until heated.

Fresh Vegetables

Add 1 pound each of small carrots and pearl onions to meat for last 30 minutes of cooking.

BOHEMIAN SALAD

1 stalk celery cabbage
1 bunch watercress
2 hard-cooked eggs, sliced
1 1-pound can salad sliced beets, drained

1 tablespoon minced chives
½ cup prepared French Dressing or French Blend Dressing (page 267)

Slice celery cabbage crosswise in ½-inch widths. Line salad bowl with watercress. Add sliced celery cabbage and arrange alternate slices of eggs and beets with minced chives and pour French Dressing over all. Toss lightly or, rather than disturb the lovely arrangement, serve portions without tossing; dressing will drizzle through. Serves 6.

VERMONT MAPLE MOUSSE

During a delightful visit, Dorothy Crandall, home economics editor of the Boston *Globe*, shared this recipe with me.

1 cup maple syrup
3 eggs, separated

⅛ teaspoon salt
1 pint heavy cream, whipped

Combine syrup and egg yolks in saucepan; heat, stirring until thickened. Remove from heat and cool. Beat egg whites with salt until stiff but not dry; fold into syrup mixture, then fold in whipped cream. Turn into 1-quart mold or tray and freeze until firm. Makes 1 quart.

DATE NUT COOKIES

1 unbeaten egg white
1 cup chopped dates

1 6-ounce package chopped walnuts or pecans (1 cup)

1 cup confectioners' sugar

Combine all ingredients and drop from teaspoon onto greased cooky sheet. Bake 10 minutes in preheated 350° oven. Remove immediately with spatula from cooky sheet — don't dally or they'll stick. Makes about 3 dozen.

May be prepared in advance. Store in airtight container.

► Beef Chop Chop

*Beef Chop Chop   Fluffy Rice   Chinese Cabbage
Sweet French Dressing
Polite Pineapples   Cheese Cubes*

COOKING COUNTDOWN

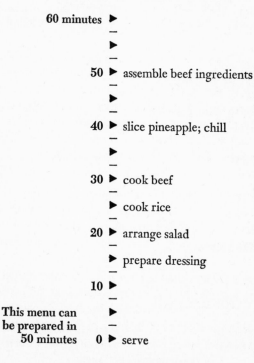

60 minutes ►
              —
              ►
              —
        50 ► assemble beef ingredients
              —
              ►
              —
        40 ► slice pineapple; chill
              —
              ►
              —
        30 ► cook beef
              —
              ► cook rice
              —
        20 ► arrange salad
              —
              ► prepare dressing
              —
        10 ►
              —
This menu can ►
be prepared in —
   50 minutes   0 ► serve

BEEF CHOP CHOP

Ground beef goes Oriental here with style and ease. Make this dish the previous day, if you wish, and just reheat.

1 pound ground beef, chuck or round
2 tablespoons sherry
¼ cup soy sauce
1 tablespoon sugar
2 medium onions, finely cut
1 4-ounce can water chestnuts, sliced

1 tablespoon peanut oil
½ cup cold water
1 teaspoon cornstarch
2 tablespoons water
2 cups cooked fluffy rice or pre-cooked rice
2 tablespoons snipped parsley

Combine beef with sherry, soy sauce, sugar; place in refrigerator. Slice onions and water chestnuts and set aside until time to cook. Heat oil in large skillet until very hot; add beef mixture and sauté until meat separates and is lightly browned. Add onions, water chestnuts and cold water; simmer 10 minutes. Combine cornstarch with water and stir into beef; cook an additional 5 minutes. Mound rice in center of platter and ring with beef. Sprinkle with parsley. Serves 4.

CHINESE CABBAGE

Chinese cabbage or celery cabbage has a firm, crisp texture, good to the bite. With a dash of salt it is a tasty appetizer or accompaniment, and it serves well as salad. With this menu, I like a sweet dressing, and the prepared Hawaiian type is fine. If you wish to keep your own dressing on hand, be a true cook, and prepare Sweet French Dressing.

The Chinese cabbage needs washing and chilling; when ready for salad service, cut the stalks into ½-inch slices using 3 for each portion. One stalk should be sufficient for 4 people. A lettuce leaf base adds a finished look, though it isn't necessary.

Sweet French Dressing

1 10-ounce can tomato soup	¼ cup sugar
½ cup white vinegar	1 teaspoon salt
½ cup salad oil	1 tablespoon grated onion
¼ teaspoon coarsely ground pepper	

Combine all ingredients in a quart jar and cover tightly. Shake thoroughly until well blended, and again before serving. Makes about 2½ cups.

POLITE PINEAPPLES

He is the very pine-apple of politeness.
— SHERIDAN, *The Rivals*

The pineapple has dignity; its sturdy beauty defies haste. Even though the end result of succulent eating has a balancing worth, peeling the tough hide and laboriously removing the "eyes" is difficult work. To avoid it, do the preparation in this fashion for informal hors d'oeuvres, dessert, or just nibbling. Remove the leaves of the pineapple with a slice of the fruit to form a firm base. (This is only for garnish.) Set it upright in the center of a small serving platter. Slice the remaining pineapple lengthwise in quarters; do not peel — remove the section of core from each and then slice each quarter further in lengths about 1-inch thick. Cut each slice into 1-inch cubes, and pile cubes around the centered leaves. The pieces may be speared with picks, or used as finger food, each piece no more than a juicy morsel, eaten from the peel.

For further glamour, tuck maraschino cherries among the leaves or spear them onto the spiked ends.

OTHER WAYS

1. For appetizer, serve with peeled, iced shrimp.

2. For dessert or appetizer, serve with cheese cubes.

3. For slices or wedges

Remove leaves by slicing across pineapple, then cut pineapple into ½-inch slices. Pare each slice, removing all "eyes." Circle core and remove. Serve in slices, half slices, or cut into inch wedges; chill. Serves 4 to 6.

QUICK ALTERNATE

Chilled canned pineapple spears or chunks make a very refreshing dessert with most menus and especially with an Oriental repast.

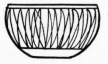

► Hamburger Pie

No Crust Hamburger Pie   Fresh Mushroom Salad
Garlic Bread and Butter
Strawberry Turnovers

COOKING COUNTDOWN

60 minutes ►

►
—

50 ► arrange turnovers

►
—

40 ► prepare hamburger pie shell

►
—

30 ► prepare garlic bread

► fill and bake hamburger pie
—

20 ► bake turnovers

► prepare salad dressing
—

10 ► arrange salad
—

This menu can   ► toast garlic bread
be prepared in   —
50 minutes   0 ► serve

May be prepared in advance:
Salad Dressing

NO CRUST HAMBURGER PIE

With a ground beef shell — quick and good young eating.

Pie Shell

1½ pounds lean ground beef
¼ cup dry bread crumbs
1 tablespoon Worcestershire
1 teaspoon celery salt
1 teaspoon salt

¼ teaspoon garlic powder (optional)
½ cup tomato juice (drained from tomatoes in filling)

Tomato Filling

1 1-pound can tomatoes, drained (Italian or whole variety)
1 teaspoon seasoned salt
¼ teaspoon oregano
¼ teaspoon sugar

¼ cup finely chopped onion, fresh or frozen
2 tablespoons snipped fresh parsley or parsley flakes
½ cup grated Parmesan cheese

Drain tomatoes and combine ½ cup of the juice with remaining Pie Shell ingredients; mix very well. Pat into greased 9-inch pie pan as evenly as possible. Refrigerate 15 minutes. Spread tomatoes in beef shell and sprinkle with remaining ingredients, with cheese as topping. Bake in preheated 375° oven 20 minutes or until meat is done and filling is piping hot. Serves 4 to 6.

FRESH MUSHROOM SALAD

Sliced fresh mushrooms are picture-pretty; coupled with subtle flavor, they make an inviting dish.

6 cups assorted greens, such as curly endive, iceberg lettuce or Boston
½ pound fresh mushrooms
¼ cup sliced green onions or scallions

2 tomatoes, sliced thinly
White Wine Dressing or prepared French Dressing

Wash greens and dry them in paper toweling or kitchen towels; store in plastic bags and refrigerate to crisp. Do not soak mushrooms; wash and dry quickly. Slice through the stem, thinly, and toss with greens in salad bowl; sprinkle with green onions and arrange slices of tomato over top. Toss with dressing, using just enough to marinate the contents, moistening each leaf. Serve to 6.

ANOTHER WAY

Make your selection of combinations for the salad. The mushrooms with lettuce are very good alone; add either one or all of the other suggested vegetables. A good addition would be radishes, sliced zucchini, watercress or cucumbers.

White Wine Dressing

Make this simple one from "scratch." It's a fine dressing for green salads; I like it too when citrus fruits are included.

1 teaspoon sugar	¼ cup white wine tarragon vinegar
½ teaspoon dry mustard	
½ teaspoon instant minced onion	½ cup dry white wine
2 teaspoons Worcestershire	1 cup salad oil
⅛ teaspoon coarsely ground or seasoned pepper	

Combine all ingredients in a jar; cover tightly and shake until blended. This is a good blender recipe; whirl for a minute until emulsified. Makes about 1½ cups.

ANOTHER WAY

To one of the many fine prepared dressings, add your personal touch to 1 cup dressing with any of the following
  1. 1 teaspoon grated onion
  2. ¼ teaspoon curry powder
  3. 1 teaspoon celery seed or poppy seed
  4. a subtle pinch of a favorite herb such as tarragon, basil, anise as a start

GARLIC BREAD

6 thick slices crusty Italian or French bread
Garlic Butter

Toast bread on one side. Spread untoasted side with Garlic Butter and place under broiler, toasting until lightly browned.

Garlic Butter

¼ cup butter or margarine
¾ teaspoon herbed garlic salt

Blend garlic salt and butter very well. Makes ¼ cup butter. Sufficient for 6 slices garlic bread.

Make a larger amount; chill in a roll; slice and serve on broiled steak or chops.

STRAWBERRY TURNOVERS

1 package refrigerator biscuits (12)
⅓ cup strawberry or raspberry jam (approximately)

Divide each biscuit in thirds and press each round to 3 inches in diameter; place ½ teaspoon jam on each and fold in half. Seal by pressing edges together with tines of a fork. Bake in preheated 375° oven 12 to 14 minutes or until lightly browned. Makes 36.

If you wish a shiny crust, brush with milk before baking.

The Golden Calf

IN EUROPE THROUGHOUT the centuries veal has been considered a delicacy but it did not enjoy great popularity in this country until quite recently. Increased interest was induced, no doubt, by our modern fast-moving means of world travel and communication. The adventure of exploring foreign cuisine brought a new approach to veal and resulted in many new and enticing recipes.

In many of the recipes that follow, cooking time is at a minimum. The delicate flavor of veal "marries" well with wines, herbs, spices and cheeses; the accompaniments are many and present no problems. The longer-cooking roasts provide convenient leftovers which may become starters for other recipes.

► Cheese Breaded Chops

Cheese Breaded Chops
Limas and Chestnuts   *Spiced Rice*
Minted Pineapple Sherbet   *Topper Brownies*

COOKING COUNTDOWN

60 minutes ► prepare and bake brownies

►

50 ►

►

40 ►

►

30 ► prepare and sauté veal chops

►

20 ► prepare limas and chestnuts

►

This menu can be   10 ► prepare rice
prepared in 30 minutes   —
if brownies are baked   ►
in advance or   —
purchased   0 ► serve

May be prepared in advance:
Topper Brownies

CHEESE BREADED CHOPS

8 veal rib chops, cut ¾ inch thick, about 2 pounds
1 teaspoon seasoned salt
½ cup flour
2 eggs, beaten
¼ cup water
½ cup dry bread crumbs

½ cup grated Parmesan or Romano cheese
1 tablespoon parsley flakes
1 teaspoon oregano
1 teaspoon salt
¼ cup vegetable oil
1 lemon, sliced
paprika

Dry chops with paper toweling; sprinkle with salt, and coat well with flour. Combine eggs and water and dip the chops in mixture, covering well. Combine bread crumbs, grated cheese, parsley, salt and oregano, and roll chops in the mixture, coating entire chop evenly. If time permits, allow to stand in refrigerator to set breading. Heat oil in skillet; add chops and sauté over moderate heat 10 minutes on each side or until nicely browned and tender. Place on platter garnished with lemon slices, edged in paprika. Serves 4.

OTHER WAYS

1. For Wiener Schnitzel, substitute 2 pounds of veal cutlets for the chops.

2. For Schnitzel Holstein, top each cutlet with a fried egg.

LIMAS AND CHESTNUTS

1 10-ounce package frozen baby lima beans
½ cup sliced water chestnuts, drained
¼ cup butter or margarine
2 tablespoons wine vinegar

2 teaspoons dill seed
½ teaspoon salt
¼ teaspoon black pepper
¼ teaspoon monosodium glutamate
2 tablespoons chopped pimientos

Cook beans according to package directions; drain. Stir in chestnuts, butter and remaining ingredients, except pimientos; heat quickly to melt butter. Sprinkle with pimientos. Serves 4.

SPICED RICE

1⅓ cups instant rice
1⅓ cups boiling water
1 teaspoon soy sauce
1 bouillon cube
1 teaspoon celery salt

¼ teaspoon oregano
dash Tabasco
¼ cup slivered almonds (optional)

Add rice to boiling water with remaining ingredients, timed according to package directions. After fluffing, toss with almonds. Serves 4.

ANOTHER WAY

Regular long-grained rice may be used. Substitute 1 cup long-grained rice for instant rice and combine with 2 cups boiling water, 2 bouillon cubes, soy sauce, celery salt, oregano and Tabasco as in preceding recipe. Cover and cook 20 minutes until liquid is absorbed. Toss with almonds. Serves 4 to 6.

MINTED PINEAPPLE SHERBET

1 pint pineapple sherbet
¼ cup green crème de menthe

1 tablespoon coarse green decorating sugar

Scoop pineapple sherbet into 4 glass serving dishes; pour 1 tablespoon crème de menthe over each serving and sprinkle with green sugar. Use the colored sugar crystals usually used for cooky decorating. Serves 4.

TOPPER BROWNIES

1 pound dark brown sugar
4 eggs, well beaten

1½ cups cake flour, sifted
1½ teaspoons baking powder
2 cups coarsely chopped pecans

Combine sugar and eggs in top of double boiler and cook while stirring until thickened. Remove from heat. Sift flour and baking powder together; blend into egg mixture, then fold in pecans very thoroughly. Pour into well-greased 9 x 13-inch baking pan. Bake in preheated 350° oven for 30 to 35 minutes. Cool on rack; cut into 24 pieces.

The brownies keep well in an airtight container and I would suggest having them on hand. Make them during a break in your activities.

QUICK ALTERNATE

A package of prepared frozen brownies.

► Veal in Clam Sauce

Veal in Clam Sauce   Sea Shell Noodles
Sunset Beet Mold   Lemon Tipped Asparagus
Golden Pears or *Frosted Berries*

COOKING COUNTDOWN

60 minutes ►
—
►
—
50 ►
—
►
—
40 ► cook veal
—
►
—
30 ► boil noodle shells
—
► prepare Lemon Cream Dressing, keep
— warm
20 ► cook or heat asparagus
—
► arrange salad
—
10 ► arrange pears; chill
—
This menu can ►
be prepared in —
40 minutes   0 ► serve

Must be prepared in advance:
Golden Pears
Beet Mold

VEAL IN CLAM SAUCE WITH SEA SHELL NOODLES

1½ pounds veal steak, cut in 4-
inch squares ¼ inch thick
¼ cup Seasoned Flour
4 tablespoons butter or other
shortening

1 cup milk or half-and-half
cream
1 7½-ounce can minced clams
Sea Shell Noodles
2 tablespoons snipped parsley

Place 2 or 3 pieces of veal at one time in paper or plastic bag with Seasoned Flour; shake to coat thoroughly. Heat butter in heavy skillet with cover and add veal; sauté over moderate heat until well browned. Reduce heat to very low and add cream or milk slowly, stirring and shaking pan. Cover and simmer 20 to 25 minutes until tender; add clams with juice and simmer an additional 5 minutes. Arrange veal and sauce on platter around mound of Buttered Sea Shell Noodles. Sprinkle with snipped parsley. Serves 4.

Seasoned Flour

¼ cup flour
¾ teaspoon salt
⅛ teaspoon coarsely ground pepper

1 teaspoon paprika
¼ teaspoon garlic powder
(optional)

Combine ingredients in paper bag for simplified coating of specified meat, fish or fowl. Sufficient for one 2-pound fryer. Any remaining Seasoned Flour is fine for thickening gravies.

Sea Shell Noodles

Cook one 8-ounce package sea shell noodles according to package directions. Drain and toss with 2 tablespoons butter or margarine.

LEMON TIPPED ASPARAGUS

**1 1-pound can asparagus or 1 10-ounce package frozen asparagus spears
Lemon Cream Dressing**

When opening can of asparagus, turn can bottom side up so as not to injure tips of asparagus. They will emerge stem end first. Heat in liquid and drain. If using frozen asparagus, cook according to package directions; drain. Place vegetable on small platter and cover tips with Lemon Cream Dressing. Serves 4.

Lemon Cream Dressing

Similar to Hollandaise with tart flavor.

½ cup sour cream
½ cup salad dressing (mayonnaise type)

2 tablespoons lemon juice
⅛ teaspoon cayenne pepper
dash salt

Combine all ingredients in saucepan and heat slowly while stirring occasionally. Makes 1 cup.

SUNSET BEET MOLD

An excellent relish.

1 3-ounce package lemon gelatin
1 cup boiling water
½ teaspoon salt
2 tablespoons lemon juice
2 cups shoestring beets, drained

2 tablespoons prepared horse-radish
1 tablespoon grated onion or 1 teaspoon onion powder
1 cup sour cream

Garnish: lettuce leaves

Dissolve gelatin in boiling water; add salt and lemon juice. Cool, then place in refrigerator until of jelly-like consistency. Fold in remaining ingredients, blending well. Pour into oiled 5-cup mold and place in refrigerator several hours until set. Unmold on bed of lettuce. Serves 6 to 8.

ANOTHER WAY

Use 4-ounce individual molds and invert onto lettuce cups. May be served individually or arranged on a platter.

GOLDEN PEARS

> I had a little nut tree, nothing would it bear
> But a silver nutmeg and a golden pear . . .
> ANONYMOUS

6 firm pears, Barlett, D'Anjou   ½ cup sugar
    or Bosc   ¼ cup lemon juice
2 cups apricot nectar   ½ cup dry sherry
           1 teaspoon grated lemon peel

Accompaniment: 1 cup whipping cream, whipped, or
                 2 cups frozen whipped topping, defrosted

Peel whole pears, allowing stem to remain if they are so equipped. Combine remaining ingredients in saucepan; bring to boiling and add pears. Reduce heat and simmer pears about 20 to 30 minutes until tender but not mushy. (Cooking time varies with type of pears and ripeness.) Baste and turn frequently while cooking to distribute color and flavor. Remove from heat and place in bowl with syrup. Chill several hours or overnight; baste and turn in syrup while chilling. To serve, place a dollop of cream on dessert plate or sherbet glass. Place each pear upright on cream and drizzle apricot syrup over each serving. Serves 6.

OTHER WAYS

1. Served without cream, the pears make a beautiful poultry or meat accompaniment.

2. For an ultra-elegant dessert, serve on slightly softened ice cream, drizzle with the apricot syrup and sprinkle with ¼ cup toasted slivered almonds. To toast almonds, heat 1 tablespoon butter or margarine in skillet; add almonds and toss over moderate heat until lightly browned.
    Refrigerated, the pears keep beautifully for several days.

QUICK ALTERNATE

Frosted Berries

Defrost one 10-ounce package berries of your choice and serve with prepared whipped topping mix or Vanilla Custard Filling (page 314).

▶ Hungarian Veal with Bohemian Noodles

Hungarian Veal Paprika   Parslied Broad Noodles
Raw Mushroom Salad
Pineapple Cheese Pie or *Lemon Sauced Pound Cake*

COOKING COUNTDOWN

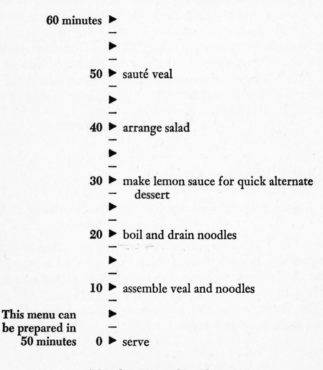

60 minutes ▶
▶
—
50 ▶ sauté veal
▶
—
40 ▶ arrange salad
—
▶
—
30 ▶ make lemon sauce for quick alternate
—   dessert
▶
—
20 ▶ boil and drain noodles
—
▶
—
10 ▶ assemble veal and noodles
—

This menu can   ▶
be prepared in   —
50 minutes   0 ▶ serve

Must be prepared in advance:
Pineapple Cheese Pie

HUNGARIAN VEAL PAPRIKA

2 pounds veal shoulder, cut into 1-inch cubes
1 teaspoon salt
¼ teaspoon coarsely ground black pepper
3 tablespoons shortening

1 onion, finely chopped
1 tablespoon paprika
2 cups dry white wine or 1 10-ounce can undiluted chicken broth and ¾ cup water
1 cup dairy sour cream
Parslied Broad Noodles

Sprinkle salt and pepper over veal. Heat shortening in skillet; add veal, brown over moderate heat about 10 minutes, stirring occasionally. Add onion and sauté about 1 minute until glossy. Stir in paprika, add 1 cup wine or broth. Cover and simmer about 30 minutes or until veal is tender. Check often, adding wine or broth if needed. Stir in any remaining liquid and blend sour cream in gradually; heat but do not boil. Arrange on platter around mounded Parslied Broad Noodles. Serves 6.

PARSLIED BROAD NOODLES

1 1-pound package broad noodles   3 tablespoon butter
¼ cup finely chopped parsley

Cook broad noodles or Bohemian noodles according to instructions on package. Rinse with cold water, drain, return to stove over low heat. Add butter and finely chopped parsley. Heat through, toss and serve with a sprinkling of paprika. Serves 6 to 8.

The Bohemian noodles are comparable to a heavy spaghetti; a good and somewhat different texture.

RAW MUSHROOM SALAD

Mushrooms, which add character to so many dishes, have a distinctive flavor and texture when they are occasionally served uncooked. This is a salad that shows them off to advantage.

1 medium head Romaine lettuce   ¼ pound curly endive
½ pound fresh mushrooms

Dressing

½ cup salad oil   ¼ teaspoon coarsely ground black
¼ cup white wine vinegar   pepper
¾ teaspoon salt   *Topping:* ½ cup prepared croutons

Wash and crisp salad greens, arrange in bowl. Rinse and dry mushrooms, cut into thin slices lengthwise through stems, and arrange on greens. To serve, pour salad dressing ingredients over salad; toss well and top with crisp croutons. Serves 6.

PINEAPPLE CHEESE PIE

1 8-ounce package cream cheese,   1 3-ounce package lemon instant
  softened   pudding
2 cups milk   1 prepared graham cracker crust
1 1-pound can pineapple pie filling, chilled

Gradually add ½ cup milk to cheese, mixing until creamy; blend in remaining 1½ cups milk and pudding. Beat with rotary beater until well blended, for about 1 minute, and pour into crust. Spread with pineapple pie filling. Chill at least 1 hour. Serves 6 generously.

ANOTHER WAY

For another touch, top cheese pie with one 1-pound can cherry pie filling, or flaky coconut.

May be prepared the previous day.

QUICK ALTERNATE

Citrus Sauced Pound Cake

Use slices of pound cake purchased at your market or any simple leftover cake. Pour Citrus Sauce over each cake serving.

Citrus Sauce

3 cups milk
2 tablespoons sugar
1 tablespoon lime juice

1 3¾-ounce package instant lemon pudding
dash salt

Combine ingredients in a bowl and beat with rotary blender 1 to 2 minutes. Let stand until slightly thickened — about 5 minutes. Makes about 3 cups.

▶ Chalet Dinner

Swiss Veal in Wine   Tiny Browned Potatoes
Carrots Marjoram
Grape Swiss Lattice Salad   Tangy Cream Dressing
Caramel Custard or Fruit with Vanilla Sauce

COOKING COUNTDOWN

60 minutes ▶
            ▶
            —
      50 ▶
            —
            ▶
            —
      40 ▶ boil potatoes
            —
            ▶ cook carrots
            —
      30 ▶ sauté veal
            —
            ▶
            —
      20 ▶ mix salad dressing; arrange salad
            —
            ▶
            —
      10 ▶ heat carrots with seasonings
            —
This menu can   ▶ brown potatoes
be prepared in   —
40 minutes   0 ▶ serve

May be prepared in advance:
Tangy Cream Dressing
Must be prepared in advance:
Caramel Custard

SWISS VEAL IN WINE

2 pounds boneless lean veal, cut in ½-inch slices

¼ cup vegetable oil or 1 tablespoon butter plus 3 tablespoons oil

3 green onions, minced, or 3 tablespoons minced dried onions

3 tablespoons cognac
3 tablespoons flour
¾ teaspoon salt
¼ teaspoon white pepper
1 cup white wine
½ cup half-and-half cream

Garnish: watercress, pimiento olives

Pound the veal with the back of a cleaver or the edge of a saucer until ¼ inch thick and meat has spread. Melt butter in large skillet; add green onions and cook slowly for 2 minutes. Add veal and sauté 5 minutes on each side; add cognac. Combine flour, salt and pepper and wine; pour over veal. Simmer, stirring until thickened, about 5 minutes. Gradually add cream and continue to simmer an additional 10 minutes or until veal is tender and sauce is blended. Garnish with a spray of watercress; spear 3 or 4 olives and arrange a bouquet. Serves 6.

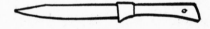

TINY BROWNED POTATOES

Very small, smooth new potatoes are a nice change and delicious when they are served in their jackets. Either the red-skinned or white-skinned variety will do nicely. Select potatoes that are fairly uniform in size and free from blemishes.

Boil 12 small new potatoes in salted water until tender but firm; drain. Melt 3 tablespoons butter in a skillet; add potatoes to butter; brown lightly over medium heat, shaking or stirring frequently. Be gentle, so potatoes remain intact and keep their nice round shape. Sprinkle with ½ tablespoon salt and ¼ teaspoon coarsely ground pepper before serving. Serves 6.

CARROTS MARJORAM

The marjoram adds a touch of glamour and a different flavor to this year-round, standby vegetable.

2 bunches carrots
3 tablespoons butter
1 teaspoon dried marjoram

¼ teaspoon white pepper
2 teaspoons fresh or bottled lemon juice

Garnish: crisp spinach leaves

Peel and slice carrots; cook in salted water about 15 minutes or until tender; drain. Combine in saucepan with remaining ingredients; heat thoroughly, tossing lightly. Serve on bed of contrasting spinach leaves. Serves 6 to 8.

GRAPE SWISS LATTICE SALAD

This salad is pretty either on individual plates or arranged on a large platter. The combination of ingredients is especially delicious with veal.

1 head Boston lettuce
1 bunch watercress
1 pound fresh white or green grapes

¼ pound sliced Swiss cheese
1 teaspoon celery seeds
Tangy Cream Dressing

Wash and crisp lettuce and watercress; trim excess stems from watercress. Wash and stem grapes. Cut Swiss cheese into thin julienne strips. Place lettuce cups on individual plates or platter. Arrange watercress in lettuce cups. Place equal amounts of grapes on watercress; top with cheese strips, lattice fashion, and sprinkle with celery seeds. Serve with Tangy Cream Dressing. Serves 6.

Tangy Cream Dressing

½ teaspoon paprika
½ teaspoon horseradish
½ teaspoon prepared mustard

½ teaspoon salt
½ cup mayonnaise
2 tablespoons half-and-half cream

Combine all ingredients, mixing thoroughly. Makes about ¾ cup.

Prepare Tangy Dressing in advance to have on hand; it is very good with seafood or fish. Try a double recipe for convenience.

CARAMEL CUSTARD

4 eggs	2¼ cups milk
⅓ cup sugar	1 teaspoon vanilla
½ teaspoon salt	⅔ cup light brown sugar

Beat the eggs until light; add sugar and salt. Scald milk and slowly stir into egg mixture; add vanilla and beat until thoroughly blended. Distribute brown sugar evenly on bottom of 4-cup baking dish or mold. Pour egg mixture over sugar. Place baking dish in a pan of warm water; bake in 325° oven for 1 hour, or until custard tests done. When a knife blade inserted in custard emerges clear, custard is done. Cool the custard thoroughly and invert on a plate or platter.

A sauce is formed in the baking and covers custard as it is turned over onto serving dish. Use a platter with a rim. Serves 6 or 7.

QUICK ALTERNATE

Fruit with Vanilla Sauce

1 1-pound can fruit cocktail or pears, drained	2 8-ounce jars junior foods vanilla custard
	nutmeg

Arrange fruit in dessert dishes; spoon custard over top and dust with nutmeg. Serves 6.

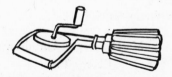

► Veal Supreme for Company

Veal Supreme   Noodles Alfredo   Artichokes Romano
Molded Garden Salad
Cherry Tart or Presto Cherry Tart

COOKING COUNTDOWN

60 minutes ►
    —
    ►
    —
50 ► cook veal
    —
    ►
40 ►
    —
    ►
30 ► hard-cook eggs for artichokes
    ► cook noodles
    —
20 ► cook artichokes; assemble
    ►
    —
10 ► unmold and garnish salad

This menu can ►
be prepared in —
50 minutes   0 ► serve

Must be prepared in advance:
Cherry Tart
Molded Garden Salad

VEAL SUPREME

8 veal cutlets	½ cup water
2 tablespoons butter	½ cup dry sherry
2 tablespoons olive or salad oil	1 ¾-ounce envelope brown gravy
1 8-ounce can mushroom pieces,	mix
drained, or ½ pound fresh	2 tablespoons snipped parsley
mushrooms, sliced	

Pat veal cutlets dry with paper toweling. Heat butter and oil in skillet (an electric skillet is fine) and add veal; sauté over moderately high heat until nicely browned, about 15 minutes; add mushrooms and sauté 5 minutes longer. Combine water, sherry and gravy mix and blend with veal; cover and simmer 30 minutes, adding a small amount of water if the liquid cooks down too much. To serve, arrange on platter and cover with pan sauce; sprinkle with parsley. Serves 6 to 8.

NOODLES ALFREDO

Serve with the flourish of an imposing fork and spoon, à la Alfredo of Rome.

1 pound egg noodles	½ cup butter
½ cup half-and-half cream	1 cup grated Parmesan cheese

Cook noodles according to package directions. Drain; add remaining ingredients and toss well. Keep warm in double boiler. Serves 8.

Nothing equals the flavor of freshly grated cheese.

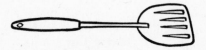

ARTICHOKES ROMANO

2 9-ounce packages frozen artichoke hearts
¾ cup mayonnaise or salad dressing
¼ cup milk

2 tablespoons parsley flakes
2 tablespoons lemon juice
1 tablespoon grated onion or
1 teaspoon instant minced
¼ teaspoon Worcestershire

2 hard-cooked eggs, chopped

Cook artichoke hearts as directed on package; drain. Heat mayonnaise or salad dressing, milk, parsley, lemon juice, onion and Worcestershire just until hot. Add eggs; pour over hot artichoke hearts. Serves 8.

MOLDED GARDEN SALAD

Pretty, for party or family, with fresh flavor.

1 3-ounce package lime-flavored
gelatin
1 cup boiling water
½ cup cold water
½ cup mayonnaise
2 tablespoons tarragon vinegar
¼ teaspoon salt

1½ cups finely shredded cabbage
½ cup sliced radishes
½ cup diced celery
¼ cup diced green pepper
(optional)
1 teaspoon grated onion, or
¼ teaspoon onion powder

Garnish: leaf lettuce, cucumber slices, quartered tomatoes,
quartered hard-cooked eggs

Dissolve gelatin in boiling water; stir in cold water, then mayonnaise, vinegar and salt. Place in refrigerator to chill until of jelly-like consistency. With rotary beater, whip until fluffy; blend in remaining ingredients. Pour into lightly oiled or greased 5-cup mold and chill in refrigerator until set. Unmold on platter lined with leaf lettuce and garnish with cucumber slices, tomatoes and quartered hard-cooked eggs. Serves 8.

QUICK ALTERNATE

Tossed Garden Salad

Toss together cabbage, radishes, celery, green pepper and grated onion in same quantities as for Molded Garden Salad. Chill. To serve, toss with ½ cup light Italian dressing; arrange on lettuce leaves with suggested garnish. Serves 6 to 8.

CHERRY TART

The flakiest kind of pastry with an added ingredient — yeast. Prepare the tart the previous day or early morning and pop it in the oven for "on schedule" dessert.

1½ cups sifted flour	1 egg yolk, beaten
dash salt	1 package active dry yeast
½ teaspoon baking soda	2 tablespoons warm water
1 tablespoon sugar	(105°)
1 cup softened shortening, butter or margarine	1 tablespoon cream
	½ teaspoon vanilla

Cherry Filling

Sift flour, salt, baking soda and sugar together; blend in shortening and egg yolk. Combine yeast, warm water, cream and vanilla, blending well. Stir into flour mixture; mix until smooth and elastic. At this point it is well to mix with hands. Form into a ball and divide in two pieces. Place one piece on wax paper; cover with second sheet of paper and roll between the two sheets until large enough to fit into 8-inch pie pan. Remove top sheet of paper and turn dough over onto pie pan. Fit loosely, pressing down on rim of pan and trim off excess dough. Pour Cherry Filling in prepared shell. Roll out second piece of dough large enough to cover filling and top the tart. Seal by moistening edges of crust with water, pressing rims of both pieces together with tines of fork. The crust is quite rich, and if there are any breaks, mend them with small pieces of trimmed dough. (Incidentally, cut leaves with leftover pieces and cover the rough spots, if any. Moisten the trim before arranging. Looks lovely too.) Brush tart with milk; carefully prick top with tines of fork and bake in preheated 350° oven about 30 minutes or until evenly browned. Remove; cool on rack. Drizzle with Confectioners' Frosting while still warm, if desired. Serves 6.

Cherry Filling

Use one 1-pound can cherry pie filling; add ½ teaspoon almond flavoring, a dash of salt and ¼ teaspoon cinnamon.

Confectioners' Frosting

Combine ½ cup confectioners' sugar, 3 tablespoons milk and ½ teaspoon vanilla.

QUICK ALTERNATE

Presto Cherry Tarts

Purchase 2 unbaked frozen pie shells. Fill one with Cherry Filling; cover with second shell and remove pan. Seal and proceed as directed for Cherry Tart. Bake in preheated 425° oven 30 to 40 minutes or until nicely browned. Makes one 8-inch pie.

▶ Veal Parmesan Dinner

Short-Cut Liver Pâté   Veal Parmesan
Spaghettini   Buttered Green Beans with Egg Sauce
Compote of Frozen Fruit   Petite Nut Cookies

COOKING COUNTDOWN

60 minutes ▶ prepare liver pâté
—
▶

50 ▶ sauté veal
—
▶ defrost fruit—refrigerate
—
40 ▶ prepare egg sauce
▶
—
30 ▶ boil and drain spaghettini
▶
—
20 ▶ cook beans
▶ arrange pâté
—
10 ▶ reheat veal
—
▶
—
0 ▶ serve

May be prepared in advance:
Short-Cut Liver Pâté
Must be prepared in advance:
Petite Nut Cookies

SHORT-CUT LIVER PÂTÉ

½ pound liver sausage
½ cup sour cream
1 teaspoon Worcestershire
½ teaspoon seasoned salt

2 tablespoons chopped green pepper or 2 teaspoons instant or frozen chopped green pepper
¼ teaspoon onion powder

Garnish: lettuce cups, sliced black olives

Combine all ingredients and blend very well. Turn into two 4-ounce orange juice glasses and chill. Slip a knife around glass to remove and cut into slices. Place lettuce cups on individual salad plates and arrange a slice of pâté in each; top with an olive slice (mock truffle). Makes 1 cup and will serve 4 to 6.

Slices of olive may be mixed with pâté for further French look.

Prepare the pâté in advance to have on hand at a moment's notice. It is sophisticated fare.

VEAL PARMESAN

2 pounds veal steak, thinly sliced
½ teaspoon salt
2 tablespoons flour
⅛ teaspoon white pepper
2 tablespoons olive or salad oil
1 clove garlic, minced, or ¼ teaspoon garlic powder

1 teaspoon oregano
1 teaspoon basil
1½ to 2 cups water
3 onion bouillon cubes
1 6-ounce can tomato paste
½ cup dry sherry
⅓ cup grated Parmesan cheese

Pound veal with edge of saucer until ¼ inch thick; cut into pieces about 2 x 4 inches. Combine salt, flour and pepper; coat veal with mixture. Heat oil in skillet, blend in garlic, then add veal and brown evenly on both sides over moderately high heat. Sprinkle with oregano and basil; bring 1 cup water to boil and stir in bouillon cubes until dissolved. Add to skillet with tomato paste. Shake pan so that all ingredients are well mixed. Cover and simmer slowly, adding remaining cup of water as needed. Watch while it cooks, as the tomato sauce may stick. Simmer 20 to 25 minutes or until tender. Stir in sherry; heat but do not allow to boil. Arrange on hot platter; sprinkle with grated cheese and serve at once. Serves 6.

ANOTHER WAY

Prepare veal in ovenproof serving ware or on an ovenproof platter. Instead of Parmesan cover with 6 slices Swiss cheese and broil for about 5 minutes until bubbly and golden brown.

These are so simple they cannot be classified as recipes, but they make a good and rounded menu.

SPAGHETTINI

Cook an 8-ounce package of spaghettini. Drain; quickly toss with 2 tablespoons of butter and dust with paprika; mound on platter. Serve with pan gravy. Serves 6.

BUTTERED GREEN BEANS

Prepare two 10-ounce packages of frozen green beans according to package directions. Drain; toss with 2 tablespoons butter and place on border of the veal platter to add color. If time permits, serve with Egg Sauce. Serves 6.

Egg Sauce for vegetables or fish

2 tablespoons butter or margarine	¼ teaspoon onion powder
1 tablespoon flour	1 teaspoon Worcestershire
1 teaspoon prepared mustard	1 cup milk
½ teaspoon salt	1 hard-cooked egg, chopped

Heat butter in saucepan; blend in flour, stirring until smooth; blend in seasonings and gradually blend in milk, stirring until sauce boils; cook 1 minute. Stir in egg. Makes 1½ cups and serves 6.

ANOTHER EASY WAY

Prepare 1 package white sauce mix; add seasonings and egg as in preceding Egg Sauce recipe.

COMPOTE OF FROZEN FRUIT

Defrost two 10-ounce packages of mixed fruits. They may be placed in refrigerator in early morning to defrost or, if at the last moment, place package in a bowl of cold water. The fruits have fine flavor when separated and still frosty. Serves 6.

Serve with an on-hand sweet, or try the following recipe for Petite Nut Cookies if you are in the mood for baking.

PETITE NUT COOKIES

2 cups ground nuts
½ cup sugar
2 egg whites, unbeaten (about 6 tablespoons)
½ teaspoon rum flavoring or brandy (optional)
15 candied cherries, halved

Mix nuts and sugar; add egg whites until sufficient amount holds mixture together. Add rum flavoring; roll with moistened palms into large marble-sized balls and place on well-greased cooky sheet. With a thimble, press an indentation in center of each ball. Place a piece of candied cherry in each hollow, or fill with currant jam. Bake in 350° preheated oven 20 minutes or until firm and lightly browned. Remove to rack to cool. Makes about 30.

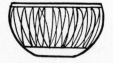

► Veal in the French Manner

Veal Parisian   Poppy Seed Noodle Shells
Brussels Sprouts with Black Butter   Spiced Apricots
Mousse au Chocolat

COOKING COUNTDOWN

60 minutes ► prepare chocolate dessert, chill

► —

50 ► —

► —

40 ► cook apricots

► sauté veal

30 ► —

► —

20 ► cook Brussels sprouts

► prepare butter

This menu can be 10 ► cook noodles and drain
prepared in 40 minutes —
if dessert is prepared ► assemble
in advance or Quick —
Alternate is used 0 ► serve

May be prepared in advance:
Spiced Apricots
Mousse au Chocolat

VEAL PARISIAN

1 pound veal scallops, sliced ⅛ inch thick
1 teaspoon salt
¼ teaspoon pepper
½ cup flour
3 tablespoons butter
8 slices thin ham

8 slices Swiss cheese, about ¼ pound
1 chicken bouillon cube
½ cup hot water
2 tablespoons dry white wine (optional)
1 teaspoon sugar

½ teaspoon onion powder

Cut veal into 8 pieces of a similar size; sprinkle with salt, pepper and flour. Heat butter in skillet; add veal and sauté about 3 minutes on each side until lightly browned. Place a slice of ham and a slice of cheese on top of each piece of veal. Dissolve bouillon cube in water and pour around veal with the wine and seasonings. Cover skillet and simmer about 10 minutes or until cheese is melted. Instead of simmering on top of stove, the veal may be prepared in ovenware serving casserole and baked the final 10 minutes in preheated 400° oven until cheese melts and browns. Either way is delicious. Serves 4.

POPPY SEED NOODLE SHELLS

Prepare one 8-ounce package noodle sea shells according to package directions. Drain and toss with 3 tablespoons butter and 2 tablespoons poppy seeds. Border veal with the noodles. Serves 6.

OTHER WAYS

Endless varieties and shapes of noodles are available in the markets, from the broad lasagne to the thin, thin spaghettini. Try others for texture and change of pace.

BRUSSELS SPROUTS WITH BLACK BUTTER

We seldom use Black Butter (Beurre Noír) in our country; in France it is a favored hot dressing for vegetables, fish and eggs, among other dishes.

1 pound fresh Brussels sprouts or
2 10-ounce packages frozen sprouts
Salt

Cook frozen sprouts according to package directions, drain. Wash fresh sprouts, removing discolored leaves; cook in 1 inch boiling salted water, ½ teaspoon salt to each cup of water, for about 8 minutes or just until tender; drain. Serve with Black Butter. Serves 6.

Black Butter

Melt butter in saucepan over moderate heat until mahogany brown. Caution: high heat will burn butter.

ANOTHER WAY

With a simple entrée, serve with Lemon Cream Dressing (page 126) or Egg Sauce (page 143). Prepared Hollandaise is available in the markets if time is limited; it is another good choice.

SPICED APRICOTS

1 1-pound 14-ounce can whole   4 cloves
  peeled apricots   ¼ teaspoon allspice
3 1-inch sticks cinnamon

Drain syrup from apricots into saucepan. Add cloves, allspice and cinnamon. Cook for 10 minutes; add apricots and let stand until cool. They may be reheated, or refrigerated to serve cold. Serves 6.

These may be prepared in advance for convenience; also use them with other meats, poultry or a contingency.

MOUSSE AU CHOCOLAT

1 6-ounce package semi-sweet chocolate pieces	2 tablespoons rum or cognac, or 1 teaspoon vanilla
6 egg yolks, well beaten	6 egg whites, stiffly beaten

Melt chocolate pieces over hot, not boiling, water in top of double boiler; when smooth, remove from heat. Add a small amount to yolks, stirring constantly; add yolks to chocolate and beat thoroughly. Cool, stirring occasionally. Blend in flavoring and fold in egg whites. Pour into 6 individual sherbet dishes or small cups and place in refrigerator to cool thoroughly. Serves 6.

May be served from 1-quart shallow dish or casserole.

QUICK ALTERNATE

Cognac Cream (page 71).

► Scallopine

Scallopine of Veal Pacifico   Herbed Rice
Italian Beans Adrian   Platter of Sliced Tomatoes
Chilled Cheese   Grapes

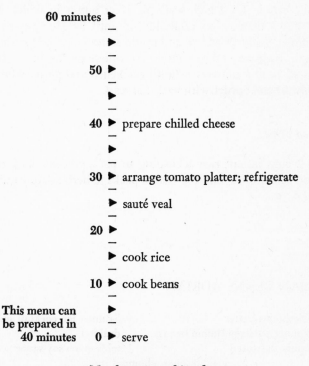

COOKING COUNTDOWN

60 minutes ►
  —
          ►
  —
    50 ►
  —
          ►
  —
    40 ► prepare chilled cheese
          ►
  —
    30 ► arrange tomato platter; refrigerate
  —
          ► sauté veal
  —
    20 ►
  —
          ► cook rice
  —
    10 ► cook beans
  —
This menu can   ►
be prepared in   —
    40 minutes   0 ► serve

May be prepared in advance:
Chilled Cheese

SCALLOPINE OF VEAL PACIFICO

With this quick menu, you can allow an hour, using the extra 20 minutes for quick clean-up and a peek in the mirror.

1 pound veal, sliced ⅛ inch thick
2 tablespoons butter
1 10-ounce can consommé
1 6-ounce can water chestnuts, drained and sliced
1 4-ounce can mushroom stems and pieces
1 tablespoon instantized flour
Herbed Rice

Cut the veal in 1 x 2-inch scallops. Heat butter in skillet; add veal and sauté 3 minutes on each side or until lightly browned. Add consommé, water chestnuts and mushrooms; cover and simmer for 5 minutes. Remove veal to platter. Add flour to pan juices, blending well, and cook 5 minutes or until thickened and clear. Mound rice on a platter and border with veal. Serves 4.

Herbed Rice

Cook 2 cups instant rice according to package directions, omitting salt and substituting one 1⅞-ounce package herb salad dressing mix. Serves 4.

ITALIAN BEANS ADRIAN

4 tablespoons butter
1 10-ounce package Italian beans, slightly defrosted
1 5-ounce jar cocktail onions, drained
1 tablespoon soy sauce
1 tablespoon chopped pimiento

Heat butter; add beans, onions and soy sauce. Cook over moderate heat, covered, for 6 minutes or until thoroughly heated. Do not overcook, as beans will become mushy. Arrange in a serving bowl and sprinkle with pimiento. Serves 4 to 6.

PLATTER OF SLICED TOMATOES

Slice 3 firm tomatoes; arrange overlapping on platter. Sprinkle with snipped parsley, chives, fresh or frozen, or thinly sliced green onions. Serves 4.

CHILLED CHEESE

Absolutely delicious, with true Italian lineage.

1 8-ounce package cream cheese, softened	¼ cup sugar
	1 tablespoon brandy
2 egg yolks	6 small bunches grapes
bowl of daisy-shaped crackers	

Whirl cheese in blender until very smooth, or force through sieve and then beat well. Combine with egg yolks, sugar and brandy and beat until smooth and creamy. Pour the mixture into a 2-cup serving bowl and chill several hours until set. Unmold on a platter and surround with bunches of grapes and crackers. Top with a center of 5 grape halves, placed like daisy petals. Serves 4.

May be prepared with ricotta cheese. Recipe may be doubled. For a quick chill, place cheese in freezer for 5 minutes.

May be made in advance if possible.

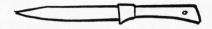

► Danish Veal

Danish Veal Birds   Spinach Plus Noodles
Senfgurken or *Watermelon Rind*
Apricot Coffee Cake Tivoli

COOKING COUNTDOWN

60 minutes ► prepare "birds"

—

►

—

50 ► cook noodles and spinach

—

►

—

40 ► cook "birds"

—

► arrange and bake spinach plus noodles

—

30 ►

—

►

—

20 ►

—

►

—

10 ► make toast points

—

►

—

0 ► serve

Must be prepared in advance:
Apricot Coffee Cake Tivoli

DANISH VEAL BIRDS

This is a basic Danish recipe with American shortcuts.

2 pounds veal steak sliced ¼ inch thick

¼ teaspoon freshly ground pepper

1½ teaspoons salt

¼ teaspoon thyme

¼ pound bacon slices, halved

1 cup coarsely chopped onions, fresh or frozen

½ cup chopped mushrooms, or 1 4-ounce can mushroom pieces (optional)

3 sweet pickles, sliced

4 tablespoons shortening

1 cup consommé or sweet white wine (Marsala)

½ cup canned tomato sauce

2 tablespoons snipped parsley, or 1½ tablespoons parsley flakes

2 tablespoons chopped green olives

Dry veal with paper toweling. Cut into scallops about 3 x 4 inches. Combine pepper, salt and thyme and spread over each piece of veal. Place a strip of bacon and a proportionate amount of onions, mushrooms and sweet pickles on each. Roll up and fasten with toothpicks or tie with string. Heat shortening in large skillet; brown veal evenly; add consommé, tomato sauce and parsley; cover and simmer 10 minutes and add chopped olives. Simmer additional 20 to 30 minutes until tender; serve on toast points. Remove fastenings from "birds" before placing on platter. Serves 6.

You may prepare "birds" in advance; refrigerate until cooking time.

SPINACH PLUS NOODLES

2 10-ounce packages frozen chopped spinach

¼ pound noodles, cooked

1 10-ounce can cream of mushroom soup

⅓ cup milk

⅛ teaspoon garlic powder or nutmeg

1 cup prepared croutons

2 tablespoons butter or margarine, melted

Cook spinach according to package directions; drain. Arrange spinach and noodles in layers in well-greased 6-cup casserole. Combine soup, milk and garlic powder; pour over noodles and spinach. Top with croutons and drizzle with butter. Bake in preheated 375° oven 30 to 35 minutes. Serves 6.

Senfgurken

These delicious pickles are obtainable in the markets; pickled watermelon would be a fine mate, either the prepared or your personal homemade stock.

APRICOT COFFEE CAKE TIVOLI

If you have time, try this simple, good and rich cake; or buy a Danish cake of your choice, if time is of the essence.

1 package active dry yeast
¼ cup warm water (about 110°)
6 tablespoons milk, scalded
½ cup (¼ pound) butter, softened
3 tablespoons sugar
½ teaspoon salt

¼ teaspoon lemon extract or ½ teaspoon grated lemon peel
1 egg, slightly beaten
2¼ cups sifted flour
1 8-ounce can apricot pastry filling
2 tablespoons butter, melted
Confectioners' Icing

Dissolve yeast in water in measuring cup (saving an extra utensil); allow the scalded milk to cool to lukewarm and combine with butter, sugar, salt, extract or lemon peel, egg and flour, blending very well. Turn out on lightly floured surface and knead 200 times or until dough is elastic and air bubbles click. Place in well-greased bowl, turning dough to grease completely. Cover and let rise in warm spot, free from drafts, for about 1 hour or until doubled in bulk. Dough will be light to the touch. Punch dough down, knead a time or two and turn out on wax paper; pat into a 12 x 10-inch rectangle; brush with melted butter and spread with apricot filling. Lift dough by raising wax paper and roll gently as for jelly roll; seal edges. Place in 8 x 8-inch well-greased baking pan, circling dough to fit. It will spread to edges of pan and form a square. Raise again for about 1 hour until dough is very light. Bake in preheated 350° oven until golden brown, about 40 to 50 minutes. Cool on rack; drizzle with Confectioners' Icing. Makes one cake; recipe may be doubled; eat one and freeze one. Change to other fillings of your choice.

Confectioners' Icing

Mix ½ cup sifted confectioners' sugar and 1 tablespoon milk until smooth.

ANOTHER WAY

After blending dough, do not knead. Place in refrigerator overnight. Remove and roll out to rectangle 12 x 10 inches and proceed as in original recipe.

Both may be made in advance. The first version may be prepared early in the day and reheated. Incidentally, coffee cakes are better when reheated. Wrap in foil and place in 400° oven about 10 minutes.

For the second version the dough must be prepared the previous day. Both may be frozen after baking.

Reheat any leftovers another time.

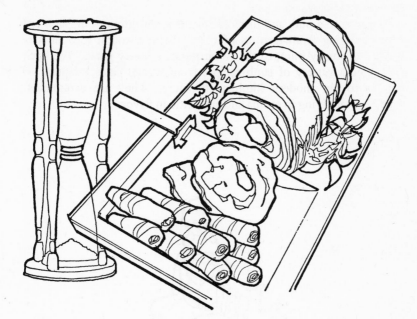

Worldly Lamb

OF ALL THE main dishes in our American "melting pot," lamb probably has the most international flavor. Through the ages lamb has been an important element in the diets of peoples from almost every corner of the world. Lamb entrées have come to us from many different cultures and are steeped in diverse history and traditions of eating. All the way from the sacrificial lamb of the Holy Lands to the stew of the Emerald Isle and on to the fragrant kabobs on the backyard barbecue, lamb is tasty fare, either unadorned or embellished with exotic spices.

Continental preparations preserve the flavor by a minimum of cooking, whereas Americans have been prone to serve it more or less well done. We now know that shorter cooking time, about three-fourths the time averaged in the past, assures finer flavor while garnering precious moments.

Prepared to a pink and luscious juiciness, the affinities of lamb are many, ranging from tartness of citrus fruits, through the conventional and sturdy mint, to the sweetness of a honey glaze. We have assembled a variety of lamb recipes from several lands, adapted, of course, to our modern kitchen efficiency. They are economical timewise, satisfying in aroma and authentic in flavor.

▶ Dinner-on-a-Chop

Lamb Steaks Plus   Hot Spiced Applesauce
French Bread and Butter
Toffee Cake

COOKING COUNTDOWN

60 minutes ▶ sauté steaks and place in oven
—
▶
—
50 ▶ cook rice
—
▶
—
40 ▶ assemble cake
—
▶
—
30 ▶
—
▶ arrange topping on steaks; bake
—
20 ▶ cook applesauce
—
▶
—
10 ▶ heat bread
—
▶
—
0 ▶ serve

May be prepared in advance:
Toffee Cake

LAMB STEAKS PLUS

6 lamb steaks or shoulder chops ¾ inch thick, about ½ pound each
2 tablespoons shortening
2 teaspoons salt
1 clove garlic, minced, or ½ teaspoon garlic powder
3 chicken bouillon cubes
1½ cups boiling water
2 tablespoons brown sugar
1 7-ounce package seasoned rice
6 slices onion, ¼ inch thick
6 slices tomato, ¼ inch thick
6 large green pepper rings, 1 inch thick

Wipe steaks with paper toweling. Heat shortening in skillet and brown steaks evenly over high heat, about 5 minutes on each side. Dust with salt and place in shallow casserole in single layer. Dissolve bouillon cubes in boiling water, blend with garlic and sugar and pour over steaks. Cover the pan with aluminum foil and seal well. Place in preheated 375° oven and bake 30 minutes. Prepare rice according to package directions and set aside. Uncover steaks and place a slice of onion on each steak, then a slice of tomato and top with a ring of green pepper. Fill each ring with about ½ cup rice. Baste rice with pan drippings and bake 15 to 20 minutes additional or until tender. Serves 6.

ANOTHER WAY

Instead of lamb steaks, prepare the recipe with pork chops, cut 1½ inches thick.

Note: bake 1½ hours, as pork requires longer cooking; the result is well worth the extra time.

HOT SPICED APPLESAUCE

1 1-pound can applesauce or 1 1-pound 5-ounce can apple pie filling
½ cup raisins
¼ cup vinegar
¼ teaspoon salt
½ teaspoon ginger
½ teaspoon dry mustard
½ teaspoon curry powder

Combine all ingredients in saucepan. Bring to a boil, stirring occasionally; reduce heat and simmer 10 minutes. Serve hot as meat accompaniment. Makes 2¾ cups.

FRENCH BREAD AND BUTTER

Wrap French bread in foil; place in oven with lamb for 10 minutes. Serve thick slices, hot, crusty, with plenty of butter.

TOFFEE CAKE

A really professional looking and tasting cake, put together with ease.

1 10-inch angel food cake
8 1⅛-ounce toffee bars, chilled
2 cups whipping cream
⅔ cup sugar

2 tablespoons instant coffee
½ cup shredded, toasted coconut
 (optional)

Bake an angel food cake (10-inch) using a mix, or purchase one at the market. Split in half horizontally, with a long sharp knife, using a sawing motion. Place bottom half on cake plate. Place toffee bars between 2 sheets of waxed paper; crush them fine with a rolling pin. Whip cream quite stiff, gradually adding the sugar and instant coffee; fold in crushed toffee bars. Spread about ⅓ of cream mixture on bottom cake half; place second half on top and completely cover sides and top of cake with remaining toffee cream. For added flavor, sprinkle top and sides of cake with toasted coconut. Refrigerate cake until serving time. Serves 10 to 12.

To toast shredded coconut, preheat oven to 300°; spread coconut on shallow baking pan. Place in oven and stir often, for about 10 minutes, until evenly browned.

Toffee Cake is equally delicious if prepared early in the day; freeze leftovers for another dinner.

If convenient, toast the coconut in advance; assemble the cake beforehand and enjoy the extra time in a relaxed evening.

▶ Island Lamb Steak

Island Lamb Steak   *Bermuda Potato Puff*
Beanomato Salad Bowl   *Simple Dressing*
Fuji Mounds

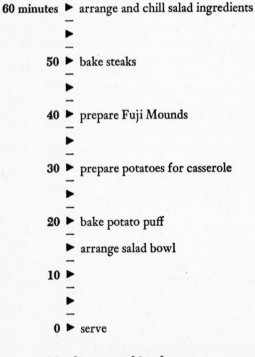

COOKING COUNTDOWN

60 minutes ▶ arrange and chill salad ingredients
— ▶
—
50 ▶ bake steaks
— ▶
—
40 ▶ prepare Fuji Mounds
— ▶
—
30 ▶ prepare potatoes for casserole
— ▶
—
20 ▶ bake potato puff
— ▶ arrange salad bowl
—
10 ▶
— ▶
—
0 ▶ serve

May be prepared in advance:
Fuji Mounds

ISLAND LAMB STEAKS

4 ¾-inch-thick lamb shoulder
   steaks (with small round bone)
3 tablespoons soy sauce
¼ teaspoon white pepper
½ cup brown sugar

½ teaspoon dry mustard
2 tablespoons wine vinegar
1 10-ounce can sliced pineapple
   (4 slices, drained)
1 orange, cut in 4 thick slices

Wipe steaks with paper toweling and place in shallow baking pan; sprinkle with soy sauce and pepper. Combine sugar, mustard, vinegar; blend well and spread ½ the mixture over steaks. Bake in preheated 400° oven 20 minutes, then turn. Top each with a pineapple and an orange slice; spread with remaining brown sugar mixture and bake an additional 20 minutes. Place each topped steak carefully on platter and pour pan sauce over. Serve piping hot to 4.

BERMUDA POTATO PUFF

4 to 5 servings instant mashed potatoes
1 tablespoon grated Bermuda onion or 1 teaspoon instant onion flakes

1 tablespoon butter or margarine
paprika

Prepare potatoes according to package directions; mix with onion and arrange in well-buttered 1-quart casserole. Dot with butter and dust liberally with paprika. Bake in preheated 400° oven 20 minutes. With this menu, place in oven with Island Lamb Steaks for last 20 minutes of baking time. Serves 4 to 5.

BEANOMATO SALAD BOWL

2 medium tomatoes, cut in ¼-inch slices
1 16-ounce can cut green beans, drained

¼ cup thinly sliced green onions or dry green onion flakes
lettuce leaves
parsley (optional)

Simple Dressing

⅓ cup salad oil
¼ cup vinegar
½ teaspoon dry mustard

½ teaspoon salt
3 tablespoons snipped parsley or parsley flakes

Combine tomatoes, beans and onions in a bowl; thoroughly blend dressing ingredients and drizzle over tomato mixture. Chill about ½ hour or more. Serve in lettuce-lined bowl, sprinkled with parsley, if you wish; it adds flavor and finish. Serves 4.

ANOTHER WAY

Substitute a sweet Italian onion in thinly sliced rings.

FUJI MOUNDS

A no-bake chocolate confection with little effort.

1 6-ounce package butterscotch pieces
1 6-ounce package semi-sweet chocolate pieces

1½ cups chow mein noodles
1 6¾-ounce can cocktail peanuts

Melt butterscotch and chocolate pieces in top of double boiler, over (not in) boiling water for about 5 minutes, stirring occasionally. Add noodles and nuts, mixing very well. Line a cooky sheet with wax paper and drop heaping teaspoons of the mixture in mounds allowing separation between. Stir mixture once or twice while forming mounds to keep ingredients well mixed. Place in refrigerator for 15 minutes to set. Store in airtight container in cool place or in refrigerator. They will be very firm in refrigerator but will soften sufficiently in the few minutes before being placed on serving plate. Makes 36 to 40 mounds.

I can only suggest these be made in advance to have on hand, and add the promise that they won't last long.

▶ Broiled Lamb Chops

Broiled Lamb Chops   *Tomatoes Provençale*
Buttered Bow Knot Noodles   *Crisp Spinach Salad*
Ginger Pie Apples   *Hard Sauce*

COOKING COUNTDOWN

60 minutes ▶
　　　　　▶
　　　　　—
　　　50 ▶ prepare hard sauce
　　　　　—
　　　　　▶ bake ginger pie apples
　　　　　—
　　　40 ▶
　　　　　—
　　　　　▶ hard-cook eggs
　　　　　—
　　　30 ▶ arrange salad bowl; chill
　　　　　—
　　　　　▶ cook noodles
　　　　　—
　　　20 ▶ cook tomatoes
　　　　　—
　　　　　▶ broil chops
　　　　　—
This menu can be 　10 ▶ toss noodles with butter
prepared in 35 minutes 　　　—
if dessert and sauce 　　　▶
are prepared in 　　　　—
advance 　　0 ▶ serve

May be prepared in advance:
　　Ginger Pie Apples
　　Hard Sauce

BROILED LAMB CHOPS

Always a reliable last-minute entrée. The paprika gives the chops a crusty finish, the flavor is subtle; the preparation a welcome change.

8 1-inch-thick lean lamb chops, rib or loin
1 tablespoon seasoned salt (approximately)

2 tablespoons paprika
Tomatoes Provençale

Preheat broiler; place chops on lightly greased rack, 3 inches below heat. See table below for timing. Broil on one side; dust with ½ tablespoon seasoned salt and 1 tablespoon paprika; turn and broil second side. Dust with remaining seasoned salt and paprika; remove to warm platter. Arrange Tomatoes Provençale around chops; cover with sauce from tomatoes or serve sauce separately. Serves 4.

Timing for Lamb Chop Broil

Size	Medium	Well Done
	(minutes each side)	
Single chops, 1 inch thick	6	7
Single chops, 1½ inches thick	9	11
Double chops, 2 inches thick	12	15

ANOTHER WAY

For simple broiled chops, reduce paprika or omit.

Tomatoes Provençale

1 1-pound can whole tomatoes
1 teaspoon sugar
4 tablespoons butter
2 cloves garlic, minced
⅓ cup coarsely chopped onion

1 green pepper cut in ¼-inch dice (optional)
2 tablespoons dry white wine
¼ teaspoon basil
½ teaspoon salt
⅛ teaspoon freshly ground pepper

Drain liquid from tomatoes and set aside; carefully place tomatoes on dish to avoid losing shape; sprinkle with sugar. Melt 2 tablespoons butter in saucepan; add garlic, onion and green pepper; sauté 5 minutes or until onions are glazed but not brown. Blend in reserved liquid from tomatoes, wine and seasonings; simmer 5 minutes. Add tomatoes carefully, pouring tomato sauce over them; heat slowly until piping hot, about 5 minutes. Add remaining 2 tablespoons butter and allow it to melt just until it floats on surface. Serves 4.

Fresh tomatoes are excellent prepared in this way. Peel 4 of medium size, cut in quarters, and proceed as for canned tomatoes.

BUTTERED BOW KNOT NOODLES

Simple as pie!

Cook one 8-ounce package bow knot noodles according to package directions. Drain and toss with 2 tablespoons butter; dust with paprika or snipped parsley and serve from a bowl or in center of entrée platter. Serves 4 to 6.

CRISP SPINACH SALAD

1 pound raw spinach	2 tablespoons finely chopped green onion
½ cup coarsely chopped salad olives	½ cup Classic French Dressing (page 247)
2 hard-cooked eggs, sliced	

Wash spinach well and remove stems, then drain and dry between paper towels; arrange in salad bowl. Toss in olives; overlap egg slices around rim and sprinkle with chopped onion; chill. To serve, moisten with dressing and toss lightly. Serves 4.

ANOTHER WAY OR TWO

There are many variations for this combination:

1. Substitute 6 anchovy fillets, cut in pieces, or 4 slices crumbled, crisp bacon for olives.

2. Add chopped egg whites and sieve the yolks for garnish.

3. Substitute parsley for onions, or use half of each.

4. Add a dash of fennel or dill to the dressing.

GINGER PIE APPLES

2 cups coarsely crushed ginger-snaps	1 1-pound can apple pie filling
1 teaspoon vanilla	1 tablespoon butter or margarine
	Cinnamon Sugar

Arrange half of crumbs in greased 1-quart casserole or baking dish; mix vanilla with apple pie filling and spread over crumbs in even layer; top with remaining crumbs, then dot with butter and sprinkle with Cinnamon Sugar. Bake in preheated 375° oven 20 to 25 minutes until piping hot. Serve warm to 4 or 6.

Cinnamon Sugar

Combine 1 teaspoon cinnamon with 3 tablespoons sugar. This will keep indefinitely, and, of course, there is the prepared mixture available in handy shaker containers.

OTHER WAYS

1. Serve with Hard Sauce.

2. To apple pie filling, add 2 tablespoons apricot or orange marmalade and 2 tablespoons brandy, mixing well.
   May be made in advance and reheated.

Hard Sauce

¼ cup butter, softened	1¼ cups confectioners' sugar
1 tablespoon light cream or milk, heated	1 teaspoon vanilla
	1 egg yolk
dash salt	

Combine all ingredients and beat with electric mixer or rotary beater until light and fluffy. Refrigerate until chilled and firm. One teaspoon cinnamon may be substituted for the vanilla.

The Hard Sauce is a small item, good to have out of the way. It may be prepared early in the day or well in advance and refrigerated.

▶ Grilled Sirloin Lamb Chops

Grilled Sirloin Lamb Chops   Vegetable Kabobs
Lettuce Wedges   Thousand Island Dressing
Meringue Nests or Chocolate Pudding

COOKING COUNTDOWN

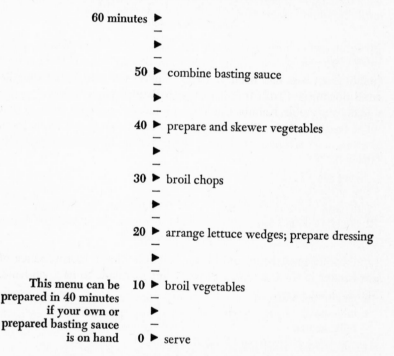

60 minutes ▶
　　　　　 —
　　　　　 ▶
　　　　　 —
　　　50 ▶ combine basting sauce
　　　　 —
　　　　 ▶
　　　　 —
　　　40 ▶ prepare and skewer vegetables
　　　　 —
　　　　 ▶
　　　　 —
　　　30 ▶ broil chops
　　　　 —
　　　　 ▶
　　　　 —
　　　20 ▶ arrange lettuce wedges; prepare dressing
　　　　 —
　　　　 ▶
　　　　 —
This menu can be 　10 ▶ broil vegetables
prepared in 40 minutes 　 —
if your own or 　　　 ▶
prepared basting sauce 　 —
is on hand 　　0 ▶ serve

May be prepared in advance:
　　　Basting sauce early in the day
Must be prepared in advance:
　　　Meringue Nests
　　　Fill meringues early in the day
　　　or on the previous day

GRILLED SIRLOIN LAMB CHOPS

Often leg of lamb is a weekend special and it is advisable to take advantage of it. A leg of lamb may be too large for your needs, but your butcher will gladly slice steaks or chops from the loin end. This recipe makes use of such an opportunity.

6 1½-inch-thick sirloin lamb
    chops (about 3 pounds)
1 teaspoon garlic salt or plain salt

½ teaspoon seasoned salt
¼ teaspoon pepper
Patio Basting Sauce
Vegetable Kabobs

Sprinkle lamb chops with garlic salt, seasoned salt and pepper; place on broiler pan. Brush chops with Patio Basting Sauce. Place 6 to 7 inches from heat and broil 12 to 15 minutes per side or until of desired doneness. Brush frequently with Patio Basting Sauce.

Add Vegetable Kabobs the last 5 minutes of broiling time so that all is ready at once. Place on platter; slide Vegetable Kabobs from skewers and arrange as border; serve remaining sauce separately. Serves 6.

Patio Basting Sauce

1 8-ounce can tomato sauce
2 tablespoon molasses

1 tablespoon cider vinegar
⅛ teaspoon dried tarragon leaves
⅛ teaspoon dry mustard

Combine all ingredients and blend well. Good as a basting sauce or as a marinade for less tender cuts. A fine marinade to have on hand. Makes about 1 cup.

VEGETABLE KABOBS

1 small cantaloupe, cut in 1-inch
    cubes, or 2 medium cucumbers,
    sliced ½ inch thick

½ pound large mushrooms
2 medium green peppers, cut in
    sixths
12 cherry tomatoes (optional)

Thread vegetables alternately on 8-inch skewers; brush with Patio

Basting Sauce and place on broiler pan 6 to 7 inches from heat. Broil
about 3 minutes on each side. Serves 6.

Preparation is frequently a matter of preference. We enjoy our
vegetables with a minimum of cooking. If you prefer, add 2 to 3
minutes to the cooking time.

Here is an and/or list of other kabob vegetables. The choice is
yours.

Vegetables	Broiling Time
small whole onions	10 to 15 minutes
zucchini, ½-inch slices	5 to 8 minutes
eggplant, 1-inch cubes	5 to 8 minutes
tomatoes, wedges or sherry tomatoes	3 to 5 minutes
corn on Cob, 2-inch pieces	3 to 5 minutes

ANOTHER WAY

May be grilled outdoors.

LETTUCE WEDGES
AND THOUSAND ISLAND DRESSING

Divide a solid, medium-sized head of iceberg lettuce into 6 wedges
and top with 2 tablespoons of dressing.

Simple Thousand Island Dressing

A good dressing with many purposes.

1 cup mayonnaise
½ cup chili sauce
2 tablespoons sweet pickle relish

2 teaspoons chopped chives, fresh
or frozen (optional)

Combine all ingredients, blending well. Makes about 1½ cups.

ANOTHER WAY

Use with seafood, vegetables, over eggs and with other greens.

MERINGUE NESTS

The versatility of these airy desserts is limitless. We will start with the suggestion for this menu, then discuss some variations. You may go on and on by using your imagination.

2 egg whites	⅛ teaspoon cream of tartar
dash salt	½ cup sugar
	½ teaspoon vanilla

Beat egg whites until frothy; add salt and cream of tartar and beat until soft peaks form when beaters are raised. Add sugar, 1 tablespoon at a time, beating until very stiff; fold in vanilla. Grease and flour a cooky sheet. Draw 6 circles in the flour using a teacup for outline; form nests inside circles; swirl meringue to hollow centers. Place in preheated 275° oven and reduce heat to 250°; bake 50 minutes or until dry to the touch. Turn off heat and allow to remain in oven to cool. They may be made well in advance and stored in airtight container. With this menu, fill with Lemon Custard. Double the recipe for an even dozen. Serves 6.

ORANGE CUSTARD

2 egg yolks (left over from meringues)	1 teaspoon grated orange peel
¼ cup sugar	½ cup whipping cream, whipped, or ¼ cup sour cream, chilled
1½ teaspoons lemon juice	green sugar
¼ cup orange juice	6 maraschino cherries

Beat yolks until thick and lemon colored in top of double boiler; beat in sugar, both juices and peel. Place over boiling water, stirring constantly until thickened. Cool; add chilled cream and pour into nests; sprinkle with green sugar and/or top with cherry. May be prepared in advance. Makes filling for 6 nests.

When filled and refrigerated in advance, the nests become Angel Pies.

OTHER WAYS

1. Fill nests with a scoop of ice cream and a compatible sauce.

Filling	*Topping*
strawberry ice cream	defrosted frozen or fresh strawberries
pineapple sherbet	shredded coconut
peppermint ice cream	chocolate sauce

2. Fill with prepared custard mix combined with an interesting addition.

Filling	*Addition*
lemon pudding and pie filling	½ teaspoon fresh lemon juice and/or ½ cup whipped cream
chocolate pudding	1 teaspoon instant coffee and/or 1 teaspoon Kahlua
banana cream pudding	sliced bananas
butterscotch pudding	¼ cup chopped nuts

QUICK ALTERNATE

1. Prepare chocolate pudding with an instant mix and add 1 teaspoon coffee-flavored liqueur. Serve with a sweet from your cooky jar.

2. Prepare lemon pudding with an instant mix and add ½ teaspoon grated lemon peel to enhance the flavor.

▶ Lamb Curry

Curry of Lamb Shoulder   Rice
Curry Accompaniments
Lemon Cream Cheese Pie or *Custard Fruit*

COOKING COUNTDOWN

60 minutes ▶ prepare cheese pie

▶

50 ▶ cook lamb

▶

40 ▶ prepare and arrange curry
accompaniments

▶

30 ▶

▶

20 ▶ cook rice

▶

10 ▶ decorate pie

**This menu can be
prepared in 50 minutes
with Quick Alternate
dessert**

0 ▶ serve

May be prepared in advance:
Lemon Cheese Pie

CURRY OF LAMB SHOULDER

Hindustani gives us its formal name — "Turcarri." Colloquial usage shortened this to "turri." Mispronunciation could account for the Anglo-Saxon, familiar "curry." Wonderful importations, curries offer exotic dining and beautiful service. An interesting arrangement of curry has the essence of a ritual. Choose as many accompaniments as you desire, but no less than three of varying color and texture. Here we have added domestic black caviar, which improves the curry, has its own elegance and adds a party flavor.

In India, curry is served on large metal trays or *thali* with the accompaniments in small metal bowls. The effect is lovely. We can have a comparable service and retain the heat of a preparation by using a modern skillet or chafing dish. I serve the accompaniments in lotus bowls, which now come in many hues, arranging them in a circle for convenience; the greater your selection, the more conversation, open sesame to a successful gathering. I must add there is nothing difficult in this performance, so proceed without hesitation.

4 lean lamb steaks or 2 pounds lamb shoulder, cut in 1-inch cubes	1 teaspoon salt
	½ teaspoon monosodium glutamate
3 tablespoons butter or margarine	½ teaspoon powdered ginger
½ cup coarsely chopped onion	½ teaspoon sugar
1 cup peeled, cored, diced apple	⅛ teaspoon pepper
2 cups consommé or 2 bouillon cubes in 2 cups boiling water	½ cup half-and-half cream or milk
1 tablespoon curry powder	2 tablespoons flour
	3 cups cooked rice

Curry Accompaniments

Pat the lamb dry with paper toweling. Heat butter in large saucepan; add lamb and brown evenly, about 10 minutes. Add onion and apples and sauté again, tossing until lightly browned, about five minutes. Add consommé, curry powder, salt, monosodium glutamate, ginger, sugar and pepper. Bring to boil, reduce heat and simmer 30 minutes or until tender. Mix cream with flour and blend into lamb; cook 5 more minutes until piping hot. Serve with instant or Fluffy Rice, and your choice of three of the Curry Accompaniments. Serves 4. Increase by one half to serve 6.

Curry Accompaniments

flaked coconut
chopped chutney
chopped salted peanuts
preserved kumquats

crumbled bacon
raisins
chopped green pepper
chopped preserved ginger

domestic black caviar

LEMON CREAM CHEESE PIE

As a bride, I found one of the magical mysteries of new products to be the combination of sweetened condensed milk and lemon juice. They become a luscious custard when combined. By adding a new ingredient, we can now have a custard lemon cheese filling.

1 8-ounce package cream cheese, softened
1 15-ounce can sweetened condensed milk
½ cup lemon juice

dash salt
1 9-inch graham cracker crumb crust, purchased or recipe (page 225)
Chocolate Curls (optional)

Allow cheese to stand at room temperature to soften, then beat until fluffy. Blend in condensed milk gradually, stirring constantly. Add lemon juice and salt; pour into prepared crust. Place in freezer to chill quickly or allow 1 hour in refrigerator. Make pie the previous day if possible and have it ready to serve when needed. Border with Chocolate Curls. Serves 6 to 8.

I suggest making the pie in advance. Preparation takes little time and having it on hand allows for a relaxing visit, especially with this menu.

Chocolate Curls

With a vegetable peeler, shave thin strips from a bar of semi-sweet baking chocolate. For easier slicing, have chocolate at room temperature.

OTHER WAYS

Instead of crumb crust, line a 9-inch pie pan with a layer of leftover cake, cut in ½-inch slices, chocolate or vanilla cookies or store-bought pound cake slices.

Leftover pie, if covered tightly, will keep well for four or five days refrigerated.

QUICK ALTERNATE

Custard Fruit

2 8-ounce jars vanilla custard   1 teaspoon sherry
  (baby food)   3 bananas, sliced, or 1 1-pound can
1 teaspoon vanilla   pears, drained

Mix vanilla custard with vanilla and sherry; place fruit in serving dish or individual dessert dishes and top with custard. Serves 6.

▶ Hurry Curry

Crab Spread Renard
Hurry Curry   Accompaniments   Rice Variations
Paludeh American Style

COOKING COUNTDOWN

60 minutes ▶ mix crab spread
          —
          ▶
          —
     50 ▶
          —
          ▶
          —
     40 ▶
          —
          ▶
          —
     30 ▶ defrost fruit
          —
          ▶ cook rice
          —
     20 ▶ combine curry dish and heat
          —
          ▶
          —
     10 ▶ arrange curry accompaniments
          —
This menu can be
prepared in 30 minutes   ▶
   if Crab Spread is   —
prepared in advance   0 ▶ serve

May be prepared in advance:
Crab Spread Renard

CRAB SPREAD RENARD

1 7-ounce can crabmeat
1 8-ounce package cream cheese,
  softened
6 green onions, green part only,
  finely snipped

2 teaspoons Worcestershire
3 tablespoons milk or cream
½ teaspoon salt
assorted crisp crackers

Drain crabmeat and remove all cartilage and bone; mash cheese with a fork until smooth and creamy, then add crabmeat, onions, Worcestershire, milk and salt. Blend very well and place in refrigerator a minimum of 1 hour. Serve in a bowl placed in center of serving platter and border with crackers. Makes 2 cups.

If you wish, Crab Spread Renard may be made early in the day. However, the dinner is so simple, the choice is a matter of your convenience.

HURRY CURRY

As the name implies, this is a quick dish — an embarrassingly easy recipe, but truly delicious!

8 to 10 slices cooked lamb
1 10½-ounce can condensed
  cream of mushroom soup

¼ cup light cream
2 teaspoons (or more to taste)
  curry powder

Heat lamb in soup mixed with cream. Add curry powder; blend well. Serves 4.

More Curry Accompaniments

toasted coconut
chopped fresh tomatoes

toasted almonds
chopped sweet pickles

Make your selection of accompaniments from these or from the list on page 176, and serve in small bowls grouped on a tray.

RICE VARIATIONS

1. *Precooked white rice* with its effective color contrast is a com-

patible curry mate. For 4 servings, prepare according to package directions.

2. *Saffron Rice.* The prepared mixture is a fine pantry item. Cook according to package directions or use quick-cooking white rice and add ½ teaspoon saffron to the boiling water.

3. *Fruited rice* is a good accompaniment for curry, too. For 4 servings, add ½ cup raisins and/or 2 tablespoons grapefruit or orange marmalade to precooked white rice.

4. *Fluffy Rice*

1 cup long-grain rice   2 cups water
½ teaspoon salt

Combine ingredients in saucepan with tight cover. Bring to boiling; cover and reduce heat. Simmer 30 minutes or until water is absorbed; remove from heat. Allow to stand 10 minutes — do not uncover while cooking. Makes 3 cups.

PALUDEH AMERICAN STYLE

A typical Persian dessert is Paludeh — fresh fruits topped with crushed ice. Our wonderful convenience foods give us this version; the ice crystals in the partially defrosted fruits effect a similar result.

1 10-ounce package frozen sliced   1 10-ounce package frozen melon
peaches, partially defrosted   balls, partially defrosted
2 tablespoons rose water (optional)

Arrange peaches in 4 shallow dessert dishes. Top with melon balls. For a truly Persian flavor, drizzle rose water over the fruit.

Note: Rose water may be purchased at Greek or Armenian groceries.

►Kabobing With Company

*Shish Kabobs   Fruit and Vegetable Kabob Collection
Bouillon Potato Tureen   City Salad Bowl
Chocolate Cups*

COOKING COUNTDOWN

60 minutes ► arrange kabobs and accompaniments

►
—

50 ►
—

► fill chocolate cups
—

40 ►
—

►
—

30 ► arrange salads
—

►
—

20 ► broil kabobs
—

► cook potatoes
—

This menu can be prepared   10 ►
in 30 minutes if Kabobs   —
are marinated and   ►
chocolate cups filled in   —
advance   0 ► serve

May be prepared in advance:
Marinate Kabobs
Must be prepared in advance:
Chocolate Cups

SHISH KABOB

There are Shish Kabobs, Kebobs, Kababs, and Shashlik en brochette in as many varieties as there are titles. But by any name or with any combination, all are interesting, delicious and quick — fun fare that is almost a complete meal.

2 pounds boneless lamb cut in
1½-inch cubes
1 cup sauce or marinade

combination of skewer accompaniments

Marinating the lamb is suggested for flavor and tenderness. A period of one hour lends a delicious result; obviously a longer period lends more flavor. Marinate the meat overnight or before you leave for your appointments; have it at hand for the next step — threading. Use 12-inch skewers and thread drained lamb with any of the suggested combinations, using 4 pieces alternated with fruit and/or vegetables. Brush with marinade and grill or broil 6 inches from heat, turning occasionally and basting until evenly browned; allow 15 to 20 minutes. Arrange in spokelike fashion on serving platter. Serve immediately with pan drippings as sauce. Serves 4.

ANOTHER WAY

Beef Kabobs may be prepared the same way; reduce broiling time, allowing 5 minutes on each side for medium and 4 minutes for rare, turning once.

SHISH KABOB SKEWER MATES

One pound of meat will make approximately sixteen 1½-inch cubes for 4 skewers. I like to thread the assortments, starting and ending with the meat cubes. Allow 4 meat cubes and 3 each of whatever selection of vegetables or fruit you use.

Suggested Vegetable or Fruit Mates

green pepper, cherry tomatoes, mushrooms
onions, quartered tomatoes, green pepper

> cucumber wedges, green pepper, onions
>
> pineapple, bananas, tomatoes
>
> cantaloupe, green pepper, mushrooms
>
> pineapple, mushrooms, small onions
>
> pineapple, peppers, mushrooms
>
> zucchini, tomatoes, green pepper

The list goes on ad infinitum and the choice is endless. Try prunes, apricots, apples, chili peppers, small cooked potatoes, preserved fruits, such as kumquats, or others of your choice. Be not afraid!

MARINADES

The simple suggestion for marinade: prepared French or Italian dressing. Either may be embellished with a personalized dash of chili powder, 1 teaspoon Worcestershire sauce or garlic powder, curry, herbs, and on and on . . .
Here is a choice of unique flavors.

1. Marinade Chinois

¾ cup salad oil
3 tablespoons soy sauce
1 teaspoon dry mustard

½ teaspoon dry ginger
½ teaspoon garlic salt
¼ cup sherry

Stir ingredients together and blend well.

2. Wine Marinade and Sauce

½ cup salad or olive oil
½ cup red wine
1 medium onion, thinly sliced
¼ cup lemon juice

1 slice lemon peel
2 garlic cloves, halved
2 teaspoons salt
1 teaspoon cloves

1 teaspoon peppercorns

Combine and blend well. After cooking lamb, drain marinade from pan, add 2 tablespoons honey and 2 tablespoons light molasses. Heat and serve as sauce.

3. Marinade Vin Rouge

¾ cup red wine
1 cup chili sauce
2 tablespoons Worcestershire
1 garlic clove (optional)

1 teaspoon chili powder
¼ cup olive or salad oil
1 teaspoon prepared mustard
2 teaspoons salt

1 tablespoon instant minced onion

Blend thoroughly. This marinade is a good sauce; if it becomes too thick, thin with additional wine. The chili powder makes the marinade zesty and is not as hot as is often implied.

BOUILLON POTATO TUREEN

Mr. Costello, maître d'hôtel of the Pearson Hotel, serves Bouillon Potatoes, a delicious specialty. He has related the recipe many times with the involved basic cooking of beef stock and the many maneuvers. I substituted canned onion soup and found the result a hearty dish, delectably flavored.

1 10-ounce can onion soup
½ cup water
1 carrot, finely grated
1 teaspoon parsley flakes

¼ teaspoon marjoram (optional)
15 frozen new potatoes or 4 large
potatoes, cut in 1-inch cubes

Combine all ingredients except potatoes and bring to boiling; add frozen potatoes, bring again to boiling and cook, uncovered, 10 to 14 minutes or until very tender. (Add fresh potatoes the same way.) The bouillon will cook down to a thickness comparable to a sauce. If necessary add a small amount of water. Serves 4 to 5.

ANOTHER WAY

Use one 10-ounce can beef bouillon instead of onion soup; add ½ cup finely diced celery. Cook until potatoes are very tender. The recipe may be doubled.

CITY SALAD BOWL

The variety of vegetables threaded with the kabobs precludes an extravagant salad. Serve chilled bowls of greens assorted if you wish and a choice of light dressing; oil and vinegar and/or French and Italian are a compatible trio. Don't forget the indispensable pepper mill.

CHOCOLATE CUPS

These are beautiful containers, simply prepared.

¼ cup sugar
6 tablespoons butter or margarine
1 1-ounce envelope no-melt unsweetened chocolate-flavored in-

gredient or 1 1-ounce square unsweetened chocolate
½ teaspoon vanilla
1 cup sifted flour

Filling: Cherry Filling, ice cream, Coffee Cream Topping (page 419) or instant pudding mix of your choice

Cream sugar and butter together until fluffy; blend in chocolate and vanilla. Stir in flour until thoroughly mixed, then knead about 1 minute until smooth. Divide into 2 balls and wrap each in wax paper. Chill in refrigerator until firm, a minimum of 2 hours. Place ½ of dough between 2 sheets of wax paper and roll out to ¼-inch thickness. Cut into circles with 3-inch cooky cutter; shape over the bottom of 2-inch, inverted muffin cups. Bake in preheated 350° oven 10 minutes or until done. Cool, then loosen gently to remove; a slight push with a fork from rim of chocolate cup will release it. Fill with filling of your choice. The ice cream goes in the last minute; if you use a pudding, fill when cool and refrigerate. Makes 12.

OTHER WAYS

1. The dough may be made the previous day and refrigerated overnight.

2. The cups may be made in advance and stored in airtight container; they keep very well.

3. Fill the cups with Cherry Filling or ice cream. Place in freezer for that special menu.

Cherry Filling for 12 Chocolate Cups

1 2⅛-ounce envelope whipped topping mix	½ cup chopped maraschino cherries
¼ cup maraschino cherry juice	6 maraschino cherries, halved

Prepare topping mix according to package directions. Fold in juice and chopped cherries. Fill cups and top each with ½ cherry, cut side down. Makes filling for 12 cups.

QUICK ALTERNATE

Cherry Filling may be served in dessert dishes; add a cooky for accompaniment.

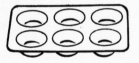

▶ Couscous Dinner in Gibraltar

Chicken and Lamb Ragoût   Couscous
Moroccan Orange Salad   Honey Lime Dressing
Almond Crescents (Kab El Ghzal) or Butterscotch Cookies

COOKING COUNTDOWN

60 minutes ▶ sauté chicken and lamb
　　　　　▶
　　50 ▶ simmer chicken and lamb
　　　　　▶
　　40 ▶ cook farina; chill
　　　　　▶ prepare dressing; chill
　　30 ▶ arrange salads; chill
　　　　　▶
　　20 ▶
　　　　　▶
　　10 ▶ add vegetables to ragoût and reheat
　　　　　▶ slice farina and sauté
　　　0 ▶ serve

Must be prepared in advance:
Almond Crescents

CHICKEN AND LAMB RAGOÛT

We once anchored at Gibraltar with the sun streaming a warm welcome and our spirits were high as we strode through exotic streets.
We encountered a gaily decorated, fringe-draped horse-drawn buggy
and climbed aboard. Within moments, the skies seemed to open and
we huddled together for protection against the downpour. As soon
as the elements permitted, we dashed indoors for coffee. Our selection of refuge proved to be a Moroccan restaurant and Couscous the
reigning menu favorite. Of course, we asked for an order and found
that Couscous is a grain of traditional, national importance, served
with a stew of meat, poultry or a combination of both, apparently
prepared with nothing but the thought of enhancing the grain. We
prefer to enhance the meat, as in this recipe.

¼ cup butter
3 onions, sliced in ¼-inch rings
1 frying chicken (about 2½ pounds), disjointed
1½ pounds boneless lamb, in 1-inch cubes
2 teaspoons salt
1 teaspoon seasoned salt
½ teaspoon onion powder
¼ teaspoon freshly ground pepper
¼ teaspoon cinnamon
dash cayenne

2 cups water
1 8-ounce can tomato sauce
1 tablespoon sugar
1 green pepper, cut in ½-inch slices
1 1-pound can garbanzos (chick peas) or kidney beans, drained
1 1-pound can sweet potatoes, drained and sliced
1 1-pound can carrots, drained
Couscous or 4 cups cooked egg barley

As a time-saver use 2 pots. Sauté chicken in a skillet and lamb in
saucepan, ready to be combined at the same time. Rub chicken
with 1 teaspoon salt, seasoned salt and onion powder. Heat 2 tablespoons butter in large skillet; add chicken and sauté until lightly
browned. While chicken is browning, heat remaining 2 tablespoons
butter in saucepan; add onions and lamb, and sauté until lightly
browned. Sprinkle with remaining salt, pepper, cinnamon and cayenne; add browned chicken, water, tomato sauce and sugar. Bring to
boil, then reduce heat and simmer, covered, 20 to 30 minutes or until
tender. Add green pepper, garbanzos, sweet potatoes and carrots;

simmer 10 minutes or until thoroughly heated. To serve, pile Couscous or egg barley in center of platter and border with chicken, lamb and vegetables. Pour some of sauce over barley and serve remainder separately. Serves 8.

Egg barley is available at most food stores; cook according to package directions. Traditional Couscous is made of farina; the following recipe approximates it.

Couscous (Farina Cubes)

Farina, our simple homespun cereal, has real resemblance to the authentic Couscous. It is a welcome addition to the dumpling family and may be used in most every menu which suggests a pasta. To add to its virtues, it may be made in advance and keeps well.

1 cup farina	1 teaspoon parsley flakes (optional)
4 cups boiling water	tional)
1 teaspoon salt	

Add farina to boiling water and salt; cook at a moderate boil for 15 minutes or until liquid is absorbed. Turn into well-greased cooky sheet or platter and spread to ½-inch thickness. Cool and refrigerate. To serve, cut into 1-inch diamond shapes.

To use for stews or ragoûts, place pieces in 2 tablespoons heated margarine in large pan in one layer and heat quickly, turning to prevent sticking.

As a soup accompaniment, place 2 or 3 pieces in soup bowl and pour boiling hot soup over. (As children, we often found our breakfast farina cut in cubes and transformed into soup dumplings.)

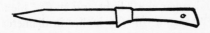

MOROCCAN ORANGE SALAD

The suggested salad with Couscous. On my shelf is a cookbook of traditional Moroccan recipes titled *Fez* and translated from Arabic to French to English. Here it is, just as I borrowed it:

"Peel a few oranges and cut them in large pieces, taking out the pips; add a few spoonfuls of orange flower water, stir, then sprinkle lightly with powdered cinnamon. Is very soothing."

For explicit directions use the following recipe; an excellent replacement. Add black olives to salad for variety.

3 oranges, peeled and sliced
1 medium-size Bermuda or Italian red onion, sliced in rings

2 heads Boston lettuce
Honey Lime Dressing

Arrange orange and onion slices over lettuce; serve with Honey Lime Dressing. Serves 8.

Honey Lime Dressing

1 6-ounce can frozen limeade concentrate
¾ cup salad oil

½ cup honey
¼ teaspoon salt
2 teaspoons celery seed

Put all ingredients except celery seed in blender and give it a 5-second whirl. Stir in celery seed. Makes 2 cups.

ALMOND CRESCENTS
(Kab El Ghzal)

2 cups butter or margarine
1¾ cups confectioners' sugar
½ pound almonds, ground (about 2 cups)

2 cups sifted flour
2½ teaspoons vanilla
confectioners' sugar or Vanilla Sugar

Cream butter and sugar until light and fluffy; blend in nuts, flour and vanilla. Shape into a roll 1½ inches in diameter and chill until firm. Slice ½ inch thick and shape each slice into a crescent. Place on cooky sheet and bake in preheated 350° oven 15 to 20 minutes or until lightly browned. Remove from pan while still hot and roll in confectioners' sugar, or Vanilla Sugar. Makes about 3 dozen.

Vanilla Sugar

Place a 2-inch stick of vanilla in a jar of confectioners' or granulated sugar. Cover tightly and allow to stand 2 or 3 days. Keeps indefinitely. Prepare about 2 cups at a time.

QUICK ALTERNATE

1 15-ounce roll refrigerated Butterscotch Cookies, quickly baked, and crisply good.

▶ Lamb Greek Style

Lamb and Eggplant Stew Greek Style
Greek Salad
Almond Slices or *Marshmallow Drops*

COOKING COUNTDOWN

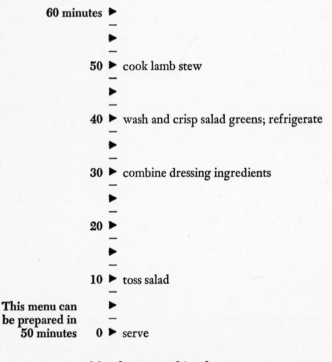

60 minutes ▶

50 ▶ cook lamb stew

40 ▶ wash and crisp salad greens; refrigerate

30 ▶ combine dressing ingredients

20 ▶

10 ▶ toss salad

**This menu can
be prepared in
50 minutes**   0 ▶ serve

Must be prepared in advance:
Almond Slices

LAMB AND EGGPLANT STEW GREEK STYLE

2 tablespoons olive oil
2 pounds shoulder lamb chops (4 chops)
1 large onion, finely diced
1 10-ounce can tomato soup

3 tablespoons lemon juice
¾ teaspoon salt
1 8-ounce can tomatoes, drained
¼ teaspoon coarsely ground pepper

1 medium eggplant, peeled, diced

Heat oil in skillet; add lamb. Brown over moderate heat on one side about 5 minutes; turn and add onions; brown again for 5 minutes. Add remaining ingredients. Cover and simmer 40 minutes or until tender. Serves 4.

ANOTHER WAY

Lamb Stew with Okra

Omit eggplant; cook 1 10-ounce package frozen okra according to package directions; omit salt. Drain and border stew.

May be prepared early in the day; freezes well.

GREEK SALAD

4 cups assorted greens
8 black olives
1 tomato, cut in wedges
¼ pound Feta cheese, crumbled
⅓ cup olive or salad oil

3 tablespoons vinegar or lemon juice
1 teaspoon oregano
¼ teaspoon paprika
½ teaspoon salt

Place greens, tomato and olives in salad bowl. Combine remaining ingredients, blending well. Pour over greens and toss lightly. Serves 4 to 6.

ALMOND SLICES

1¼ cups butter	2½ cups sifted flour
1¼ cups sugar	2½ cups almonds, ground fine
	¾ teaspoon ground cinnamon

Cream butter with sugar; add flour, ground almonds and cinnamon, blending thoroughly. Divide dough in half; form each half into a roll about 1½ inches in diameter. Wrap each roll in wax paper and refrigerate for at least 2 hours. Preheat oven to 375°. Remove dough from refrigerator, one roll at a time, and slice about ¼ inch thick. Place on greased cooky sheets, 1½ inches apart, and bake until set, not brown, about 12 to 15 minutes. Watch carefully; overbaking destroys the delicate flavor. Makes about 8 dozen.

ANOTHER WAY

Bake only one roll of cooky dough. Place other roll in freezer; take it out whenever you want fresh cookies. No need to defrost dough before slicing and baking. Allow 2 or 3 minutes additional baking time if you use frozen dough.

QUICK ALTERNATE

Marshmallow Drops

Really no recipe. Take a simple cooky, homemade or bakery prepared. Top each with a large marshmallow and place in 250° oven for 2 minutes; press down on marshmallow to spread and return to oven for another minute or two. If you wish, top with a chocolate bit when removing from oven the first time.

▶ Caraway Lamb Stew

Caraway Lamb Stew
Pineapple and Cottage Cheese Salad
Oven Pancakes

COOKING COUNTDOWN

60 minutes ▶ cook lamb
—
▶
—
50 ▶
—
▶
—
40 ▶ prepare dressing
—
▶
—
30 ▶ chill greens
— drain and chill pineapple
▶
—
20 ▶ bake pancakes
—
▶
—
10 ▶ arrange salads
—
This menu can be
prepared in 40 minutes ▶
if lamb is prepared —
in advance 0 ▶ serve

May be prepared in advance:
Casserole of lamb; store in freezer

CARAWAY LAMB STEW

Caraway was used by primitive man, and the seeds scattered, over the centuries, throughout the world. Its definite flavor, so often associated with rye bread, adds interest to many foods. Paradoxically, I must add, in this instance, the lamb stew without the seeds is flavorful. It's good either way.

For convenience, the meat is in small cubes for quick cooking and is seasoned with a soup mix.

1½ pounds boneless lamb, cut in ¾-inch cubes
2 slices bacon, minced
1 1½-ounce package onion soup mix
½ teaspoon monosodium glutamate
¼ teaspoon oregano
½ teaspoon salt
2 teaspoons sugar
1 1-pound 13-ounce can tomatoes
1 teaspoon caraway seeds
4 medium potatoes, halved, or 8 frozen new potatoes
1 10-ounce package frozen mixed vegetables

Remove all fat from lamb. Sauté bacon in large saucepan until about 1 tablespoon fat is rendered. Add lamb and brown lightly. Sprinkle with onion soup mix and toss with lamb in the drippings. Add remaining ingredients, except potatoes and frozen vegetables. Cover and simmer slowly 20 minutes. Add potatoes; bring to boiling and cover. Simmer another 20 minutes or until tender. Add vegetables, and when stew comes to a boil again, cover and simmer 10 minutes. Serves 4 to 6.

If using frozen potatoes, add with other vegetables.

ANOTHER WAY

Make a double portion and freeze one half; freeze leftovers for another day. The "freezer to oven ware" is especially convenient here. Add other vegetables or substitute your preference. Defrost; heat in 350° oven 30 minutes.

May be prepared early in the day and reheated.

PINEAPPLE AND COTTAGE CHEESE SALAD

Almost traditional, but so acceptable.

1 1-pound can sliced pineapple drained
romaine or leaf lettuce

1 pint cottage cheese
1 teaspoon grated orange peel (optional)

Chill drained pineapple. To serve, line individual plates with lettuce; place slice of pineapple on each and center with a scoop of cottage cheese. (An ice cream scoop is fine for this purpose.) Sprinkle with orange peel or dust with paprika. May be served with salad dressing if desired. Honey Lime Dressing (page 190) is very good. Serves 6.

OVEN PANCAKES

These are scheduled pancakes and eliminate the last minute of standing over the stove. They are light and cakelike in texture.

1 cup pancake mix
1 cup milk
1 egg

1 tablespoon melted butter
cinnamon sugar or 1 10-ounce package frozen berries, defrosted

Combine ingredients, beating until smooth. Pour into oiled 9 x 9-inch baking pan; place in preheated 425° oven and bake 15 to 20 minutes until lightly browned. Cut into squares, serve with cinnamon sugar or berries. Makes nine 3-inch pancake squares.

OTHER WAYS

1. Double the recipe and bake in 15 x 10-inch jelly roll pan; cut into 15 squares.

2. *Apple Pancakes.* Use 1 cup sliced apples for each cup of pancake mix; spread batter in oiled pan, top evenly with apples and bake as above. Cut into squares. Serve dusted with cinnamon sugar.

3. Or mix batter with sliced apples.

4. *Corn Pancakes.* Add ½ cup well-drained kernel corn to each cup of pancake mix. Bake as above and serve with pancake syrup.

▶ Sauced Lamburger Meatballs

Sauced Lamburger Meatballs
Dressed Up Scalloped Potatoes
Asparagus in Green Pepper Rings   *Bread and Jelly Pudding*

COOKING COUNTDOWN

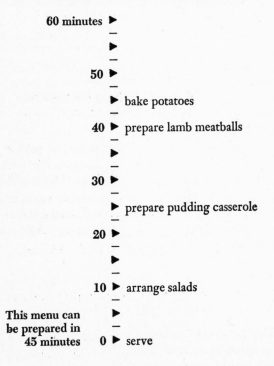

60 minutes ▶
 —
 ▶
 —
50 ▶
 —
 ▶ bake potatoes
 —
40 ▶ prepare lamb meatballs
 —
 ▶
 —
30 ▶
 —
 ▶ prepare pudding casserole
 —
20 ▶
 —
 ▶
 —
10 ▶ arrange salads
 —
This menu can ▶
be prepared in —
45 minutes   0 ▶ serve

SAUCED LAMBURGER MEATBALLS

Meatballs

1½ pounds lean ground lamb   ¼ cup chili sauce
1 egg slightly beaten   ¼ cup water
¼ cup dry bread crumbs   1 teaspoon salt
¼ teaspoon garlic powder   1 teaspoon onion flakes
2 tablespoons flour

Place lamb in bowl; combine remaining ingredients except flour and mix thoroughly. Shape into 18 balls. Roll meatballs in flour. Set aside.

Sauce

2 tablespoons shortening   3 tablespoons brown sugar
2 tablespoons flour   2 tablespoons lemon juice
1½ cups water   ¾ cup sliced pimiento salad
½ teaspoon salt   olives
1 teaspoon paprika

Heat shortening in large skillet; add meatballs and brown evenly. Remove from pan; pour off shortening, reserving 2 tablespoons. Return the 2 tablespoons shortening to skillet and blend in flour, stirring until smooth. Add water, salt, paprika, brown sugar and lemon juice; cook until thick, stirring constantly. Add meatballs, cover pan and simmer about 20 minutes stirring occasionally. Add olives and cook 2 or 3 minutes, to heat. Serves 4.

DRESSED UP SCALLOPED POTATOES

A new twist to the classic scalloped potato, and the anchovies add a nice flavor contrast to the lamb entrée.

1 5¾-ounce package scalloped   1 2-ounce can anchovy fillets,
potato mix   drained

Prepare scalloped potato mix according to package directions. Remove from oven 10 minutes before they are done (about 25 minutes in preheated 400° oven). Arrange fillets over top of potatoes; return to oven and bake remaining 10 minutes. Serves 4 to 6.

ASPARAGUS IN GREEN PEPPER RINGS

1 1-pound can white asparagus,   1 head Boston lettuce
drained and chilled   ¾ cup French Dressing (made
4 ¼-inch rings green pepper   from a mix or bottled)

Open can of asparagus from bottom, thus removing asparagus, stalk first. With careful handling, tips remain intact. Drain. Place ring of green pepper on bed of lettuce on individual salad plates; slip 3 spears through each ring. Drizzle 2 tablespoons French Dressing on each serving. Serves 4.

BREAD AND JELLY PUDDING

1 3-ounce package vanilla pud-   ½ teaspoon vanilla
ding mix   2 slices bread
¼ cup raisins   1 tablespoon jelly
2 cups milk   nutmeg

Prepare pudding according to package directions, adding raisins with the milk; remove from heat and stir in vanilla. Spread bread with jelly and cut in quarters; layer in bottom of 1-quart casserole. Pour prepared pudding with raisins over bread, and sprinkle with nutmeg. The bread and jelly may be layered alternately with the pudding. Serve warm to 4.

Versatile Pork

PORK IS PLENTIFUL at the markets all year round; often quite economical and is second only to beef as a favorite meat in the United States. Pork may be found on the menu for any of the three meals a day from breakfast bacon to an impressive banquet of roast suckling pig. One of the advantages of this meat, from a cook's point of view, is that it not only has a distinctive taste when left on its own but also has great affinity for blending with other flavors. Pork combines happily with vegetables or fruits and can be sauced with innumerable combinations.

A large portion of the smoked pork is favored meat, enthusiastically consumed as bacon and ham. Since fresh pork requires lengthy and thorough cooking, we have minimized menus for roasts, and have concentrated on recipes for several cuts which stay within the limits of the Cooking Countdown.

A casserole dish can be an original preparation when inspired by the creativity of an ingenious cook and the leftover bonus of Versatile Pork.

▶ Pork and Green Bean Dinner

Pork Strips with Green Beans   *Salad Zuban*
Waffles à la Mode

COOKING COUNTDOWN

60 minutes ▶ prepare salad

—

▶

—

50 ▶ prepare ice cream scoops; place in freezer

—

▶

—

40 ▶ cook pork strips

—

▶

—

30 ▶ cook rice

—

▶

—

20 ▶

—

▶

—

This menu can be   10 ▶
prepared in 40 minutes   —
if salad and ice cream   ▶
scoops are prepared in   —
advance   0 ▶ serve

May be prepared in advance:
Salad Zuban
Ice cream scoops for waffles

PORK STRIPS WITH GREEN BEANS

A quick-cooking unusual pork recipe with a different flavor.

2 pounds boneless pork, cut in strips, 2 x ¼-inch
2 tablespoons butter or vegetable shortening
½ cup chopped onions, fresh or frozen
1 teaspoon salt
½ teaspoon freshly ground pepper
2 cups boiling water
2 beef bouillon cubes

½ teaspoon ground cloves
1 tablespoon lemon juice
½ cup currant jelly
2 teaspoons cornstarch
2 tablespoons sherry
1 1-pound can whole green beans, drained
2 cups cooked rice, precooked or long grain

Add pork to heated shortening in saucepan (with cover); stir in onions and sauté about 10 minutes until evenly browned. Dust with salt and pepper. Dissolve bouillon cubes in hot water and add 1 cup of the mixture; cover and simmer 15 minutes or until tender. Shake pan while cooking and add bouillon mixture if liquid boils down. Add cloves, lemon juice and any remaining bouillon. Add jelly to pan liquid, stirring until dissolved. There should be about 1 cup of liquid; add water if necessary. Make a paste of cornstarch and sherry; stir into pan juices. Add green beans and cook five minutes until sauce is clear and thickened and beans are heated. Serve over rice. Serves 4 to 6.

If liquid boils down while cooking or more sauce is desired, make additional liquid with 1 cup water and 1 bouillon cube and add sufficient amount.

May be prepared early in the day; freezes well.

SALAD ZUBAN

1 1-pound can garbanzos (chick-peas), drained
4 small zucchini, scrubbed and sliced ¼ inch thick

¾ cup prepared Italian dressing
2 tomatoes, each cut in sixths
watercress sprigs

Combine garbanzos and zucchini slices in bowl and toss with dressing.

Refrigerate to chill. Serve from bowl, garnished with tomato wedges and watercress. Serves 6.

WAFFLES À LA MODE

4 frozen waffles   1 pint vanilla ice cream
1 5½-ounce can chocolate syrup

Pop the waffles in your toaster; be certain they are nicely browned. Place each on individual dessert plate, top with scoops of ice cream. Spoon the sauce over the delicious combination. Serves 4.

Substitute any sauce you like for the chocolate syrup. Maple syrup or butterscotch sauce are good alternates, or use defrosted frozen peaches, strawberries or any other fruit.

Suggestion: Put scoops of ice cream into freezer ahead of time so that they will be ready when it is time to assemble dessert.

▶ Pork Chops for Company

Pork Chops Bercy   *Wide Egg Noodles*
Frosty Marinated Vegetables   *Brown and Serve Rolls*
Minted Ambrosia   *Praline Cookies*

COOKING COUNTDOWN

60 minutes ▶ prepare vegetables
—
▶ sauté chops
—
50 ▶
—
▶ add sauce to chops, continue cooking
—
40 ▶ assemble ambrosia; chill
▶
—
30 ▶ bake pralines
▶
—
20 ▶ heat rolls
—
▶ cook noodles
—
10 ▶ arrange vegetables
▶
—
0 ▶ serve

May be prepared in advance:
    Minted Ambrosia
    Frosty Marinated Vegetables

PORK CHOPS BERCY

4 large pork chops
1 tablespoon butter or margarine
1 teaspoon seasoned salt
¼ teaspoon paprika
¼ cup finely chopped green onions or dry minced onions
1 tablespoon flour
¾ cup hot water
1 chicken bouillon cube

½ teaspoon caraway seed
2 tablespoons claret or dry white wine
1 teaspoon Italian seasoning or oregano
½ cup light cream
4 ounces wide egg noodles, cooked according to package directions

Remove fat from chops and place fat in a large covered skillet with butter. Sauté slowly until lightly browned, and sufficiently rendered to sauté the chops. Discard browned pieces; dust chops with seasoned salt and paprika; place in heated fat. Sauté over moderate heat until evenly browned, about 5 minutes on each side. Remove chops from pan and drain off pan drippings (reserving two tablespoons). Add onions to reserved fat; brown lightly, and stir in flour until lightly browned. Add water, bouillon cube, caraway and wine, blending until smooth. Return chops to skillet; dust with Italian seasoning or with oregano. Cover the pan and simmer about 30 minutes, or until very tender. If the sauce dries in cooking, add a small amount of water at a time. Just before serving, remove chops from skillet, and arrange on heated serving platter. Stir cream into sauce, and heat gently, but do not boil. Pour sauce over chops, and serve immediately over cooked noodles. Serves 4.

The original recipe browns the chops, then adds the Sauce Bercy. This takes an extra pot and makes unnecessary work, but you may prefer to make the sauce separately to use with other recipes or with leftover meats.

Sauce Bercy

4 tablespoons butter
2 tablespoons chopped shallots or green onions

2 tablespoons flour
1 cup beef stock or canned beef consommé
¼ cup dry white wine

Melt butter in skillet, add shallots and brown lightly. Blend in flour, then add beef stock and wine and stir until smooth and well heated. Add salt and pepper to taste, if necessary. Yield: About 1 cup sauce.

FROSTY MARINATED VEGETABLES

¼ cup cider vinegar
¼ cup water
3 tablespoons sugar
¼ teaspoon salt
¼ teaspoon paprika

¼ teaspoon onion flakes (optional)
1 10-ounce package frozen mixed vegetables
8 thinly sliced water chestnuts
lettuce cups

Combine vinegar, water, sugar, salt, paprika and onion flakes in saucepan; bring to a boil. Add frozen vegetables; bring to boiling again, and cook 5 minutes. Remove from heat and add water chestnuts; refrigerate until chilled. Serve in individual lettuce cups, or in a serving bowl as a relish. Serves 4 to 6.

If you wish, double the amount and keep some on hand, using a 3-ounce can of chestnuts. This is a fine recipe to make in advance; the flavor improves as it stands.

ANOTHER WAY

To serve, arrange lettuce cups, fill with the relish and nestle tomato wedges in the leaves. Marinate tomato wedges in the vinegar mixture from the relish.

BROWN AND SERVE ROLLS

A large variety of brown and serve rolls are available at the market. Bake according to package directions and serve hot with plenty of chilled butter.

MINTED AMBROSIA

1 10-ounce can pineapple chunks, drained
1 11-ounce can Mandarin oranges, drained
¼ cup flaky coconut
1 tablespoon crème de menthe or 1 teaspoon mint flavoring

Toss all ingredients together lightly; chill thoroughly. Serves 4.
This quick preparation may be made in advance and chilled.

OTHER WAYS

1. Serve the fruit as a sauce over ice cream.

2. Serve as a compote with meat or poultry.

PRALINE COOKIES

12 graham crackers
½ cup butter
1 cup dark brown sugar, firmly packed
pinch of salt
½ cup chopped pecans

Arrange graham crackers in 1 layer on ungreased, foil-lined cooky sheet. Combine butter, sugar and salt in saucepan; heat to boiling, stirring constantly. Boil an additional 2 minutes, then stir in pecans and spoon over crackers. Bake in preheated 350° oven 10 minutes. While warm, cut each cracker in fourths and remove from pan to cool. Makes 4 dozen.
The cookies keep well, stored in airtight container.

ANOTHER WAY

If you wish a larger cooky, cut graham crackers in halves.

▶ Skillet Chop Dinner

Delta Pork Chops   Vermicelli
Red Cabbage and Apple Slaw
Raisin Cream Ring

COOKING COUNTDOWN

60 minutes ▶ start chops
—
▶
—
50 ▶ prepare and bake raisin cream ring
—
▶
—
40 ▶
—
▶
—
30 ▶ prepare slaw dressing and assemble salad;
— refrigerate
▶
—
20 ▶
—
▶
—
10 ▶ cook vermicelli
—
▶
—
0 ▶ serve

DELTA PORK CHOPS

Use either electric skillet or pan on top of stove.

6 pork chops, ¾ inch thick
2 tablespoons vegetable shortening
1 teaspoon salt
6 thin slices onion
6 thin slices lemon
6 slices green pepper, ¼ inch thick

2 tablespoons light brown sugar
½ cup chili sauce
¼ cup water
1 8-ounce package vermicelli, cooked

Dry chops with paper toweling; trim any excess fat. Heat shortening in skillet; add chops and sprinkle with salt, then sauté on both sides until evenly browned. Top each chop with a slice of onion, lemon and green pepper and sprinkle each with a teaspoon of sugar. Combine chili sauce and water and pour over prepared chops. Cover and simmer over moderate heat 50 minutes to 1 hour until tender. Serve from tableware skillet with bowl of vermicelli at hand. Serves 6.

The electric skillet should be set to 350°; check the sauce so that it does not cook down. Reduce heat, if necessary and add a small amount of water.

ANOTHER WAY

Use shoulder lamb chops; simmer 35 minutes or until tender.

RED CABBAGE AND APPLE SLAW

4 cups red cabbage, shredded
1 large sweet onion, sliced and separated into rings

2 red Delicious apples, cored and sliced
Cole Slaw Dressing

Combine all ingredients and toss lightly until cabbage and apples are evenly coated with dressing. Chill. Pile into a salad bowl and sprinkle with freshly snipped parsley or chives. Serves 6 to 8.

The slaw keeps well; prepare an extra amount in advance and refrigerate to have on hand.

Cole Slaw Dressing

½ cup sour cream   1 tablespoon sugar
  2 tablespoons white vinegar   dash salt
              ⅛ teaspoon turmeric (optional)

Combine ingredients and blend well.

RAISIN CREAM RING

  2 3-ounce packages cream cheese,   2 tablespoons orange peel
    softened   ½ cup raisins
½ cup sugar   2 cups biscuit mix
              ¼ cup honey

Blend cream cheese and sugar; stir in orange peel and raisins. Prepare biscuit mix according to package directions for biscuits. Roll into 12 x 18-inch oblong. Spread cream cheese mixture on dough; roll up, starting at wide end. Form ring and place on cooky sheet. With scissors, make cuts three-quarters through ring at 1-inch intervals, turning each cut section on its side. Bake in preheated 450° oven 15 minutes. Brush with honey for a shiny glaze and bake 5 minutes longer.

▶ Oriental Dinner for Six

White Coral Cocktail
Pork and Pineapple Hawaii   Bean Sprouts Vinaigrette
Sherry Custard Cake

COOKING COUNTDOWN

60 minutes ▶ start pork
—
▶ chill bean sprouts
—
50 ▶ prepare custard sauce
—
▶
—
40 ▶ mix vinaigrette dressing and toss with
— bean sprouts; refrigerate
▶
—
30 ▶ arrange cake; refrigerate
—
▶
—
20 ▶ arrange salad
—
▶ complete pork
—
10 ▶
—
▶
—
0 ▶ prepare and serve cocktails

May be prepared in advance:
Sherry Custard Cake

WHITE CORAL COCKTAIL

2 jiggers Kahlua   2 jiggers cream
2 jiggers Cointreau   2 jiggers grenadine

Place 3 or 4 ice cubes in cocktail shaker. Pour cocktail ingredients over ice, cover shaker and shake quickly to chill. Pour into cocktail glasses. Serves 6.

PORK AND PINEAPPLE HAWAII

1½ pounds lean pork tenderloin, cut in 1-inch cubes
1 tablespoon shortening
⅓ cup water
½ cup brown sugar
3 tablespoons cornstarch
⅓ cup vinegar
1 1-pound can pineapple chunks, drained (reserve ½ cup liquid)
¼ cup soy sauce
1 teaspoon salt
1 green pepper, cut in ½-inch squares
1 green onion, thinly sliced
1 8-ounce can water chestnuts, drained and sliced
2 tomatoes, cut in sixths
2 3-ounce cans Chinese chow mein noodles or 3 cups cooked rice

Add pork to heated shortening in skillet; brown evenly and add water. Cover and simmer 40 minutes. Check often that it does not stick. Drain off fat. Combine sugar and cornstarch in a bowl; add vinegar, liquid from pineapple, soy sauce and salt; blend well. Add to meat, reduce heat and simmer, stirring until smooth and thickened, for about 5 minutes. Add green pepper, onion, pineapple chunks, water chestnuts and tomatoes; cook 3 minutes. Serve with chow mein noodles or rice. Serves 6.

BEAN SPROUTS VINAIGRETTE

Crisp, cold bean sprouts, for a change.

2 1-pound cans bean sprouts

Vinaigrette Dressing

3 tablespoons vinegar (cider or wine variety)
⅔ cup vegetable oil
¼ cup parsley flakes
1 tablespoon chopped green onion tops or dried chives

1 tablespoon pickle relish
1 tablespoon chopped capers (optional)
1 teaspoon salt
¼ teaspoon seasoned black pepper
Boston lettuce
paprika

Rinse and drain bean sprouts; place in bowl. Combine all ingredients for dressing; mix together thoroughly, or shake vigorously in a jar. Pour dressing over bean sprouts, toss gently and refrigerate until chilled; one hour. Drain off excess dressing before serving. Serve from bowl, or place mounds of marinated sprouts in beds of lettuce, either on a large platter or individual salad plates. Sprinkle with paprika. Serves 6.

SHERRY CUSTARD CAKE

Worthy of a fresh start, though made to order for leftover yolks and that extra layer of cake in the freezer. An emergency guest dessert.

2 tablespoons light rum
1 8- or 9-inch cake layer, sponge, butter or chiffon

1 cup whipping cream, whipped
6 maraschino cherries, sliced
Sherry Custard Sauce

Drizzle rum over cake, spread with whipped cream and decorate with a sprinkling of cherries. Cut into 6 portions and pour Sherry Custard Sauce, Vanilla Custard Sauce or Quick Sherry Sauce over each serving. Serves 6.

Sherry Custard Sauce

3 egg yolks, beaten
¼ cup sugar

⅛ teaspoon salt
2 cups milk, scalded
1 tablespoon sherry

Combine yolks, sugar and salt in top of double boiler; add milk gradually, stirring constantly. Place over heat and cook, stirring continually, until custard thickens and coats a silver spoon. Remove from heat and add sherry. Refrigerate until chilled. Makes about 2 cups.

Vanilla Custard Sauce

Omit the sherry and substitute 1 teaspoon vanilla. For a simpler dessert for children, just pour the Vanilla Custard Sauce over slices of cake.

Quick Sherry Sauce

1 3¾-ounce package vanilla instant pudding

¾ cup corn syrup
1 5⅓-ounce can evaporated milk
1 tablespoon sherry

Combine vanilla pudding mix and corn syrup; blend well. Add milk, stirring constantly, and add sherry. Let stand 10 minutes to set. Refrigerate until needed; it keeps well. Makes 2 cups.

▶ Ribs and Rice

Oriental Ribs   Fluffy Rice with Pimientos
Preserved Kumquats and Celery Sticks
Fortune Teller Pineapple Sherbet

COOKING COUNTDOWN

60 minutes ▶ boil and simmer ribs
—
▶
—
50 ▶ make sherbert balls; place in freezer
—
▶
—
40 ▶ prepare kumquats and celery
—
▶
—
30 ▶
—
▶
—
20 ▶
—
▶
—
10 ▶ cook rice
—
▶
—
0 ▶ serve

ORIENTAL RIBS

This is an unusual treatment for spareribs — cooked on top of the stove, quick and delicious.

2 pounds pork spareribs	¼ cup sugar
1 tablespoon salad oil	¼ teaspoon dry mustard
1 small piece ginger root or ½ teaspoon ground ginger	½ teaspoon salt
	2 tablespoons soy sauce
1 clove garlic	3 tablespoons vinegar

1 cup water

Cut spareribs in one-rib pieces and place in large skillet. Cover with hot water; bring to boiling, then reduce heat; simmer 30 minutes. Drain and dry. Heat oil in skillet and add spareribs; brown. Peel ginger root and chop fine. Crush garlic and place in bowl with ginger root. Add remaining ingredients and stir until smooth. Pour mixture over spareribs in skillet and simmer 30 minutes. Serve hot. Serves 4.

FLUFFY RICE WITH PIMIENTOS

A colorful tasty accompaniment.

Cook precooked rice according to package directions, making 2 cups cooked rice. Drain a 2-ounce jar pimientos; chop coarsely and toss gently with the hot rice. Serves 4.

PRESERVED KUMQUATS AND CELERY STICKS

4 stalks celery
1 8-ounce jar preserved kumquats

Prepare celery stalks by cutting into sticks about ¼ inch wide and 3 inches long. Crisp in cold water, drain and chill in refrigerator. Chill a jar of preserved kumquats, and drain a number of them equal to the number of celery sticks. Insert celery sticks in one end of each kumquat and arrange upon a plate. This is a novel and attractive-looking relish; a perfect complement to the other dishes on the menu. Serves 4 to 6.

FORTUNE TELLER PINEAPPLE SHERBET

Form 4 scoops from 1 pint pineapple sherbet and place in sherbet glasses or dessert bowls. Allow to set in freezer until serving time. Just before serving, top each sherbet ball with a fortune cooky. Serves 4.

This is an easy and fitting finale — the entire menu requiring very little effort from the cook!

Fortune cookies are a packaged item, available in most markets.

▶ Pilaf Combination

Olive Pilaf
Grapefruit and Avocado Salad
Upside Down Apple Pancake

COOKING COUNTDOWN

60 minutes ▶ cook rice for pilaf
▶
–
50 ▶ assemble and arrange salad platter;
–   refrigerate
▶
–
40 ▶ prepare apples for pancake
▶
–
30 ▶ cook pilaf
▶
–
20 ▶ prepare and bake pancake
▶
–
10 ▶
–
▶
–
0 ▶ serve

OLIVE PILAF

It can be made with any variety of leftovers including rice, vegetables, meats or poultry.

3 tablespoons vegetable oil	2 cups boiling water
¾ cup chopped onion, fresh or frozen	¼ teaspoon saffron
	3 bouillon cubes
3 cups cooked rice (1 cup raw rice)	¾ cup sliced pimiento-stuffed olives or salad olives
¼ teaspoon salt	½ pound frankfurters or choice of sausage, sliced ¼ inch thick
⅛ teaspoon pepper	
½ teaspoon garlic powder	2 cups diced, cooked pork
½ cup slivered almonds (optional)	

Heat oil in large skillet, add onion, cooking until lightly browned. Add rice, salt, pepper and garlic powder, blending well. Add saffron and bouillon cubes to boiling water, stirring until bouillon cubes are dissolved. Add to rice mixture with olives, sausage and cooked meat; mix well, and cook 10 to 15 minutes until liquid is absorbed. Serve on large platter; sprinkle with almonds. Serves 6.

ANOTHER WAY

When adding meat, stir in one 10-ounce package of frozen peas, which have been cooked 2 minutes less than package directions.

GRAPEFRUIT AND AVOCADO SALAD

1 medium head curly endive, washed and crisped	2 cans frozen grapefruit sections, thawed and drained, or 3 large grapefruit, sectioned
2 ripe avocados, peeled and sliced	
2 tablespoons lemon juice	paprika

Arrange a bed of endive pieces on serving platter; sprinkle avocado slices with lemon juice and place on endive alternating with grapefruit sections. Dust with paprika, and serve with Creamy French Dressing mix made according to directions. Serves 6.

UPSIDE DOWN APPLE PANCAKE

For breakfast, luncheon entrée or dessert.

2 tablespoons butter
2 tablespoons sugar
1 teaspoon cinnamon
¼ cup flour
¼ teaspoon baking powder
⅛ teaspoon salt

2 egg yolks, slightly beaten
¼ cup milk
2 egg whites, beaten stiff
2 tablespoons sugar
3 apples, pared, cored and thinly
   sliced

Melt butter in 10-inch ovenproof skillet, add sugar and cinnamon; then simmer 5 minutes. Combine dry ingredients, stir in egg yolks and milk; mix thoroughly. Beat remaining 2 tablespoons sugar into egg whites very gradually, beating until sugar is dissolved. Spread evenly over apples in pan. Place in preheated 400° oven and bake 10 minutes until golden. Loosen edges with spatula and invert on serving plate. Serves 4 to 6.

▶ Elegant Baked Ham Dinner

Rose-Colored Ham   Saucy Sweets
Vegetable Cole Slaw
Chocolate Orange Torte

COOKING COUNTDOWN

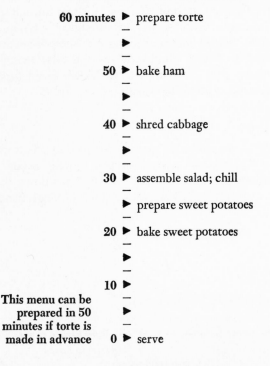

60 minutes ▶ prepare torte
—
▶
—
50 ▶ bake ham
—
▶
—
40 ▶ shred cabbage
—
▶
—
30 ▶ assemble salad; chill
▶ prepare sweet potatoes
—
20 ▶ bake sweet potatoes
—
▶
—
10 ▶
—
This menu can be   ▶
prepared in 50   —
minutes if torte is
made in advance   0 ▶ serve

May be prepared in advance:
Vegetable Cole Slaw
Chocolate Orange Torte

ROSE-COLORED HAM

It tastes as good as it looks.

1 2- to 3-pound canned ham	¼ cup maple-flavored syrup
1 teaspoon ground cloves	1 3-ounce package strawberry- or
½ teaspoon dry mustard	lemon-flavored gelatin
6 maraschino Cherry Flowers	

Remove all gelatin coating from ham and sprinkle with cloves and mustard. Place on large sheet of heavy-duty foil, sufficient to enclose ham completely, allowing air space. Pour syrup over top and sprinkle with gelatin. Seal securely. Place in preheated 400° oven and bake 20 minutes; open foil and arrange opened Cherry Flowers in a pattern; baste with drippings. Return to oven and bake an additional 20 minutes or until glazed. Serves 4 to 6. When sliced makes approximately 12 sandwiches.

Cherry Flowers

Cut each cherry from stem end to, but not through, bottom, first in half, then in quarters and then in eighths, forming petals. Open them when arranging on the glazed ham and press down to form flowers. They can be secured with whole cloves through the center.

SAUCY SWEETS

A simple, yet sophisticated, combination.

2 1-pound cans sweet potatoes or yams	1 cup light brown sugar
	1 tablespoon flour
1 cup sour cream	

Drain potatoes and place in ovenproof dish. Combine sugar, flour and sour cream in saucepan and heat until thickened and bubbly, stirring to prevent sticking. Pour sauce over potatoes and bake in a preheated 400° oven for 20 minutes. Serves 6.

VEGETABLE COLE SLAW

½ medium cabbage, shredded
½ green pepper, diced
1 teaspoon grated onion
1 carrot, grated or minced
½ cup mayonnaise

¼ cup sour cream
¼ cup sugar
½ teaspoon celery salt
freshly ground pepper
½ teaspoon salad herbs (optional)

Combine cabbage, green pepper, onion and carrot; toss well to mix. Blend together mayonnaise, sour cream, sugar, celery salt, pepper and herbs. Add to drained vegetables and toss until all vegetables are coated with dressing. Chill. Serves 6.

Make in advance so that slaw may stand while flavors "marry."

CHOCOLATE ORANGE TORTE

The chocolate and orange flavors are especially good together.

1½ cups milk
1 3¼-ounce package orange tapioca pudding
½ cup orange juice
½ teaspoon grated orange peel or 1 tablespoon orange liqueur (optional)

dash salt
1 8-inch Chocolate Crumb Crust
Chocolate Curls (page 176)

Heat milk; add pudding mix and bring to rolling boil. Remove from heat and add orange juice, peel or liqueur and salt. Pour into prepared crust; cool. Cover surface with wax paper to prevent crust forming and refrigerate. To serve, garnish with border of Chocolate Curls. Serves 6.

Make the torte in advance, if you prefer.

Chocolate Crumb Crust

12 chocolate sandwich cookies
¼ cup butter or margarine, softened

Place cookies between 2 sheets of wax paper; crush with a rolling pin to make 1 cup crumbs. Combine crumbs and butter; mix well and press against bottom and sides of 8-inch pie plate, forming an even shell. The sandwich cookies have a sweet confectioners' filling, and need no sugar.

OTHER WAYS

For other crusts — graham cracker, vanilla wafers, or gingersnap:

1¼ cups crumbs ¼ cup butter or margarine, soft-
¼ cup sugar ened

Combine crumbs and sugar; blend in butter with fork or fingers and press against bottom and sides of 9-inch pie plate. Chill 1 hour for positive firmness. For a baked crust; bake in 375° oven 8 minutes. Cool and fill.

▶Southern Ham Dinner for Four

Raisin Ham Slice   Sweet Potatoes
Salad Topped Salad   Corn Sticks
Strawberry Shortcake

COOKING COUNTDOWN

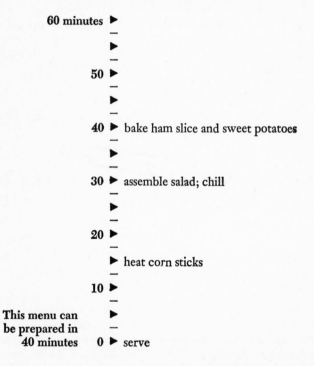

60 minutes ▶
—
▶
—
50 ▶
—
▶
—
40 ▶ bake ham slice and sweet potatoes
—
▶
—
30 ▶ assemble salad; chill
—
▶
—
20 ▶
—
▶ heat corn sticks
—
10 ▶
—
This menu can ▶
be prepared in —
40 minutes   0 ▶ serve

Strawberries may be defrosted in advance

RAISIN HAM SLICE WITH SWEET POTATOES

1 2-pound slice smoked ham, about 1½ inches thick	½ teaspoon curry powder
20 whole cloves (approximately)	¼ teaspoon allspice
1 tablespoon prepared mustard	½ cup raisins
½ cup brown sugar	1 1-pound can sweet potatoes, drained and sliced ½-inch thick
1 cup orange juice	

Score the fat around ham and stud with cloves. Place on greased baking pan; spread with prepared mustard and brown sugar. Combine orange juice, curry powder, allspice and raisins; pour over the ham. Bake uncovered in a preheated 350° oven for 30 minutes, basting frequently with the pan juices. Place sweet potato slices around the ham to cook at the same time. Serves 3 to 4.

ANOTHER WAY

If you prefer, this recipe can be prepared in an electric skillet, set at 300°, instead of in the oven.

Corn Sticks

Prepared frozen corn sticks are delicious. They may be heated, direct from the freezer, in toaster or broiler, and covered with plenty of butter.

SALAD TOPPED SALAD

4 ½-inch-thick slices iceberg lettuce	½ cup mayonnaise
4 ½-inch-thick slices large tomato	⅓ cup chili sauce
1 cup finely diced celery	¼ teaspoon onion powder
½ cup finely diced green pepper	⅛ teaspoon garlic powder (optional)

Shred lettuce slices and place on 4 salad plates; top each with tomato slice. Combine remaining ingredients mixing well, then spread ¼ of mixture over each tomato slice. Chill before serving, but no longer than 30 minutes in advance. Serves 4.

STRAWBERRY SHORTCAKE

(Effortless)

4 individual sponge cake cups   Whipped topping from pressurized
1 10-ounce package frozen straw-   can
  berries, defrosted

Arrange cake on individual dessert plates and spoon strawberries into
each cavity; swirl prepared whipped cream or other topping lightly
over berries. You may dot each with a fresh berry or sprinkle with
colored sugar. Serves 4.

▶ Eggplant Entrée

Deviled Ham Eggplant   Noodle Pancakes
Bottoms Up Fruit Cake

COOKING COUNTDOWN

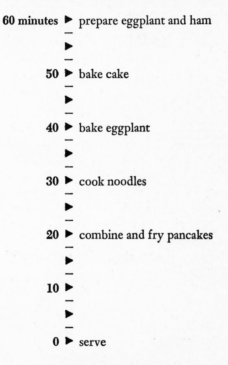

60 minutes ▶ prepare eggplant and ham
— ▶
—
50 ▶ bake cake
— ▶
—
40 ▶ bake eggplant
— ▶
—
30 ▶ cook noodles
— ▶
—
20 ▶ combine and fry pancakes
— ▶
—
10 ▶
— ▶
—
0 ▶ serve

May be prepared in advance:

Bottoms Up Fruit Cake
Deviled Ham Eggplant

DEVILED HAM EGGPLANT

Your guests will never guess the elements of the delicious flavor. Here's the answer.

2 small eggplants
boiling salted water
1 10-ounce can tomatoes, drained and cut in chunks
1 small onion, coarsely chopped (½ cup)
1 4½-ounce can deviled ham

1 teaspoon sugar
1 teaspoon salt
dash cayenne
¾ to 1 cup dried bread crumbs or cracker crumbs
2 tablespoons cracker crumbs
1 tablespoon butter
paprika

Cut eggplants in half lengthwise. Remove pulp, leaving a ½-inch shell. Be careful not to pierce the eggplant shells. (A grapefruit knife does the job efficiently.) Cut pulp into ½-inch cubes and place in saucepan. Add boiling water to 1-inch depth, allowing ½ teaspoon salt to each cup water, and cook, covered, for 5 minutes. Drain and combine with tomatoes, onion, ham, sugar, salt and cayenne, blending well. Add bread crumbs sufficient to make a thick mixture. Fill eggplant shells and top with cracker crumbs dotted with bits of butter; sprinkle with paprika. Place in casserole and fill with hot water to one half the height of eggplant. Bake in preheated 375° oven 35 minutes. Serves 4.

Freezes very well; double the recipe to have on hand. Two large eggplants will do it.

NOODLE PANCAKES

Though they're really worthy of a fresh start, you may use your leftover noodles.

1 8-ounce package fine noodles (3 to 4 cups)
2 eggs, lightly beaten
¾ teaspoon salt

1 tablespoon poppy seeds (optional)
⅛ teaspoon freshly ground pepper
¼ cup butter or other shortening

Cook noodles according to package directions, rinse with cold water and drain thoroughly. Combine with eggs, salt, poppy seeds and pepper. Heat half of shortening in skillet; place small mounds of noodle mixture, about ¼ cup each, in skillet or griddle. Sauté over moderate heat until lightly browned and reverse to brown second side, adding shortening as needed. Serve very hot as quickly as possible. Makes 6 to 8.

BOTTOMS UP FRUIT CAKE

The old upside-down cake rejuvenated.

2 generous cups sliced raw apples
2 tablespoons butter
⅓ cup light brown sugar, firmly packed
½ teaspoon cinnamon

1 tablespoon lemon juice
1 9-ounce package yellow cake mix
whipped cream, whipped dessert topping, or Orange Sauce

Pare, core and slice apples in ¼-inch wedges. Heat butter in 8-inch baking pan. Combine sugar and cinnamon; sprinkle over butter. Arrange apples in close rows over sugar mixture and sprinkle with lemon juice. Prepare cake mix according to package directions and spread evenly over apples. Bake in preheated 350° oven 25 to 30 minutes or until cake is browned and pulls away from sides of pan. Place on rack for 10 minutes, then turn out on cake plate, bottom side up. Serve warm or cold; topped with whipped cream, prepared dessert topping mix or Orange Sauce. Makes 9 pieces.

For breakfast dust with powdered sugar.

If you have time to plan, make the cake early in the day.

Orange Sauce

1 3¾-ounce package instant lemon pudding
1½ cups orange juice

dash salt
1 teaspoon orange-flavored liqueur (optional)

Combine pudding mix, orange juice and salt; beat slowly just until blended, about 2 minutes; add liqueur. Chill. Makes 1¾ cups.

OTHER WAYS

1. Use one 1-pound can sliced peaches, apricots or plums, drained; omit apples.

2. Use gingerbread mix with apples; yellow cake with plums; or make your original selections.

3. If using a larger package of cake mix, check for pan size and make an extra cake layer for another day.

▶ Ham Casserole Dinner for Eight

Ham and Cheese Casserole   Chilled Vegetables
Bread Sticks and Sweet Butter
Lemon Custard Meringue Rice

COOKING COUNTDOWN

60 minutes ▶ marinate vegetables
—
▶
—
50 ▶ assemble ham casserole
—
▶
—
40 ▶ make lemon custard meringue rice; bake
—
▶
—
30 ▶ bake ham casserole
—
▶
—
20 ▶ arrange vegetables in lettuce cups
—
▶
—
10 ▶ spread and bake meringue topping

This menu can be
prepared in 50 minutes
if vegetables are
prepared in advance   0 ▶ serve

May be prepared in advance:
Chilled Vegetables

HAM AND CHEESE CASSEROLE

A wonderful dish for using leftover ham.

2 packages frozen artichoke hearts	¼ cup sherry
2 cups smoked ham, diced	¼ teaspoon garlic salt
1 10½-ounce can mushroom soup	½ teaspoon salt
1 10½-ounce can Cheddar cheese	8 hard-cooked eggs, quartered
soup	4 slices Cheddar cheese
1 tablespoon instant minced onion	pepper to taste

Cook artichoke hearts as directed on package, drain. Combine ingredients, except Cheddar cheese, in 3-quart casserole. Top with slices of cheese, and bake at 350° for 30 minutes. Serves 8.

BREAD STICKS AND BUTTER

The bread sticks are available in the markets. Arrange them like a bouquet in a mug or low pitcher and serve with piled whipped butter, in a companion mug, or low bowl.

CHILLED VEGETABLES

The lemon juice and olive oil are an epicurean combination.

2 1-pound cans carrots or green beans,
chilled, or vegetables of your choice

Lemon Marinade

½ cup lemon juice	¼ teaspoon freshly ground black
½ cup olive oil	pepper
2 teaspoons salt	2 teaspoons dried dill weed or 1
2½ teaspoons sugar	tablespoon chopped fresh dill
½ teaspoon garlic powder	lettuce cups

Drain carrots and allow them to remain in can or jar; pour combined marinade ingredients over and allow to stand a minimum of 1 hour in refrigerator. Cover jar or can and rotate it so carrots are well marinated. Serve as a relish, or in lettuce cups as a salad. Serves 8.

ANOTHER WAY

Fresh or frozen vegetables may be used. Cook until almost tender; then marinate. The variety of vegetables you may use is great: Brussels sprouts, cauliflower and asparagus are good subjects for a lemon bath.

Suggestion: Buy fresh dill in season; cut off coarse stems and wash thoroughly. Shake off moisture and place dill in plastic container to freeze for out-of-season use. The flavor holds very well.

LEMON CUSTARD MERINGUE RICE

2 cups hot milk	grated rind of 1 lemon
4 tablespoons butter	1/8 teaspoon salt
1 cup cooked rice	1/4 cup sugar
2 egg yolks, well beaten	lemon meringue

Combine hot milk, butter and rice in a large bowl; stir in egg yolks gradually. Blend in lemon rind, salt and sugar. Pour into greased 4-cup casserole, place in pan of water; bake 20 to 30 minutes in preheated 350° oven. When custard is set (test by cutting with silver knife; when done knife will be clean when it emerges), remove from oven; cover with meringue. Raise oven heat to 400° and bake an additional 5 minutes or until golden brown. Serve warm. Serves 8.

Lemon Meringue

1/2 cup sugar	juice of 1 lemon or 3 tablespoons
2 egg whites	lemon juice

Beat egg whites until foamy. Gradually beat in sugar until whites are glossy and form stiff peaks. Fold in lemon juice. Spread over Lemon Rice Custard as directed.

►Day-Ahead Dinner

Pork Chops Extraordinaire
Pickled Plums   Tomato-Potatoes
Jelly Roll Trifle

COOKING COUNTDOWN

60 minutes ► brown and bake chops
—
►
—
50 ► prepare trifle; chill
—
►
—
40 ► prepare tomato-potatoes
—
►
—
30 ► bake tomato-potatoes
—
►
—
20 ►
—
►
—
10 ►
—
►
—
0 ► serve

Must be prepared in advance:
Pickled Plums
Marinate pork chops

PORK CHOPS EXTRAORDINAIRE

Extraordinary in that they are simple, but still unusual gourmet fare. Marinating them the previous day makes this recipe an exception to the 60-minute Countdown. The cooking time itself fits well.

8 ½-inch-thick pork chops	½ cup olive oil
2 teaspoons seasoned salt	2 tablespoons shortening
¼ teaspoon garlic powder	2 beef bouillon cubes
½ cup lemon juice	spiced apple rings or Pickled Plums

Season chops with seasoned salt and garlic powder and place in shallow dish; pour in lemon juice and oil, turning chops to marinate well. Allow to stand in refrigerator a minimum of 3 hours. Drain, reserving marinade. Heat shortening in ovenproof skillet; add chops and brown evenly over moderate heat. Add marinade; cover skillet tightly and place in preheated 350° oven; bake 25 minutes, basting once or twice. Add bouillon cubes, stirring to dissolve, and bake an additional 20 minutes, basting once. Remove chops to heated platter; garnish with spiced apple rings, available at all markets, or with Pickled Plums if you have time to prepare them. Serves 4 to 6.

Pickled Plums

This recipe may be cut in half or doubled for "on hand" stock.

1 quart large, firm plums	1 3-inch stick cinnamon
1¾ cups sugar	1 teaspoon whole allspice
1 cup white vinegar	1 teaspoon whole cloves

Tie spices in cheesecloth or other bag and place in kettle with sugar and vinegar. Bring to a boil and cook 5 minutes. Add plums; cook gently 20 to 25 minutes or until tender. Refrigerate until needed; they keep very well. Makes 3 pints.

If you would like to have the Pickled Plums on hand, pour them into hot sterilized jars and seal tightly.

TOMATO-POTATOES

4 cups cooked instant mashed potatoes (8 4-ounce servings)
1 egg, well beaten
¼ teaspoon onion powder
½ cup shredded Cheddar or American cheese (3 ounces)

6 ½-inch tomato slices
2 tablespoons melted butter or
margarine
¼ cup dry bread crumbs
½ teaspoon seasoned salt

Combine mashed potatoes, egg and onion powder, mixing well. Shape into 6 patties and place on well-greased baking pan. Make a depression in top of each patty and fill with cheese. Cover with tomato slice and top with combined butter, bread crumbs and seasoned salt. Bake 30 minutes in 350° oven. Serves 6.

Cook instant mashed potatoes according to package directions; check amounts as quantities of brands vary. Of course, you may boil and mash potatoes from scratch, using about 2 pounds for 4 cups.

JELLY ROLL TRIFLE

1 8½-ounce package small jelly
rolls (about 3)
2 tablespoons sherry
1 3¾-ounce package instant vanilla pudding

½ teaspoon vanilla
1 cup whipped frozen topping,
defrosted, or dessert topping
mix, prepared according to
package directions

Slice jelly rolls about ½ inch thick, saving 2 pieces for decoration. Line a 4-cup bowl (glass, if you have it), with cake slices; sprinkle with sherry. Prepare pudding according to package directions and add vanilla. Pour into cake-lined bowl. Spread with topping and arrange the 2 reserved jelly roll slices in the middle, standing at angles, butterfly-like. Chill. Serves 4 to 6.

If time permits, make the Trifle in advance and simplify last-minute assembling.

Poultry, P.D.Q.

POULTRY IS A GRADUATE with a P.D.Q. degree — Pretty, Delicious, Quick. Such a vast variety is available in our supermarkets that one could literally put a "chicken in every pot" every day, prepare it in a new way, and come up with endless nuances of flavor and texture. There's something for everyone.

Turkeys, which were once primarily year-end holiday fare, are now abundant for the Fourth of July picnic as well as for the Thanksgiving feast. How about roast turkey roll for a midweek supper? It's no longer a far-out idea. Succulent ducks and capons can be put on our menus anytime, just for the cooking. Delicate and elegant Rock Cornish game hens are always available in the freezer case at your market.

The old standby 2½- to 3-pound broiler-fryer has come a long way. Advances in breeding have assured us of juicy, tender chicken every time. There's no need to despair that a chicken has only two legs; purchase the parts of your choice — drumsticks, breasts or wings. Packaged backs and necks can be made into luscious and nourishing soups.

Not to be overlooked is the fact that poultry fits into the tightest of budgets. Economical year-round, turkeys and chickens appear frequently on the lists of specials at your market.

We have concentrated on recipes that fit with ease into the 60-minute cooking countdown. That 2½- to 3-pound broiler-fryer can be transformed quickly into the focal point of a thrifty, delicious and glamorous meal. Many of the chicken dishes we present are based on the cuisines of different ethnic groups. The flavors are authentic, but again, we utilize convenience foods and shortcut methods for producing gourmet dining. Almost any fruit or vegetable is compatible with poultry; this chapter offers recipes for traditional unadorned dishes and others that include new and unusual combinations. Try several and add some of your own devising.

▶ Chicken Mandarin

Chicken Mandarin   Brown Rice
Pimiento Green Beans   Relish Tray
Zabaglione

COOKING COUNTDOWN

60 minutes ▶
         —
              ▶ sauté chicken
              —
     50 ▶ prepare sauce for chicken
              —
              ▶ cook brown rice
              —
     40 ▶ bake chicken
              —
              ▶
              —
     30 ▶ assemble relish tray, chill
              —
              ▶
              —
     20 ▶ prepare beans
              —
              ▶
              —
     10 ▶ prepare Zabaglione
              —
              ▶
              —
       0 ▶ serve

CHICKEN MANDARIN

1 cup flour
1 tablespoon salt
1 teaspoon pepper
1 teaspoon monosodium glutamate
1 cup half-and-half cream

4 whole breasts of chicken, boned
(about 8 ounces each)
vegetable shortening
Mandarin Sauce
unpeeled orange slices
parsley

Combine flour, salt, pepper and monosodium glutamate. Dip breasts in cream, drain and dredge with flour mixture. Pour vegetable shortening in skillet to depth of ¼ inch; add prepared breasts and sauté over medium heat until evenly browned on both sides. Drain on paper toweling, then place on baking sheet. Coat with Mandarin Sauce and bake in preheated 350° oven, basting frequently with pan drippings, adding additional sauce if necessary. Bake 40 minutes or until tender. Serve with Brown Rice. Garnish with orange slices and crispy parsley. Pour heated sauce over breasts or serve separately. Serves 4.

MANDARIN SAUCE

1 cup chicken stock
½ cup orange juice
2 tablespoons apricot preserves
1 11-ounce can Mandarin oranges
1 tablespoon cornstarch or arrow-
root

¼ cup cold water
2 tablespoons Cointreau or orange
liqueur

Combine stock, orange juice, preserves and Mandarin orange juice (reserve sections) in saucepan and bring to boiling; simmer about 5 minutes. Dissolve cornstarch in cold water and add to orange liquid; simmer until clear and thickened. Add reserved, drained Mandarin oranges and liqueur, adjust seasoning. Makes 1½ cups sauce.

This sauce candies the chicken breasts and the edges become crunchy. Mandarin Sauce is delicious over sautéed chicken, dessert pancakes or puddings.

For chicken stock, substitute 1 cup canned chicken broth, un-diluted.

BROWN RICE

Brown rice is richer in taste and has more value nutritionally than polished or processed rice.

1 teaspoon salt	1 cup brown rice
	2½ cups water

Combine ingredients in saucepan; cook, covered, over very low heat until liquid is absorbed and rice is fluffy, about 45 minutes. Serves 4.

QUICK ALTERNATE

Instant rice or a prepared herbed packaged rice is good; they are quick substitutes. Long-grain rice and wild rice, a packaged combination, are party mates.

GREEN BEANS PIMIENTO

3 tablespoons butter	2 tablespoons chopped pimiento
1 1-pound can whole green beans	¼ cup slivered almonds

Heat butter in saucepan; add almonds and sauté slowly until lightly browned. Shake the pan frequently to avoid scorching the almonds. Heat the beans and drain well. Place in serving dish and cover with almonds and butter drippings from the pan; top with pimiento. Serves 4.

RELISH TRAY

Create a colorful pattern with an assortment of the many zesty accompaniments available in the markets. On a serving platter, arrange spokes of drained, marinated asparagus, white or green. Use them as dividers separating the following relishes or others you select: mixed pickles, red pickled beets or red spiced apples, minted green pears and perky radish roses. Consider adding black or pimiento olives, other spiced fruits and antipasto peppers. There are many other possibilities and it is fun looking and choosing. Don't forget crisp sprigs of parsley or watercress and perhaps some bright strawberries tucked here and there.

Marinated Asparagus

Drain a 1-pound can of asparagus — about 8 stalks. Place in flat, shallow dish; cover with French Dressing. Chill about 1 hour, turning occasionally.

Minted Pears

Make your own minted pears.

1 1-pound 13-ounce can pears,	½ teaspoon mint extract
2 dozen whole cloves	4 or 5 drops green vegetable
¼ cup sugar	coloring
3 tablespoons lemon juice	

Drain syrup from pears into saucepan; stud pears with 2 or 3 cloves for each half and arrange in 9 x 9-inch pan, hollow side down. Add sugar and lemon juice to reserved syrup and bring to boiling, stirring until sugar is dissolved. Add extract and coloring and pour over pears. Refrigerate overnight or a minimum of 4 hours. Serves 6 to 8.

ZABAGLIONE

6 egg yolks	¼ cup light rum
6 tablespoons sugar	1 tablespoon grated orange peel

Combine egg yolks, sugar and rum in top of double boiler. Beat until well blended. Place over hot, not boiling, water and beat constantly with rotary beater or wire whisk 5 to 10 minutes or until the sauce thickens. Pour into 6 parfait glasses or dessert dishes; top with a sprinkling of orange peel. May be served at once as a hot dessert or may be chilled and served cold. Serves 6.

ANOTHER WAY

This is an excellent sauce to serve over drained, canned fruit or fresh berries in season.

▶ Blackhawk Chicken

Collop of Chicken Breast Blackhawk
Parslied Rice   Salad Catalina
Celery Seed Dressing or Classic French Dressing
Kahlua Sundae

COOKING COUNTDOWN

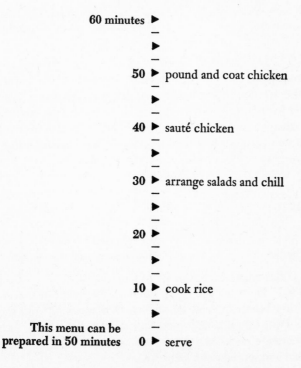

60 minutes ▶
—
▶
—
50 ▶ pound and coat chicken
—
▶
—
40 ▶ sauté chicken
—
▶
—
30 ▶ arrange salads and chill
—
▶
—
20 ▶
—
▶
—
10 ▶ cook rice
—
▶
This menu can be —
prepared in 50 minutes 0 ▶ serve

May be prepared in advance:
Celery Seed Dressing

COLLOP OF CHICKEN BREAST BLACKHAWK

Don Roth, gracious host and restaurateur, featured recipes from *Cooking with Love* in his menus. He requested a new chicken dish for following menus and I was delighted to share this one. So, when I prepared the chicken breasts on the televised Jim Conway Morning Show, I named the dish for Mr. Roth's famed Blackhawk Restaurant in Chicago. It is as attractive to the eye as to the palate.

6 double chicken breasts	½ pound fresh mushrooms, sliced
1½ teaspoons salt	1 cup light cream or milk
¼ teaspoon white pepper	3 or 4 tablespoons milk
⅓ cup flour	⅓ cup Chablis or other dry white wine
1 teaspoon monosodium glutamate	6 toast triangles
¼ cup butter or margarine	6 mushroom caps (optional)
¼ cup vegetable oil	1 tablespoon butter

Garnish: pimiento olives

Have your meatman bone the chicken breasts and remove skin; cut each in half. Dry with paper toweling. Place the boned chicken collops between sheets of wax paper and pound with the edge of a saucer or back of meat cleaver until quite thin. Use care not to tear the flesh. Combine salt, pepper, flour and monosodium glutamate in paper bag. Drop 2 or 3 chicken collops in bag at a time and shake well to coat each piece thoroughly. Heat butter and oil in heavy skillet (preferably one with a cover) and add collops in one layer. Sauté over moderate heat until lightly browned; turn often, using tongs to insure even browning and cooking, for about 20 minutes. Using a broad spatula, scrape brown bits from under the chicken to prevent sticking. Add sliced mushrooms; cover skillet and steam over moderate heat for 5 minutes. Again, check with spatula to prevent sticking. Pour cream over chicken and mushrooms; simmer 5 minutes. If sauce is too thick, stir in sufficient milk; add the Chablis. Heat well, but do not boil. Place a slice of toast on each dinner plate, then overlap with 2 collops for each portion. Top each collop with mushroom cap sautéed in butter and a mound of Parslied Rice. Add a sprig of watercress and pimiento olives for garnish. Serves 6.

Parslied Rice

Cook 2 cups precooked rice according to package directions; add 2 tablespoons parsley flakes to salted boiling water before adding rice. Serves 6.

SALAD CATALINA

2 large grapefruit
1 large ripe avocado
1 apple

1 head leaf or Boston lettuce
Celery Seed Dressing (page 268)
or Classic French Dressing

Peel grapefruit and separate into sections; reserve juice. Peel and slice avocado about same width as grapefruit segments; drop slices into grapefruit juice to prevent discoloration. Thinly slice unpeeled apple (that's for color); brush with grapefruit juice. Arrange lettuce on individual salad plates; alternate grapefruit segments and avocado slices in a row through center and slip apple slices in between for contrast. Serve with Celery Seed Dressing. Serves 4.

To cut grapefruit (or oranges) into segments, peel fruit completely, exposing pulp. Beginning at the core, slip a paring knife between the separating membrane and one segment of grapefruit, cutting them apart. Now slip the knife between the other side of the segment and the membrane; bring the knife up, quickly releasing the section. Continue until all segments are removed.

Classic French Dressing

¾ cup salad oil or olive oil
¼ cup cider vinegar or lemon juice
1 clove garlic, minced (optional)

1½ teaspoons salt
⅛ teaspoon freshly ground pepper

Combine all ingredients very well; chill thoroughly. It's wise to double the quantity to have on hand as it keeps very well.

KAHLUA SUNDAE

1 quart vanilla ice cream
Kahlua

Since liqueur is a matter of personal taste let each guest serve himself. Allow approximately ½ cup for 6 servings, poured from an interesting pitcher. Serves 6 to 8.

► Chicken Gardner

Chicken Gardner   *Buttered Fine Noodles*
Artichokes Hollandaise   *Cauliflower Pimiento Salad*
Pears à la Hélène or *Icy Pears*

COOKING COUNTDOWN

60 minutes ► cook cauliflower

► combine salad ingredients; refrigerate

50 ► bake chickens

►

40 ► cook artichokes

►

30 ►

►

20 ► cook noodles

► arrange pears; place in freezer

10 ► assemble salad

► heat chocolate sauce

0 ► serve

May be prepared in advance:
Chicken Gardner
Golden Pears for Pears Hélène

CHICKEN GARDNER

Roast chicken with a slightly different gourmet flavor.

6 chicken breasts or 2 2½-pound fryers, disjointed
2 teaspoons salt
½ teaspoon coarsely ground pepper
½ teaspoon dry ginger

½ cup butter or margarine
2 tablespoons butter
2 tablespoons water
½ pound mushrooms, sliced
½ cup light cream
1 cup white wine

1 cucumber, peeled and diced

Place breasts or chicken pieces in roasting pan; sprinkle with salt, pepper and ginger. Dot with ½ cup butter. Place in preheated 450° oven and bake until brown, about 15 minutes. Baste with pan juices; reduce heat to 350° and cover tightly. Bake 30 minutes or until tender. Heat 2 tablespoons butter with water and add mushrooms. Cover and steam 5 minutes. Strain all pan drippings into mushroom mixture; add cream, wine and cucumber cubes; heat well. Place chicken on serving platter and cover with mushroom cucumber sauce, reserving some for requests for "seconds." Serves 6.

Chicken Gardner may be made in advance. To serve, place chicken in casserole, cover with sauce and reheat for 30 minutes in a 350° oven.

BUTTERED FINE NOODLES

Cook one 8-ounce package of fine noodles, according to package directions. Drain and toss with 2 tablespoons butter and 1 tablespoon snipped parsley. Serves 6.

ARTICHOKES HOLLANDAISE

The artichoke is a beautiful flower-like vegetable with extensive versatility. Indulge when it is in season, for then its price takes a nose dive. Its basic preparation can take many forms, but as a vegetable accompaniment the artichoke is incomparable — an adventure in dining.

6 artichokes	3 tablespoons Italian style
boiling salted water	dressing
Hollandaise Sauce or melted butter	

Slice about 1 inch from top of artichokes and cut brown tips from each leaf, in even lines. Cut stems so artichokes will stand erect when cooked. Place closely together in saucepan, so they support each other and will not tip. Add sufficient salted water (½ teaspoon salt per cup) to a depth of 1 inch. Pour 1 tablespoon dressing into water and drizzle remainder over artichokes. Cover pan tightly and cook 30 to 45 minutes until a bottom leaf pulls out easily. Remove and drain; open gently to the heart and remove "choke," the fuzzy growth from within at the base. Scrape out with a spoon if necessary. Serve with prepared Hollandaise or melted butter. Serves 6.

Charming individual colored butter servers are available in specialty shops and add a conversational note.

Prepared Hollandaise is available in the markets; serve it according to directions on the jar.

CAULIFLOWER PIMIENTO SALAD

1 small head cauliflower, divided in flowerets	3 finely chopped green onions
boiling salted water	¼ cup vinegar
½ can anchovies, drained	½ cup salad oil
12 stuffed green olives, sliced	lettuce, small tomatoes and watercress

Cook cauliflowerets in boiling salted water 6 minutes. Flowerets should be still firm. Drain; blanch with cold water. Place in bowl; cut anchovies in ½-inch slices and add with sliced olives, green onions. Combine vinegar and oil and toss with cauliflower mixture. Cover and refrigerate. To serve, pour into lettuce-lined bowl; garnish with small tomatoes and watercress. Serves 6.

ANOTHER WAY

If you have time, prepare salad several hours in advance; the flavors improve as they blend.

PEARS À LA HÉLÈNE

Golden Pears (page 127)
1 6-ounce can chocolate sauce
½ teaspoon vanilla or Kahlua

1 pint vanilla ice cream, slightly softened

Prepare pears according to recipe for Golden Pears or in simple syrup as listed below. Heat chocolate syrup and add vanilla or Kahlua. Spoon ice cream into individual dessert plates and stand chilled pear upright in ice cream. Serve the hot syrup separately as the pears are too pretty to cover too soon. Serves 6.

OTHER WAYS

The Golden Pears are lovely, but for true Pears Hélène a simple syrup is used. Here it is.

Pears in Simple Syrup

6 fresh pears, pared whole with stems
1¼ cups water

¾ cup sugar
1 1-inch piece vanilla bean or 1 teaspoon vanilla extract

Pare the fruit, and if you wish, core from bottom; do not cut too deeply as the pears may lose form. Combine water, sugar and vanilla bean (if using vanilla extract, add after pears are cooked). Bring to boiling and cook 5 minutes; add pears and simmer slowly about 20 minutes until tender, but not mushy. Turn frequently to cook evenly. Allow to cool in syrup; chill. Serves 6.

QUICK ALTERNATE

Icy Pears

When fresh pears are not available, a substitute dessert may be prepared with drained canned pears. Place halves on ice cream and serve with hot chocolate sauce. Serves 6.

▶ Red Lemon Broiled Chicken

Red Lemon Broiled Chicken
Sauced Mushrooms   Nutty Rice
Tomato Aspic in a Cylinder or *Aspic Madrilène*
Chocolate Mint Pie or *Minute Mint Pie*

COOKING COUNTDOWN

60 minutes ▶ prepare basting sauce

▶ broil chickens

50 ▶

▶

40 ▶

▶

30 ▶

▶ turn and baste chicken

20 ▶ cook rice

▶

10 ▶ broil mushrooms

▶

0 ▶ serve

Must be prepared in advance:
    Chocolate Mint Pie
    Tomato Aspic in a Cylinder

RED LEMON BROILED CHICKEN

1 2½-pound broiler, quartered
Red Lemon Basting Sauce

Dry broiler with paper toweling; brush with Red Lemon Basting Sauce and place on foil-lined shallow pan, skin side down. Place in preheated broiler oven, 7 inches from heat source. Broil 30 minutes on one side, basting twice. Turn over and brush again with basting sauce, broiling 15 to 30 minutes or until fork tender, or until tested for doneness. Place on platter and serve pan drippings over chicken or in separate bowl. Serves 4.

Red Lemon Basting Sauce

1 cup sweet red wine (such as Concord grape)	1 teaspoon paprika
¼ cup soy sauce	½ teaspoon garlic powder
3 tablespoons lemon juice	½ cup butter
	3 drops hot pepper sauce

Combine all ingredients in saucepan; bring to boil, and remove from heat; keep warm. Makes about 1¾ cups.

To test chicken for doneness

The thigh should feel tender "to the touch." Be careful to cover fingers with towel when testing (to prevent a burn). Also the leg joint should move very easily when your broiled chicken is ready for the table.

SAUCED MUSHROOMS

Allow 3 to 4 mushrooms per person; remove stems and save them for another recipe. About 5 minutes before removing chicken from oven, add mushrooms to pan, hollow side up. Brush with Red Lemon Basting Sauce and broil with chicken.

NUTTY RICE

1½ cups water	1 tablespoon parsley flakes
1 teaspoon salt	1½ cups precooked rice
2 chicken bouillon cubes	1 tablespoon butter
¼ cup chopped walnuts	

Combine water, salt, bouillon cubes and parsley flakes in saucepan; bring to boiling, stirring until bouillon cubes are dissolved. Add rice, butter and nuts, blending well. Cover tightly and remove from heat. Let stand 5 minutes. Toss with a fork to fluff the kernels. Serves 4.

My grandmother used to place a Turkish towel over the pot of cooked rice to keep the rice fluffy and hot, the secret being that the towel absorbs the moisture.

TOMATO ASPIC IN A CYLINDER

1 1-pound can tomato juice (2 cups)	½ teaspoon seasoned salt
1 3-ounce package lemon- or lime-flavored gelatin	1½ tablespoons tarragon or white vinegar
	dash Tabasco

Pour 1 cup of the tomato juice into saucepan and bring to boiling; remove from heat and add gelatin, stirring until dissolved. Pour back into can, mixing with remaining juice; add salt, vinegar and Tabasco. Chill in refrigerator until firm. To unmold, puncture bottom of can slightly to loosen gelatin. Remove onto moistened plate as it will slide more easily. Cut in slices and place in lettuce cups or serve from relish dish. Will serve 6 as a salad or 8 to 10 as relish. To hasten the setting of gelatin, set in the freezer for the first ½ hour.

QUICK ALTERNATE

Aspic Madrilène

Chill a 13-ounce can prepared red consommé madrilène. Remove from can and cut in slices or cubes. Serve in lettuce cups. Serves 5 to 6.

CHOCOLATE MINT PIE

1 8-ounce package cream cheese
½ cup sour cream
¼ cup sugar
2 envelopes liquid chocolate-flavored ingredient

2 2-ounce packages dessert topping mix
2 tablespoons crème de menthe
½ teaspoon peppermint flavoring
3 to 4 drops green food coloring

1 Chocolate Crumb Crust (page 224)

Soften cream cheese; add sour cream, sugar and chocolate. Beat until smooth and fluffy. Prepare 1 package dessert topping mix according to package directions. Fold chocolate mixture into whipped topping. Prepare second package of topping, substituting crème de menthe for 2 tablespoons milk. Fold in peppermint and coloring. Swirl chocolate mixture into crust. Top with mint mixture. Chill. Serves 6 to 8.

QUICK ALTERNATE

Minute Mint Pie

Fill a prepared crumb crust with one 1¾-ounce package chocolate whipped dessert mix, prepared according to package directions, substituting 2 tablespoons crème de menthe for 2 tablespoons milk.

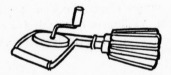

► Honey Glazed Chicken

Honey Glazed Chicken   Toasted Egg Barley
Special Salad
Meringue Spice Cake or *Apple Strudel*

COOKING COUNTDOWN

60 minutes ►
—
►
—
50 ► bake chickens
—
►
—
40 ► hard-cook eggs; fry bacon
—
►
—
30 ► cook barley
—
►
—
20 ► arrange salad bowl
—
►
—
10 ► toss salad

This menu can ►
be prepared in —
50 minutes   0 ► serve

Must be prepared in advance:
Meringue Spice Cake

HONEY GLAZED CHICKEN

I hope you try this recipe, for it is a favorite of mine. Use the recipe for Honey Glaze with leftover poultry or lamb and make them as delicious as the first time around.

1 2½- to 3-pound frying chicken disjointed, or 3 pounds of selected pieces	1 teaspoon seasoned salt Honey Glaze

Season chicken; set aside. Prepare Honey Glaze.

Honey Glaze

¼ cup butter 6 tablespoons honey 3 tablespoons prepared mustard	2 teaspoons (or more to taste) curry powder

Garnish: shredded lettuce

The glaze is made right in the roasting pan, thus eliminating one saucepan cleaning job. Place butter in 9 x 13-inch roasting pan in preheated 375° oven; let stand until melted. Remove from oven; add honey, mustard and curry powder, stirring until well blended. Place chicken in sauce, turning to coat evenly. Arrange in one layer and return to 375° oven; bake 45 minutes or until tender. Baste and turn the pieces several times while baking and be rewarded with beautifully glazed, succulent portions. Spread a thick bed of shredded lettuce on serving platter and arrange chicken on it. The combination of textures and flavors is deliciously different. Serves 4.

ANOTHER WAY

Place cooked leftover poultry or meat in roasting pan as for Honey Glazed Chicken. Heat the dish in 325° oven for 35 to 40 minutes, basting often. Note difference in oven temperature.

TOASTED EGG BARLEY

Cook 4 ounces toasted egg barley according to package directions. Toss with 1 tablespoon butter and salt. Serves 6.

SPECIAL SALAD

Special because it's an especially good combination and sufficiently hearty for a main course.

1 quart torn lettuce, iceberg, Bibb or Boston	3 hard-cooked eggs, sliced
1 cup sliced celery	¼ cup grated Parmesan cheese
6 slices crisply cooked bacon, crumbled	¾ cup prepared creamy French dressing or French Blend Dressing (page 267)
2 tomatoes, sliced	

Use a combination of 2 or 3 varieties of lettuce. Wash and drain well. Refrigerate in plastic bag to chill and crisp. Toss in salad bowl with celery. Border the lettuce with alternate rings of tomatoes and egg slices and sprinkle with crumbled, crisp bacon. Dust with grated cheese. To serve, pour over your selected dressing, tossing lightly until well marinated. Serves 4 generously.

The salad is a most attractive one and usually I present it for a modest display before tossing. It has eye and appetite appeal!

MERINGUE SPICE CAKE

A baked-on topping over such good baked-in flavor.

¾ cup butter	1 teaspoon baking soda
2 cups light brown sugar	1¼ cups buttermilk
2 egg yolks, beaten	1 teaspoon vanilla
2⅓ cups cake flour	1 cup brown sugar, firmly packed and sifted
1 teaspoon baking powder	2 eggs whites, stiffly beaten
1 teaspoon powdered cloves	½ cup coarsely chopped pecans or walnuts
1 teaspoon cinnamon	
¾ teaspoon salt	

Cream butter and sugar until light and fluffy; beat in egg yolks. Sift flour, baking powder, cloves, cinnamon and salt together; mix baking soda with buttermilk. Add flour mixture to butter mixture, beginning and ending with flour, one-fourth at a time, alternating with buttermilk mixture. Beat well after each addition; blend in vanilla. Turn into greased and floured 9 x 13-inch baking pan. Add 1 cup brown sugar to beaten egg whites, 2 tablespoons at a time, beating well until blended and stiff. Spread over cake batter, pushing into corners, and sprinkle with chopped nuts. Bake in preheated 350° oven for 50 to 60 minutes until done when tested with a toothpick or tester. (If pick is dry after piercing cake, baking is completed.) Remove to cake rack and cool thoroughly. Cut into squares, approximately 2 inches each way. Makes 24.

Note: This old recipe once called for sour milk but today's homogenized product will not work. Instead use buttermilk as a substitute or make your own sour milk. For each cup of sour milk, pour 1 tablespoon white vinegar into a cup, add sweet milk to fill balance of the cup measure. For the 1¼ cups buttermilk in the above recipe substitute 1 tablespoon plus ¾ teaspoon vinegar with sufficient sweet milk for the remainder.

QUICK ALTERNATE

Bake a quick batch of frozen apple or cherry strudel (those which come in a 14-ounce package).

▶ Chicken Gloriana

Breast of Chicken Gloriana   Saffron Rice
Braised Celery   Melba Toast
Coconut Ice Cream Balls   Pecan Wafers

COOKING COUNTDOWN

60 minutes ▶ assemble ice cream balls
—
▶
—
50 ▶ cook chicken
—
▶
—
40 ▶ slice and bake chilled cooky dough
—
▶
—
30 ▶ braise celery
—
▶
—
20 ▶ arrange toast and butter
—
▶ cook rice
—
10 ▶ complete chicken preparation
—
This menu can be
prepared in 50 minutes ▶
if ice cream balls are —
shaped and frozen 0 ▶ serve

Must be prepared in advance:
Cooky dough

BREAST OF CHICKEN GLORIANA

3 chicken breasts, halved
1 teaspoon salt
1 teaspoon seasoned salt
¼ teaspoon parsley flakes
4 tablespoons butter or margarine
6 slices ham

1 1-pound 13-ounce can apricots, pitted and drained
¼ cup slivered almonds
¼ cup brandy
½ cup apricot liquid
1 teaspoon meat extract paste

1 tablespoon butter or margarine

Season breasts with salt, seasoned salt and parsley. Heat butter in skillet; add chicken. Brown and cook over moderate heat, 30 to 40 minutes or until tender. Remove chicken to another pan and keep warm. If necessary, add 1 tablespoon butter to same skillet; sauté ham quickly. Remove and keep warm with chicken. Now add apricots and almonds to pan and heat; ignite warmed brandy; pour over apricots, allowing flame to burn out. Stir in apricot liquid. Heat but do not boil. Arrange ham on platter and place one breast on each slice of ham; border with apricots. Add meat extract and 1 tablespoon butter to sauce in pan. Stir and heat quickly. Pour over chicken and ham. Serves 6.

SAFFRON RICE

Prepare one 8-ounce package Saffron Rice Mix according to package directions. A very good accompaniment for poultry and fruit. Serves 4 to 6.

BRAISED CELERY

Try this recipe, proof that celery deserves attention in the hot vegetable category.

3 tablespoons butter
1 small onion, diced
6 large stalks celery, pared and cut in 2-inch diagonal slices
½ cup beef consommé or ½ cup

boiling water and 1 beef bouillon cube
½ teaspoon salt
¼ teaspoon white pepper
paprika

Melt butter in skillet; add diced onion and sauté until transparent. Add the celery and consommé to the skillet, cover and simmer gently for 20 minutes. Add the salt and pepper, and continue to simmer about 10 minutes, or until most of the liquid has been absorbed. Transfer to serving dish, dust with paprika, and serve very hot. Serves 6.

ANOTHER WAY

Prepare 3 Belgian endives, sliced lengthwise in halves, this same way. Serves 6.

MELBA TOAST AND BUTTER

As a simple departure from the usual rolls and butter, we suggest, as an accompaniment to this menu, crisp whole-wheat Melba toast and whipped sweet butter. Half-pound cartons of the whipped butter are available at most markets. Let the butter come to room temperature and pile into a small bowl placed in the center of a plate or tray. Surround with Melba toast.

COCONUT ICE CREAM BALLS

1 pint ice cream
1 4-ounce package flaked coconut (1½ cups)

Shape the balls ahead of time with an ice cream scoop until well rounded; roll in coconut. Quickly wrap each in wax paper and into the freezer to be on hand for dessert time. Serves 4.

ANOTHER WAY

Shape any flavor of ice cream into balls, wrap and keep in the freezer to serve at a moment's notice with a topping of sauce or liqueur.

For a last-minute dish, scoop ice cream from the package to serving dishes.

PECAN WAFERS

Make the Pecan Wafers at your convenience, they are simple and very good to have on hand.

1 egg, slightly beaten	1 teaspoon baking powder
¾ cup brown sugar	1 9½-ounce package pie crust
½ cup pecans, finely chopped	mix

Combine egg, sugar, pecans and baking powder in a bowl. Add pie crust mix and blend thoroughly. Divide into 2 rolls about 1½ inches in diameter. Wrap in waxed paper and chill until firm. When in haste, place in freezer to chill. Slice in ¼-inch slices and bake on an ungreased cooky sheet in a preheated 400° oven for about 10 to 12 minutes or until delicately brown. Makes about 5 dozen.

► Chicken Madelon

Chicken Madelon   Asparagus Romanoff
Citrus Salad   French Blend Dressing
Sauced Raisin Rice   Fattening Cookies

COOKING COUNTDOWN

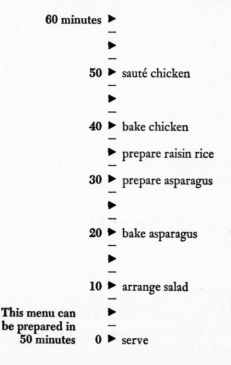

60 minutes ►
—
►
—
50 ► sauté chicken
—
►
—
40 ► bake chicken
—
► prepare raisin rice

30 ► prepare asparagus
—
►
—
20 ► bake asparagus
—
►
—
10 ► arrange salad
—
This menu can   ►
be prepared in   —
50 minutes   0 ► serve

Must be made in advance:
Fattening Cookies
French Blend Dressing

CHICKEN MADELON

¼ pound butter
4 chicken breasts, halved and skinned
2 small onions, sliced
½ cup sherry
½ cup tomato juice

½ teaspoon paprika
½ teaspoon powdered ginger
1 teaspoon salt
½ teaspoon pepper
1 cup chicken bouillon
crisp watercress

Heat half of the butter; add chicken breasts and brown evenly until golden on both sides; remove and place in baking dish. Add remaining butter to skillet; add onions and sauté until lightly browned. Stir in remaining ingredients except watercress; bring to boiling and cook 1 minute; pour over chicken. Place in 400° preheated oven and bake 30 minutes; turn breasts, skin side up, and baste with pan drippings. Reduce heat to 375° and bake 10 minutes or until tender. To serve, place on platter and dress with pan sauce; garnish with watercress. Serves 4 to 6.

OTHER WAYS

1. If chicken bouillon is not available, dissolve 1 chicken bouillon cube in 1 cup boiling water.

2. This recipe can be adapted very successfully to veal. Three and one-half pounds veal steak will serve 6. It is a light, flavorful preparation and freezes well.

ASPARAGUS ROMANOFF

The noodles make this a two-course dish. It stands alone as an entrée or doubles as an accompaniment to meat, fish or fowl. Gourmet flavor with a minimum of effort.

1 10-ounce package frozen asparagus
1 5¾-ounce package noodles with prepared sour cream sauce

¼ cup milk (additional to package directions)
2 slices aged Cheddar cheese, cut in 1-inch pieces
paprika

Cook asparagus 1 minute less than package directions and turn into greased 9-inch ovenware skillet or baking dish. Prepare noodles and sauce according to package directions, adding the ¼ cup milk to the prescribed ⅓ cup milk to make a thinner sauce. Pour over asparagus, then cover with sliced cheese and bake in preheated 375° oven about 20 minutes until bubbly and cheese has melted. Dust with paprika. Serves 4.

May be assembled in advance; bake before serving.

ANOTHER WAY

Use frozen broccoli, spinach or beans.

CITRUS SALAD

2 cups grapefruit segments or 1 1-pound can, drained and chilled

1 8-ounce can Mandarin oranges, drained and chilled

2 tablespoons shredded coconut

lettuce cups

¾ cup French Blend Dressing

Lightly toss together grapefruit, oranges and coconut. Chill thoroughly. Mound in lettuce cups and spoon 2 tablespoons French Blend Dressing over each serving. Serves 6.

ANOTHER WAY

A clear French Dressing of a prepared variety is very good on citrus fruits, and is always available.

FRENCH BLEND DRESSING

A delicious dressing in itself and a great base for embellishments.

1 egg

¼ teaspoon pepper

1 teaspoon salt

1 teaspoon dry mustard

1 clove garlic, minced or ¼ teaspoon powdered garlic

½ cup lemon juice or white vinegar

1½ cups salad oil

Combine all ingredients except salad oil in blender or bowl of electric mixer. Cover blender when starting (or set mixer at low speed), for it will splash at first. Beat until very well combined, then add oil in very slow stream until dressing is completely blended. It will be quite thick, a creamy type of French dressing. Makes 2 cups.

OTHER WAYS

To 1 cup French Blend Dressing:

Blue Cheese Dressing — add ¼ cup crumbled Blue or Roquefort cheese

Anchovy Dressing — add 2 tablespoons anchovy paste

Celery Seed Dressing — add 1 teaspoon celery seed and ¼ teaspoon onion powder

Lemon Fruit Dressing — add 2 tablespoons honey and 1 teaspoon lemon juice

Lorenzo Dressing — add ½ cup chili sauce and ½ cup chopped watercress

Calcutta Dressing — add 2 tablespoons chopped chutney and ¼ teaspoon curry powder

Calcutta Plus — to Calcutta dressing add 2 hard-cooked eggs, chopped

Vinaigrette Dressing — add 2 tablespoons sweet pickle relish, 1 finely chopped hard-cooked egg, and 1 tablespoon chopped pimiento

SAUCED RAISIN RICE

1 cup precooked instant rice
1 cup boiling water
¼ teaspoon salt
1½ cups milk
2 egg yolks, slightly beaten
½ cup sugar
½ cup seeded, plumped raisins

¼ teaspoon cinnamon
1 tablespoon butter or margarine
½ teaspoon vanilla
½ teaspoon lemon extract
whipped cream or topping mix (optional)

Add rice to boiling water, stirring until mixed. Stir in salt and remove from heat; cover and let stand 5 minutes. Combine milk, egg yolks, and add to rice. Blend in remaining ingredients except flavorings and mix well. Bring to boiling, stirring constantly; remove from heat and add vanilla and lemon extract. Cover and let stand 30 minutes to one hour in saucepan. It will become creamy and will thicken. To serve add a swirl of cream, if desired. Serves 4.

FATTENING COOKIES

Had to include these for you to bake in an expected lapse of time. They are layer on layer rising to an irresistible sweet; a foolproof recipe, the gift of a Palm Springs, California, hostess.

½ cup butter
1 cup graham cracker crumbs
1 3½-ounce can flaky coconut
1 4-ounce package semi-sweet chocolate pieces

1 4-ounce package butterscotch pieces
1 cup chopped pecans
1 15-ounce can sweetened condensed milk

Heat oven to 350°. Place butter in 8 x 12-inch shallow baking pan and set in oven until melted. Remove and add crumbs, mixing until well blended, then spread mixture evenly over bottom of pan. Sprinkle coconut evenly over crumb base, add a layer of the chocolate pieces, top with a layer of the butterscotch pieces and last a layer of the pecans. Pour the milk over all, spreading with a spatula if necessary. Bake 30 minutes in the preheated 350° oven. Remove and cool thoroughly. Cut into 1-inch squares and allow to set overnight before removing from pan. If they are not eaten at once, they will keep for a month in an airtight container. In our home, we never have enough left to warrant unearthing the container. I leave them out on a cake plate covered with plastic wrap. Makes about 8 dozen.

ANOTHER WAY

Cut the pan of "fudgy" cake into 3-inch squares and serve as a cake dessert. A scoop of mocha or vanilla ice cream adds sufficient glamour for a party. Sprinkle the tops with chopped pecans or shredded coconut.

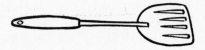

▶ Cherry Chicken

Cherry Chicken   Potato Dumplings
Broccoli with Hollandaise Sauce
Cinnamon Chocolate Cream or *Cinnamon Chocolate Pudding*

COOKING COUNTDOWN

60 minutes ▶ bake chicken

     ▶

50 ▶ prepare cherry sauce

     ▶

40 ▶ prepare dumpling batter

     ▶

30 ▶ cook broccoli; drain

     ▶

20 ▶ cook dumplings

     ▶

10 ▶ prepare Hollandaise

     ▶

0 ▶ serve

May be prepared in advance:
Cherry Chicken
Potato Dumpling batter

Must be prepared in advance:
Cinnamon Chocolate Cream

CHERRY CHICKEN

1 2½- to 3-pound frying chicken, disjointed, or your selection of pieces	½ teaspoon powdered ginger
	½ teaspoon salt
1½ teaspoons seasoned salt	1 teaspoon Worcestershire
½ teaspoon paprika	½ teaspoon rosemary
½ cup white wine or sherry	¼ cup coarsely chopped onion, fresh or frozen
1 1-pound can pitted red sour cherries, drained (reserve ½ cup cherry syrup)	

Wash chicken, but do not dry; sprinkle evenly on both sides with seasoned salt and paprika. Arrange in 9 x 9 x 1-inch pan; the pieces very close together. Place in preheated 375° oven; bake ½ hour without peeking. Pour off pan juices. Combine wine, cherry syrup, ginger, salt, Worcestershire and rosemary; baste chicken with ½ cup of this mixture. Add onions to pan sauce around the chicken; bake 10 minutes and baste with remaining ½ cup cherry syrup mixture. Bake an additional 10 minutes or until tender. Add cherries and bake about 5 minutes, long enough to heat cherries. Arrange chicken on platter; cover with cherries and dress with pan juices. Border with potato dumplings. Serves 4.

May be partially prepared early in the day; reheat, adding cherries, and bake 5 minutes additional.

ANOTHER WAY

The recipe may be increased proportionately as needed. If a thicker sauce is preferred, pour pan juices into the saucepan. For each 2 cups of sauce, make a paste of 1 tablespoon cornstarch and ¼ cup liquid. Add to pan juices and simmer about 5 minutes until sauce is thickened and clear.

POTATO DUMPLINGS

Similar to the Italian Gnocchi, these dumplings contain less flour and may be dropped from a spoon.

¾ cup instant mashed potatoes	¼ teaspoon nutmeg
1¼ cups boiling water	1 teaspoon parsley flakes
1 teaspoon salt	24 packaged seasoned croutons
2 eggs	(optional)
¾ cup flour	

Combine instant mashed potatoes (from package) in saucepan with boiling water and salt. Beat in eggs until blended, then beat in flour. Sprinkle croutons over batter. Heat 8 cups water to boiling and add 4 teaspoons salt. Drop batter by tablespoons in gently boiling water, enclosing a crouton with each spoonful. Cook about 10 minutes; dumplings will come to the surface. Toss with melted butter or serve with entrée gravy. Makes about 2 dozen.

It may be convenient to mix the batter early in the day and cook just before serving.

BROCCOLI WITH HOLLANDAISE

Cook 2 packages frozen broccoli according to package directions and serve with your choice of Hollandaise sauce.

Mock Hollandaise #1

1 10-ounce can cream of chicken soup	¼ cup mayonnaise
	1 tablespoon lemon juice
	dash cayenne

Cook over moderate heat, stirring occasionally. Makes 1½ cups. Add lemon juice to taste if you like the tart sauce.

Mock Hollandaise #2

1 cup sour cream	¼ cup lemon juice
1 cup mayonnaise	dash cayenne

Combine ingredients; heat slowly, stirring occasionally. Do not boil. Makes 2¼ cups.

Mock Hollandaise #3

2 3-ounce packages cream cheese, softened
2 egg yolks

2 tablespoons lemon juice
⅛ teaspoon salt
dash cayenne

Add egg yolks to cream cheese, one at a time, in top of double boiler, stirring and blending well after each addition. Add lemon juice, salt and cayenne. Place over hot water and heat thoroughly; stir occasionally. Makes a generous cup.

CINNAMON CHOCOLATE CREAM

We tried this south of the border "trick" and found it had merit — cinnamon does nice things to chocolate. We combined several convenience foods and came up with a rich and elegant dessert.

½ cup unsweetened cocoa
¼ cup boiling water
2 cups frozen whipped dessert topping, defrosted, or 1 cup whipping cream, whipped

1 cup miniature marshmallows
½ cup red hot cinnamon candy drops, powdered in a blender
½ cup chopped walnuts

Dissolve cocoa in boiling water; combine with all ingredients and mix together thoroughly. Pour into a 4-cup container; cover and freeze for at least 4 hours. Because this is a very rich dessert, plan on small portions. Serve in *pots de crème*, demitasse cups, or other small dessert dishes. Serve 8.

QUICK ALTERNATE

Cinnamon Chocolate Pudding

2 cups milk
2 tablespoons red cinnamon candies

1 4-ounce package chocolate pudding and pie filling mix
whipped cream topping

Combine 1 cup milk and cinnamon drops in saucepan; heat, stirring until cinnamon drops have dissolved. Remove from heat. Combine pudding mixture with remaining cup of milk and stir until blended. Mix into milk and candy mixture; place over medium heat and stir until pudding comes to a rolling boil. Pour into bowl or 6 individual dessert dishes. Place in refrigerator to chill. Serves 6.

Top with cream from a pressurized can.

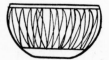

▶ Curried Chicken

Curried Chicken
Curry Accompaniments   Fluffy Rice
Magic Lemon Pie

COOKING COUNTDOWN

60 minutes ▶ prepare lemon pie
         –
         ▶
         –
    50 ▶
         –
         ▶
         –
    40 ▶
         –
         ▶
         –
    30 ▶ arrange curry accompaniments
         –
         ▶
         –
    20 ▶ prepare chicken
         –
         ▶
         –
    10 ▶ cook rice

This menu can be
prepared in 30 minutes   –
if Quick Alternate   ▶
dessert is used   0 ▶ serve   –

May be prepared in advance:
Magic Lemon Pie

CURRIED CHICKEN

This is a delightful dish, lovely to look at and delicious to eat. And so simple you'll be embarrassed to accept the compliments. Wonderful for leftovers.

4 chicken breasts, broiled or boiled
4 10-ounce cans chicken à la king
2 teaspoons curry powder

½ teaspoon celery salt
1 diced apple
4 cups fluffy rice, long grain or precooked

Curry Accompaniments

Remove cooked chicken from bones in large pieces. Add to remaining ingredients and heat thoroughly. Serve in chafing dish with bowl of rice, and Curry Accompaniments bordering the burner. Serves 8. With sufficient variety and amounts of accompaniments, no salad is really necessary. The dessert and beverage complete an ample dinner.

Curry Accompaniments

This is a list of suggestions. Let your imagination run away with you here, for you may offer as many adjuncts to the curry as you have little bowls to put them in. Don't worry if the bowls don't match. An attractive table for a curry menu exhibits the accompaniments in containers of many interesting sizes and shapes.

chopped hard-cooked eggs
chopped parsley
chopped orange peel
shredded canned pineapple
chopped cucumber

chopped peanuts
chopped green onions
toasted coconut
dried currants
chopped mango chutney

Another assortment will be found on page 176. Fluffy Rice (page 180).

MAGIC LEMON PIE

This pie has the surprise element of a sorcerer's trick and is simple to perform.

Graham Cracker Crust

1 cup fine graham cracker crumbs   Magic Lemon Filling
¼ cup butter or margarine, softened

You may purchase a prepared graham cracker crust or prepare it if you have time. Combine cracker crumbs and butter, mixing with fork or fingers until smooth and blended. Press firmly against bottom and sides of 9-inch pie pan until smooth and even. Pour Magic Lemon Filling into prepared crust and place in refrigerator to chill. It will set in about 30 minutes but can stand longer. It is a good "keeper." Serves 6 to 8.

Magic Lemon Filling

1 15-ounce can sweetened condensed milk   2 egg yolks, well beaten
                                            ½ cup lemon juice
              2 egg whites, stiffly beaten

Combine milk, egg yolks and lemon juice; fold in beaten egg whites carefully, blending well. Makes filling for one 9-inch pie shell.

QUICK ALTERNATE

Mandarin Ambrosia

Toss drained Mandarin oranges, miniature marshmallows and coconut together.

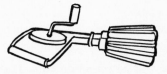

▶ Teriyaki Chicken

> *Teriyaki Chicken*   *Tomatoes Polonaise*
> *Wilted Spinach Salad*   *Hot Rye Bread*
> *Banana Mousse*

COOKING COUNTDOWN

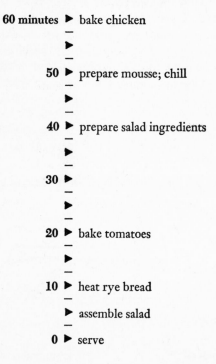

60 minutes ▶ bake chicken

▶

50 ▶ prepare mousse; chill

▶

40 ▶ prepare salad ingredients

▶

30 ▶

▶

20 ▶ bake tomatoes

▶

10 ▶ heat rye bread

▶ assemble salad

0 ▶ serve

TERIYAKI CHICKEN

Unusually delicious Teriyaki Chicken may be used for an entrée or cut into bite-sized pieces to serve as an appetizer.

3 2½-pound fryers, quartered or ½ cup softened butter
   pieces disjointed   Teriyaki Sauce
½ teaspoon Tabasco   parsley

Dry fryers with paper toweling; place close together in shallow pan, brush with combined Tabasco and butter. Bake in 350° preheated oven 30 minutes, basting frequently with Tabasco butter. Baste with Teriyaki Sauce and continue to bake an additional 20 to 30 minutes or until tender. Baste frequently with Teriyaki Sauce or pan drippings. Serve on platter garnished with bouquets of parsley; border with tomatoes. Serves 6 to 8.

Teriyaki Sauce

¼ cup sugar   2 teaspoons finely grated or pow-
½ cup soy sauce   dered ginger
½ cup sake or sherry

Combine and blend ingredients thoroughly. Makes 1¼ cups.

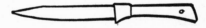

TOMATOES POLONAISE

3 tomatoes, halved   2 tablespoons bread crumbs
1 teaspoon seasoned salt   2 tablespoons butter

Place tomatoes on baking sheet, sprinkle with salt, bread crumbs; dot with butter. Bake in preheated 350° oven 10 to 15 minutes until piping hot. If crumbs need more browning, place them under the broiler for a minute or two. Serves 6.

WILTED SPINACH SALAD

A delicious dish.

1 pound fresh young spinach	½ teaspoon paprika
4 slices bacon	⅛ teaspoon coarsely ground pepper
2 tablespoons flour	
4 teaspoons sugar	⅓ cup cider vinegar
½ teaspoon salt	¼ cup water

2 hard-cooked eggs, sliced in rings

Wash spinach and tear into bite-size pieces, discarding tough stems; drain well. Cook bacon until crisp, then remove and drain on paper toweling; crumble coarsely and set aside. Blend flour with bacon grease in skillet and add remaining ingredients, except eggs; simmer, stirring until thick and smooth. To serve, place spinach in salad bowl; sprinkle with crumbled bacon and garnish with rings of hard-cooked eggs. Pour hot dressing over all and toss lightly until all leaves are coated. Serves 6.

ANOTHER WAY

Wilted lettuce may be prepared the same way; a fine accompaniment to cold cuts, it is a Pennsylvania Dutch recruit.

HOT RYE BREAD

Wrap sliced rye bread tightly in foil and place in oven with chicken for 15 minutes. Serve with sweet butter.

BANANA MOUSSE

This dessert is today's banana bonanza! It's delicious, quick and easy; a plus reward — the topping mix cuts the calories.

1 2-ounce package whipped topping mix

pinch of salt
2 cups thinly sliced bananas
1 sliced banana

Garnish: 3 maraschino cherries, halved

Beat topping mix according to package directions. Fold in salt and bananas, mixing lightly. Pour into sherbet glasses. Place in refrigerator about 30 minutes or until set. To serve, top with freshly sliced banana and/or cherries. Serves 6.

▶ Arkansas Chicken

Arkansas Chicken
Artichoke Hearts   Curry Waldorf Salad
Peanut Crunch Cream Pie or *French Chocolate Cream*

COOKING COUNTDOWN

60 minutes ▶ bake chicken

▶

50 ▶ crisp greens

▶

40 ▶ prepare salad; chill

▶

30 ▶

▶

20 ▶ add artichokes to chicken

▶

10 ▶ arrange salad on greens

▶

0 ▶ serve

May be prepared in advance:
Arkansas Chicken
Must be prepared in advance:
Peanut Crunch Cream Pie

ARKANSAS CHICKEN

Recipes are born travelers. While on a trip through Arkansas, we thoroughly enjoyed this dish cooked by our Little Rock hostess, liking it so much that we brought the recipe back to Chicago.

2 2½-pound fryers or 4 pounds selected pieces
¼ cup flour
1 teaspoon salt
¼ teaspoon pepper
1 teaspoon monosodium glutamate
¼ cup melted butter

1 10-ounce can cream of celery or mushroom soup
¼ cup dry white wine
2 14-ounce cans artichoke hearts, drained
1 3-ounce can mushrooms broiled in butter

Dry chicken with paper toweling; combine flour, salt, pepper, and monosodium glutamate in paper bag. Drop chicken, a few pieces at a time, into flour mixture and shake until evenly coated. Place in 1 layer in shallow baking pan; pour butter over all and place in preheated 350° oven. Bake ½ hour. Combine soup and wine in saucepan; heat and pour one half over chicken.

Bake 15 minutes. Baste with remaining soup and wine; add artichoke hearts and mushrooms, and bake an additional 15 minutes, or until tender. Serves 4 to 6.

May be prepared early in the day. Reheat, add artichokes and bake last 15 minutes as directed.

CURRY WALDORF SALAD

1 small head romaine lettuce, washed and chilled
1½ cups diced red apples (Jonathan or Delicious)

1 cup celery, diced
½ cup broken walnut meats
1 cup mayonnaise
2 teaspoons curry powder

½ teaspoon salt

Line bowl with crisp lettuce leaves. Combine all other ingredients and mix gently but thoroughly. Pile into bowl and chill before serving. A few sprigs of celery leaves make a nice garnish. Serves 6.

PEANUT CRUNCH CREAM PIE

The filling for this pie is rich and delicious, and it takes a very knowledgeable guest to guess the ingredients.

1 8- or 9-inch baked pie shell	2 cups whipping cream, whipped
1½ cups (about ½ pound) crushed peanut brittle	2 tablespoons instant coffee
	1 teaspoon vanilla

Use a pie crust mix, your favorite recipe or a frozen pie shell available at the markets. Set baked pie shell aside to cool. Prepare early in the day.

Crush candy on waxed paper with a rolling pin, or whirl it for a second in a blender. Remove 2 tablespoons for topping; set aside. Combine whipped cream with instant coffee, vanilla and crushed peanut brittle. Blend thoroughly and spoon into pie shell, mounding evenly. Sprinkle the reserved 2 tablespoons of crushed brittle around the edge of pie. Freeze for at least 3 hours. Serves 6 to 8.

QUICK ALTERNATE

French Chocolate Cream

Canned convenience with a French accent.

1 1-pound can chocolate pudding	2 tablespoons chopped pistachio nuts
1 tablespoon cognac	
1 cup whipped frozen topping mix, defrosted, or ½ cup whipping cream, whipped	

Combine pudding and cognac, then fold into whipped cream. Pour into individual serving dishes or pot de crème cups; chill. The small lotus cups make lovely service. Decorate with a sprinkling of pistachio nuts. Serves 6.

► Chicken Country Captain

Chicken Country Captain   Rice Mound
Raw Vegetable Plate
Apple Fritters

COOKING COUNTDOWN

60 minutes ► cook chickens
—
►
—

50 ►
—

► prepare and crisp vegetables
—

40 ►
—

► fry fritters
—

30 ►
—

►
—

20 ► arrange vegetables
—

►
—

10 ► cook rice
—

► arrange platter
—

0 ► serve

CHICKEN COUNTRY CAPTAIN

The source of a recipe is always of interest. When I first heard of Chicken Country Captain I questioned the martial sound of the title, thinking it might have been a wartime improvisation. But interestingly, "Captain" is a corruption of the word "capon," and the recipe is an import from India, adjusted to American cooking. It is exotically delicious and is an invariable success. A beautiful platter for a buffet dinner! The recipe may be doubled or tripled to suit the number of guests.

1 3-pound fryer, disjointed, or 3 pounds legs, thighs and breasts
⅓ cup flour
1½ teaspoons salt
2 teaspoons curry powder
¼ teaspoon white pepper
2 tablespoons butter or margarine
2 tablespoons salad oil
1 cup coarsely chopped onion, fresh or frozen

1 1-pound can tomatoes
1 8-ounce can tomato sauce
1 tablespoon sugar
½ teaspoon monosodium glutamate
1 teaspoon seasoned salt
¼ cup currants or raisins
1 green pepper, cut in ¼-inch strips
3 cups hot fluffy rice (prepared from 1½ cups precooked rice)
¼ cup slivered almonds

Dry chicken with paper toweling; combine flour, salt, curry powder and pepper in paper bag. Add chicken, a few pieces at a time, and shake in bag until well coated. Heat butter and oil in large skillet; add chicken and sauté over moderate heat until lightly browned. Remove from pan; add onions and sauté until limp but not browned. Add tomatoes, tomato sauce, sugar, monosodium glutamate, seasoned salt, any remaining seasoned flour from bag and bring to boiling, stirring. Add chicken and currants; cover and simmer about 30 minutes or until just tender. Add green pepper strips and cook an additional 5 to 10 minutes. Mound rice in center of platter and border with chicken; pour sauce over rice and chicken; sprinkle with slivered almonds. Serves 4 to 6.

RAW VEGETABLE PLATE

This is a particularly agreeable accompaniment to the chicken dish. The contrasts of texture and color are just right.

1 cup of cauliflowerettes
2 carrots, peeled and cut into narrow 3-inch sticks
1 medium green pepper, pared and cut into thin rings

1 cucumber, peeled and sliced thin
3 stalks Pascal celery, cut into diagonal chunks
1 teaspoon seasoned salt

Chill vegetables and arrange them in sunburst fashion on a round plate or platter, starting with the cauliflower in the center and surrounding it with circles of the other vegetables. Dust with seasoned salt. As a relish serves 6.

APPLE FRITTERS

These old-time favorites are a quick dessert or a breakfast or brunch treat.

4 medium-sized tart apples, peeled and cored
1 tablespoon lemon juice

6 tablespoons vegetable shortening for frying

Batter

1 cup prepared biscuit mix
¾ cup milk

1 egg
¼ teaspoon nutmeg (optional)

Accompaniments: confectioners' sugar, lemon slices

Cut apples in ⅓-inch slices, sprinkle with lemon juice. Combine batter ingredients and beat with rotary beater until smooth. Heat shortening in 10-inch skillet. Dip apples in batter, coating evenly, and place in hot shortening; fry until nicely browned; turn and brown reverse side. Place on paper toweling to drain, and repeat with remaining slices. Arrange on platter; dust with confectioners' sugar, and serve with lemon slices. The lemon juice adds a piquant flavor. Makes about 12 to 16 fritters, depending on size of apples. Serves 4.

If arranged on heatproof platter, fritters may be placed in warmed oven before serving.

OTHER WAYS

Canned peaches, apricots, plums or other fruits may be drained and "frittered." Slice fresh pineapple, sprinkle with sugar and let stand 30 minutes before frying.

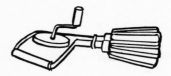

► Chicken Marengo

Chicken Marengo   Crisp Celery Hearts
Lime Sherbet
Confection Pound Cake or *Toasted Pound Cake*

COOKING COUNTDOWN

60 minutes ► prepare chicken
—
►
—
50 ►
—
►
—
40 ►
—
►
—
30 ► heat peas
—
►
20 ► cook sauce for chicken
—
►
—
10 ► arrange platter
—
►
—
0 ► serve

Must be prepared in advance:
Confection Pound Cake

CHICKEN MARENGO

1 2½- to 3-pound broiler-fryer chicken, quartered
1½ teaspoons salt
¼ teaspoon pepper
⅓ cup flour
2 tablespoons vegetable oil
2 tablespoons butter or margarine
2 tablespoons flour
1 cup chicken stock
1 4-ounce can sliced mushrooms, drained
1 tomato, cut in sixths
½ cup sliced stuffed olives
2 tablespoons dry white wine
1 4-ounce can shoestring potatoes or Chinese fried noodles
1 6-ounce can peas, drained and heated
¼ cup toasted slivered almonds

Sprinkle chicken quarters with salt and pepper; dredge with ⅓ cup flour. Heat oil in skillet; add chicken and sauté until tender, 30 to 40 minutes. Remove from pan; place on platter and set in warm spot. To same pan, add butter; heat, and mix in 2 tablespoons flour, stirring until lightly browned. Blend in chicken stock; add sliced mushrooms, tomato, olives and wine. Let simmer about 10 minutes until well blended and heated, pour over chicken. Center platter with shoestring potatoes, border with chicken and sprinkle peas and almonds over all. Serves 4.

Chicken Marengo is just as flavorful when prepared early in the day.

The perfect complement to Chicken Marengo: a scoop of lime sherbet in your prettiest compote dishes.

CONFECTION POUND CAKE

Dusted with confectioners' sugar this big beauty is complete. A real "keeper," it slices evenly and easily. Serve with ice cream, with fruit sauces or a soft custard for topping.

1 pound confectioners' sugar
1 pound margarine
6 eggs
1½ cups all-purpose flour
1½ cups cake flour
⅛ teaspoon salt
1 teaspoon butter flavoring
1 teaspoon vanilla
sifted confectioners' sugar

Cream sugar and margarine together until light and fluffy; add eggs, one at a time, beating well after each addition. Sift all-purpose flour, cake flour and salt together, and beat into margarine mixture until very well blended. Add butter flavoring and vanilla. Pour into a well-greased 10-inch tube pan, and bake in preheated 350° oven 50 minutes. Increase heat to 375°, and bake an additional 25 minutes. Dust with confectioners' sugar. Serves 12 or more.

ANOTHER WAY

Marble Pound Cake

To ⅓ of the batter, fold in 1 envelope premelted chocolate; to ⅓ batter add 3 to 4 drops red food coloring to tint the batter a rosy pink. The third part is left plain. Pour the plain batter into cake pan in one layer, next pour in the chocolate batter, then the pink. Do not mix them, they will marbleize themselves, a do-it-yourself idea. Bake as for the Confection Pound Cake.

QUICK ALTERNATE

Toasted Pound Cake

On your way home, purchase a pound cake at the market. Cut it in ½-inch slices and toast them just before serving.

► Paprika Chicken

Paprika Chicken   Buttered Noodles or *Noodles Polonaise*
    Zucchini Strips   Country Salad   Lemon Dressing
Frozen Peppermint or *Chocolate Peppermint Sundaes*

COOKING COUNTDOWN

60 minutes ► prepare salad; chill
— ►
—
50 ► cook chicken
— ►
—
40 ► coat zucchini
— ►
—
30 ► mix salad dressing
— ►
—
20 ► cook noodles
— ► sauté zucchini
—
10 ►
—
► assemble salad
—
0 ► serve

May be prepared in advance:
Paprika Chicken
Must be prepared in advance:
Frozen Peppermint

PAPRIKA CHICKEN

1 frying chicken, about 3 pounds, disjointed
2 tablespoons butter or margarine
2 tablespoons vegetable oil
2 tablespoons onion flakes or 1 medium onion, chopped
2 tablespoons instantized flour
2 tablespoons paprika
2 teaspoons salt
1 10-ounce can beef consommé
1 1¼-ounce package sour cream sauce mix
¼ cup milk
1 8-ounce package medium noodles, cooked and drained

Dry chicken pieces with paper toweling; heat butter and oil in large skillet and add chicken. Sauté until lightly browned. Add onions and flour to drippings in pan; sprinkle chicken with paprika and salt; add beef consommé. Cover tightly and simmer 30 minutes or until tender. Just before serving, combine sour cream sauce mix and milk; beat thoroughly with rotary beater and add to pan drippings. Heat well but do not boil. Mound noodles in center of platter and border with chicken and gravy. Sprinkle noodles with paprika or snipped parsley. Serves 4.

It is good, though not essential, to make this in advance.

ZUCCHINI STRIPS

6 zucchini
¼ cup flour
½ teaspoon salt
¼ teaspoon basil
¼ cup butter
paprika
freshly ground pepper

Quarter zucchini lengthwise; dip in flour and coat evenly; sprinkle with salt and basil. Heat butter in skillet; add zucchini, one layer at a time, and sauté until golden, about 10 minutes. Dust with paprika and freshly ground pepper. Serves 6.

ANOTHER WAY

Omit flour; just brown zucchini in butter and add seasoning.

BUTTERED NOODLES

8 ounces fine egg noodles   2 tablespoons butter
½ teaspoon paprika

Cook noodles according to package directions; drain and toss gently with butter. Turn onto serving dish or platter around chicken; dust with paprika. Serves 6.

ANOTHER WAY

Noodles Polonaise

Melt 2 tablespoons butter in a small skillet; add ½ cup bread crumbs and ½ teaspoon seasoned salt and stir over low heat until crumbs are nicely browned. Sprinkle crumb mixture over cooked noodles before serving.

COUNTRY SALAD

Without oil in the dressing, the salad is simple and refreshing.

2 cucumbers, peeled, sliced ⅛   Lemon Dressing
   inch thick   1 head leaf lettuce, torn in bite-
1 sweet red onion, sliced   size pieces
1 green pepper, cut in ¼-inch   ¼ cup yogurt
   slices   3 hard-cooked eggs, quartered

Combine cucumbers, onion slices and green pepper slices in bowl; cover with Lemon Dressing and refrigerate until chilled. To serve, combine in salad bowl with lettuce, adding Lemon Dressing. Dot with dollops of yogurt and garnish with hard-cooked eggs; toss just before serving. Serves 4 to 6.

Lemon Dressing

3 tablespoons lemon juice
1 tablespoon wine vinegar
3 tablespoons sugar
1 teaspoon salt

½ teaspoon celery seed
⅛ teaspoon coarsely ground pepper
½ cup water

Combine all ingredients and chill.
   Keeps well and may be made in advance. Makes ¾ cup.

FROZEN PEPPERMINT

1 3½-ounce package strawberry-flavored gelatin
1 cup boiling water
1 pint vanilla or peppermint ice cream

¼ pound peppermint stick candy, crushed
1 9-ounce jar hot fudge ice cream topping

Dissolve gelatin in hot water. Add ice cream; stir until blended. Mix in crushed candy. Pour into greased 4-cup mold and refrigerate until firm, about 2 hours. Turn out on cold platter and serve with fudge topping, if desired. May be poured into 6 individual molds or dessert dishes. Serves 6.

QUICK ALTERNATE

In a rush? Serve ice cream or chocolate sundaes.

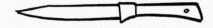

► Hunter's Italian Chicken

Hunter's Italian Chicken
Celery Cabbage and Green Pepper Rings
Oil and Vinegar Dressing
Mozzarella Garlic Bread
Lime Sherbet Melba

COOKING COUNTDOWN

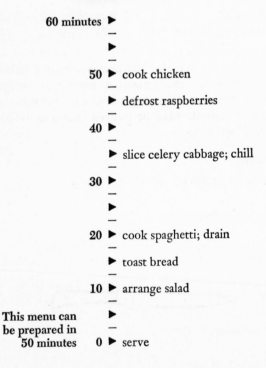

60 minutes ►
—
►
—
50 ► cook chicken
—
► defrost raspberries
—
40 ►
—
► slice celery cabbage; chill
—
30 ►
—
►
—
20 ► cook spaghetti; drain
—
► toast bread
—
10 ► arrange salad
—
This menu can ►
be prepared in —
50 minutes   0 ► serve

HUNTER'S ITALIAN CHICKEN

Cans make for convenience, and early preparation, if you wish, leaves time for other activities.

4 to 5 pounds chicken, disjointed or your choice of pieces	½ teaspoon oregano
¼ cup Seasoned Flour (page 300)	1 1-pound can stewed tomatoes
¼ cup salad or olive oil	1 4-ounce can mushroom stems and pieces
¾ cup diced onion	1 1-pound jar boiled onions, drained
1 garlic clove, minced	
½ cup water	1 8-ounce package spaghetti, cooked
½ cup dry red wine	

Wipe chicken with paper toweling and dust evenly with Seasoned Flour. Heat oil in large skillet; add chicken pieces and sauté over moderate heat until evenly browned. Remove from pan as pieces are browned, and set aside. To same pan add onions and garlic; sauté until onions are lightly browned. Blend in water, wine, oregano and stewed tomatoes; add chicken pieces. Cover pan and simmer about 30 minutes, shaking occasionally to prevent sticking. Add mushrooms and boiled onions; heat thoroughly, about 10 minutes. Arrange spaghetti on platter and cover with chicken pieces and sauce, all piping hot. Serves 6.

SIMPLE CELERY CABBAGE

1 green pepper, sliced in ¼-inch rings
1 head celery cabbage, cut in 18 slices about ½-inch thick

Celery cabbage does not need a great deal of preparation. Wash it thoroughly, drain and chill. To serve, slice in ½-inch slices, 3 to a portion, top with green pepper rings and drizzle with your favorite oil and vinegar dressing. Serves 6.

ANOTHER WAY

If the celery cabbage is not available, use thick slices of iceberg lettuce.

MOZZARELLA GARLIC BREAD

½ large loaf Vienna bread
¼ cup melted butter or margarine
1 large clove garlic, minced

½ teaspoon paprika
1 8-ounce package sliced Mozzarella cheese (8 slices)

Cut bread into 16 slices and place on a cooky sheet. Combine melted butter, garlic and paprika. Brush mixture on bread and toast for about 10 minutes in preheated 375° oven. Remove from oven, top with half slice of cheese and place under broiler until browned and bubbly, about 3 to 4 minutes. Serve immediately. Makes 16 slices.

LIME SHERBET MELBA

1½ pints lime sherbet or fruit ice
1 10-ounce package frozen raspberries, thawed

Place scoop of lime sherbet into sherbet or champagne glasses. Spoon thawed raspberries over sherbet; top with a sprig of fresh mint, if you have it. This is a lively medley of fruit flavors and a very inviting combination of colors, especially when served in clear glass or crystal. Serves 6.

▶ Hazel's Fried Chicken

Hazel's Fried Chicken
Green Cheese Noodles   Boston Tomato Salad
Watermelon Bowl or *Ruth's Brownies*

COOKING COUNTDOWN

60 minutes ▶ cook noodles
—
▶
—
50 ▶ fry chickens
—
▶
—
40 ▶
—
▶
—
30 ▶ bake noodles
—
▶
—
20 ▶ arrange watermelon bowl
—
▶
—
10 ▶ assemble salad
—
▶
—
0 ▶ serve

May be prepared in advance:

assemble Green Cheese Noodles
carve Watermelon Bowl
bake Brownies

HAZEL'S FRIED CHICKEN

Hazel Kennedy is our housekeeper and friend of many years and is the best fried-chicken cook I know. Her execution of the ritual was inherited from her Southern mother, and I have recorded the procedure as I watched her perform it.

2 2½-pound fryers, disjointed
2 teaspoons seasoned salt
1 teaspoon monosodium gluta- mate

½ cup Seasoned Flour
vegetable shortening or peanut oil
   sufficient for frying
parsley sprigs

Dry chicken with paper towels and sprinkle evenly with combined seasoned salt and monosodium glutamate. Mix Seasoned Flour in paper or plastic bag and drop 3 or 4 pieces of chicken in at one time, coating well by shaking in flour mixture. Heat shortening in heavy skillet, a sufficient amount for 1½-inch depth. (It will be the correct temperature when a stale cube of bread browns in about 60 seconds.) Place dark meat in pan and fry five minutes. Add white meat, and continue cooking over moderately high heat in uncovered pan about 20 minutes, until well browned on both sides. Use 2 pans, or remove chicken pieces when they are browned and set aside in warm place. When all are browned, arrange again in skillet with small amount of shortening; cover and cook over low heat for 10 to 20 minutes until tender when tested with a fork. Serves 6.

Seasoned Flour

½ cup flour
1 teaspoon paprika

1½ teaspoons salt
¼ teaspoon pepper

Combine in paper or plastic bag; blend well. This will make enough for 2 chickens. Halve the amounts for one.

GREEN CHEESE NOODLES

1 8-ounce package green noodles   2 tablespoons snipped fresh or
1 pint sour cream   frozen chives
2 6-ounce packages Swiss cheese,   ½ teaspoon salt
   diced

Cook noodles according to package directions; about 25 minutes in boiling salted water; drain. Grease 6-cup casserole; layer noodles, sour cream, and cheese, alternately, starting with noodles and topping with cheese; sprinkle chives and salt over repeated layers. Bake in preheated 350° oven 20 to 25 minutes until cheese is melted and casserole well heated. Serves 6 to 8.

OTHER WAYS

1. Layers may be seasoned with a sprinkling of oregano, garlic powder, onion powder or nutmeg.

2. The casserole may be assembled in advance and refrigerated, ready to pop in the oven. Add 15 minutes to baking time.

BOSTON TOMATO SALAD

2 heads Boston lettuce   ⅓ cup finely sliced green onions
4 medium tomatoes, thickly sliced   ½ cup Vinaigrette Dressing

Wash lettuce, separating leaves. To crisp, drain well; wrap in paper toweling, then place in plastic bags. Refrigerate until serving time. Arrange cuplike on individual salad plates, with 2 or 3 tomato slices in each lettuce cup. Serve with Vinaigrette Dressing and sprinkle with sliced green onions if desired. Serves 6.

Vinaigrette Dressing

¼ cup salad oil   3 tablespoons pickle relish
3 tablespoons wine vinegar   ¼ teaspoon dry mustard
1 teaspoon sugar   ⅛ teaspoon seasoned salt
        dash freshly ground pepper

Combine all ingredients and blend well.

WATERMELON BOWL

One fourth of a watermelon will do nicely for 6 persons. Scoop balls from the fruit with the tablespoon measure, rolling it around to make balls symmetrical. Remove the surface seeds and place in a bowl (crystal is particularly pretty for transparency). Border the bowl with bunches of grapes and/or smaller balls of honeydew melon, cut with the teaspoon measure. Serves 6.

When preparing the fruit bowl for 12 or more, the shell of the watermelon makes a beautiful container. Use one half, cut horizontally. Scoop out the meat with the tablespoon measure, then remove all pink and turn shell upside down to drain. Cut the rim in zigzag notches or scallops as a finishing touch and fill as for the crystal bowl. Add other fruits in season or those colors which will add contrast.

QUICK ALTERNATE

Serve sliced watermelon.

RUTH'S BROWNIES

The best I ever ate and I'm certain you will agree.

½ cup butter	½ cup walnuts (3-ounce package)
1 cup sugar	½ cup flour
2 eggs	
2 packets liquid chocolate-flavored ingredient or 2 1-ounce squares unsweetened chocolate, melted	

Cream butter and sugar together until fluffy; add eggs, chocolate and nuts, mixing well. Stir in flour and pour into well-greased 9 x 13-inch baking pan. Bake in preheated 350° oven 15 to 20 minutes until set and dough springs back when pressed with finger. Cool and cut in 2 x 1-inch bars. Makes about 4 dozen.

►Yankee Doodle Rock Cornish Game Hens

Cantaloupe Cream Cups
Yankee Doodle Rock Cornish Game Hens   Tangy Carrots
Whizz Bang Chocolate Cake or Strawberry Tarts

COOKING COUNTDOWN

60 minutes ► bake hens

► —

50 ► assemble garnish

— ► make cantaloupe cups

—

40 ►

— ►

—

30 ►

— ►

—

20 ► cook carrots

— ►

—

10 ► blend melon mixture and fill cantaloupe
cups

— ►

—

0 ► serve

Must be prepared in advance:

Whizz Bang Chocolate Cake
Stuffing for Cornish hens

CANTALOUPE CREAM CUPS

A frothy fluff with subtle flavor, particularly cooling for summer dining.

2 small cantaloupes	1 tablespoon sugar
1½ cups dry white wine	⅓ cup non-fat dry milk
¼ teaspoon salt	grated nutmeg
4 lime wedges	

Have cantaloupes and wine chilled. Cut cantaloupes in halves, in zig-zag fashion so that edges are notched when melon is separated. (It is a good idea to draw the lines before cutting.) Remove meat, leaving sufficient shell of about ½ inch; cut meat into small pieces (about 3 cups of melon), then place in blender with wine, salt, sugar and dry milk. Whirl at high speed until smooth and frothy; pour into prepared cantaloupe cups and dust lightly with nutmeg. Fasten lime wedges at the rim with a toothpick, and if you feel festive, spear a bright cherry to the pick. Serves 4.

YANKEE DOODLE ROCK CORNISH GAME HENS

As American as Yankee Doodle and the prepared macaroni mix with which it is stuffed. The hens need only an hour's roasting time; allow an extra 15 to 20 minutes to stuff them.

1 8-ounce package Spanish rice and macaroni mix	1 tablespoon lemon juice
	½ cup softened butter
4 1-pound Rock Cornish hens	½ cup dry white wine
3 teaspoons salt	½ cup canned beef bouillon
2 teaspoons poultry seasoning	1 teaspoon Worcestershire
½ teaspoon white pepper	4 bunches watercress sprigs
1 1-pound jar spiced apple slices	

Prepare rice and macaroni mix according to package directions; set aside. Pat hens dry with paper toweling and rub well with salt, poultry seasoning and pepper. Stuff each with approximately ⅓ cup macaroni mixture; skewer and lace cavities; fasten neck skin to bodies with lacing pins or toothpicks and fold wings under so birds lie flat in pan. Combine lemon juice and 6 tablespoons butter; spread over hens and place in roaster. Bake in preheated 450° oven 30 minutes; combine wine, bouillon, Worcestershire and remaining 2 tablespoons butter and baste hens liberally; reduce heat to 350° and bake, basting twice, about 20 minutes additional, or until done. When tender, thigh moves easily and flesh is soft to the touch. Protect your fingers with a paper napkin. Don't forget to remove pins and lacing. Place in spokelike fashion on heated platter around a mound of Tangy Carrots. Garnish with watercress placed between hens and border with spiced apple slices. Serve pan drippings separately. Makes 4 generous servings.

OTHER WAYS

1. Omit wine, substitute ½ cup undiluted beef bouillon. Garlic Butter (page 59) is a delicious coating; use it instead of ½ cup softened butter, then proceed with combined butter, wine and bouillon, basting as in the recipe. Though the stuffed hens look plump and beautiful, time may be saved by serving the macaroni mix separately as an accompaniment.

2. Prepare macaroni-rice mixture according to package directions, make an attractive arrangement by mounding it in center of platter and border with Tangy Carrots.

3. Omit stuffing; substitute by placing ½ medium-sized onion and 1 rib of celery in the cavity of each hen, thus eliminating the extra time needed for stuffing and lacing. The flavor is delicious either way.

TANGY CARROTS

A newer shortcut; really good.

2 1-pound cans baby carrots, drained
¼ cup liquid from carrots
1 tablespoon butter or margarine
3 teaspoons instant powdered citrus drink

½ teaspoon salt
1 teaspoon snipped chives, fresh or frozen (optional)

Combine all ingredients except carrots in large skillet; heat and blend. Add carrots; heat, tossing lightly so carrots do not mash. Shake pan to blend well. Serves 4.

WHIZZ BANG CHOCOLATE CAKE

So named because it is prepared in a whizz and goes over with a bang — every time.

1½ cups sifted flour	1 cup sugar
3 tablespoons cocoa	1 tablespoon vinegar
½ teaspoon salt	1 cup water
1 teaspoon baking soda	1 teaspoon vanilla

6 tablespoons melted butter

Sift flour, cocoa, salt, soda and sugar into an ungreased 8-inch square baking pan. Combine vinegar, water, vanilla and butter; pour over dry ingredients in pan and stir with a fork until blended. Bake in preheated 350° oven 35 minutes or until done when tested. Allow to stand in pan until cool, then cut into squares. Serve with whipped cream or ice cream. Makes 9 pieces 2½ x 2½ inches. Delicious served warm with prepared marshmallow sauce.

QUICK ALTERNATE

Strawberry Tarts

4 baked tart shells	¼ cup currant jelly
1 pint strawberries, washed and hulled	

Topping: 4 unhulled large strawberries

The tart shells may be purchased in the market. Fill each with the strawberries. Melt currant jelly over moderate heat and pour over strawberries as a glaze. Top with unhulled berries. Serves 4.

Fish and Seafood

THE THOUGHT OF fish brings many pictures to mind. Lazy lolling on a riverbank, pole in hand; wading in a rushing stream; catapulting through the sea on the trail of a deep-water denizen. The catch is always an exciting climax.

With modern packaging and shipping, the kitchen has benefited from commercial development of the sport. Cleaned, packaged, and fresh or quick-frozen, this delicate food has untold possibilities.

Follow these few simple rules, and with experience and creativity, you will enjoy many hours of new and delightful cooking:

1. Fish cooks quickly; overcooking toughens the flesh.

2. Boned fish will serve about 3 persons per pound.

3. Bake fish at about 350°; high heat gives it a dry texture.

4. Allow 24 hours for defrosting 1 pound of raw fish in refrigerator.

5. Do not defrost at room temperature or in warm water.

6. For quick defrosting, place packaged fish under cold running water.

7. Cook fish as soon as possible after thawing.

8. Do not refreeze defrosted raw fish.

9. Frozen fish may be cooked without defrosting; allow approximately ⅓ additional time.

10. Handle fish carefully, whether raw or cooked, as it will break easily.

11. Store cooked fish in refrigerator. Do not keep fish longer than 2 or 3 days, unless otherwise indicated, as for pickled fish.

12. To freeze cooked fish, pack in airtight moisture-vapor proof containers; do not keep longer than two months at 0° F.

To test fish for doneness

1. For fillets: test with a fork; if fish flakes easily, it is done. (Test at a point where the contour will not be disturbed.)

2. For fish with bones: when cooked the fish will separate easily from the bones.

3. Raw fish has a translucent, watery look; cooked fish becomes opaque and white in color. If the fish is thick, test it from within, near the bone.

▶ Crabmeat Pantry Shelf

Crabmeat Pantry Shelf   French Pan Fries
Cucumbers in Dill Marinade
Deep Dish Cherry Swirl

COOKING COUNTDOWN

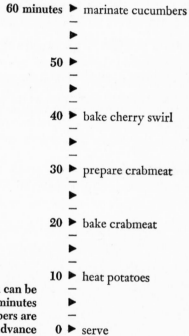

60 minutes ▶ marinate cucumbers

50 ▶

40 ▶ bake cherry swirl

30 ▶ prepare crabmeat

20 ▶ bake crabmeat

10 ▶ heat potatoes

**This menu can be
prepared in 40 minutes
if cucumbers are
marinated in advance**

0 ▶ serve

May be prepared in advance:

Cucumbers in Marinade

CRABMEAT PANTRY SHELF

This is the quick version of a classic recipe.

1 10-ounce can cream of celery soup
¼ teaspoon dry mustard
1 teaspoon Worcestershire
¼ cup dry sherry

1 cup of crabmeat, fresh, canned or frozen, defrosted
1 4-ounce can sliced mushrooms and liquid

Topping

½ cup bread crumbs
2 tablespoons melted butter

4 lemon slices, halved
½ teaspoon paprika

Combine all ingredients, blending well, and pour into buttered 1-quart casserole or 4 individual ramekins. Combine butter and bread crumbs; spread over crabmeat mixture and circle with lemon slices. Sprinkle with paprika and bake in preheated 375° oven 20 minutes or until brown. If necessary, place under broiler for 5 minutes, browning well. Serves 4.

ANOTHER WAY

For crabmeat, substitute 1 7-ounce can tuna, drained, or 2 cups diced, cooked chicken.

FRENCH PAN FRIES

1 9-ounce package frozen French fried potatoes
3 tablespoons vegetable oil
½ teaspoon salt
paprika

Arrange potatoes in heated oil in large skillet; cook about 10 minutes, stirring frequently until well heated. Drain on paper toweling, then dust with salt and paprika. Serves 4.

CUCUMBERS IN DILL MARINADE

Not too tart, not too sweet — a real keeper, too.

1 sweet onion, sliced in rings, or	2 large cucumbers
½ cup sliced scallions	Dill Marinade

Score unpeeled cucumbers with tines of a fork; slice thinly and place in bowl or covered jar with sliced onions or scallions, when in season. Pour Dill Marinade over and refrigerate a minimum of 1 hour; toss occasionally to marinate evenly. Serve from salad bowl. Serves 4 to 6.

May be prepared on the previous day; to have an extra batch on hand, you may double or triple the recipe without hesitation.

Dill Marinade

½ cup white wine vinegar	1 teaspoon dill salt
½ cup water	¾ teaspoon seasoned salt
3 tablespoons sugar	¼ teaspoon paprika

Combine ingredients and mix very well until blended. Prepare early in the day. Makes about 1¼ cups.

ANOTHER WAY

Omit dill salt; substitute ½ teaspoon salt and ½ teaspoon dill seed.

DEEP DISH CHERRY SWIRL

1 1-pound can cherry pie filling	½ teaspoon cinnamon
½ teaspoon anise or almond flavoring	1 9½-ounce package refrigerated cinnamon rolls, with icing

Butter a 1-quart casserole; combine cherry pie filling with flavoring and cinnamon (mix the combination in the can). Pour into prepared casserole and top with a border of rolls. Bake in 375° oven 30 minutes. While still warm drizzle with icing from package. Serve hot or cold. Serves 4.

▶ Bright Pink Shrimp

Bright Pink Shrimp   Peas and Rice
Grapefruit Tossed with Greens
Boston Cream Pie on the Square

COOKING COUNTDOWN

60 minutes	▶ fill and glaze Boston cream pie
—	
	▶
—	
50	▶
—	
	▶
—	
40	▶ chill salad ingredients
—	
	▶ prepare shrimp and vegetables
—	
30	▶
—	
	▶ cook peas and rice; keep warm
—	
20	▶
—	
	▶ assemble salad
—	
10	▶ cook shrimp
—	
	▶
—	
0	▶ serve

**This menu can be
prepared in 40 minutes
if dessert is prepared
in advance**

Must be prepared in advance:

cake layer for Boston Cream Pie

BRIGHT PINK SHRIMP

1 pound raw shrimp in shells	6 green onions, cut in 2-inch
2 green peppers, sliced in ¼-inch	lengths
strips	2 tablespoons peanut or salad oil

2 teaspoons salt

Wash shrimp; remove legs and point of head only. Prepare vegetables and set aside. Heat oil in skillet and stir in salt; add shrimps and cook just until pink, then add vegetables. Stir-fry, tossing vegetables and shrimp for 6 minutes until shrimp are bright pink. Serves 4 as an entrée, 6 as an appetizer.

ANOTHER WAY

As an appetizer, the shrimp may be served from the serving ware skillet, but they need the comfort of a plate, fork and napkin, as they do drip a little. (Every drop a delicious delight.)

PEAS AND RICE

1⅓ cups precooked rice	1 8-ounce can peas,
1 teaspoon onion flakes	drained

Cook rice according to package directions, adding onion flakes to water before cooking. When cooked, toss with peas and keep warm. Serves 4.

GRAPEFRUIT TOSSED WITH GREENS

1 1-pound can grapefruit seg-	4 cups torn salad greens
ments, chilled and drained	¼ cup prepared French dressing

Combine chilled grapefruit segments with torn greens; add French dressing. Toss lightly and well. Serves 4.

BOSTON CREAM PIE ON THE SQUARE

The old and the new blend well in this descendant of the Spanish Tipsy Cake.

3 egg yolks	¼ teaspoon salt
1 teaspoon vanilla	½ cup sugar
¼ teaspoon lemon extract or ½ teaspoon grated lemon peel	½ cup sifted all-purpose flour
	Vanilla Custard Filling
3 egg whites	Simple Chocolate Glaze

Combine egg yolks with vanilla and lemon extract, mixing lightly until blended. Beat egg whites with salt until foamy, then beat in sugar very gradually until sugar is dissolved and mixture is very stiff. Fold into yolk mixture until blended; fold in flour gently but thoroughly. Spoon into greased and floured 8 x 8-inch baking pan, spreading batter well into corners. Bake in preheated 325° oven about 40 minutes or until lightly browned and cake pulls away from sides of pan. Cool in pan then remove, loosening with spatula; if it sticks place a hot wet cloth over bottom of pan and it will loosen, like magic. Split crosswise, cutting with a long-bladed sharp knife. Spread bottom half with Vanilla Custard Filling; cover with other half and spread with Simple Chocolate Glaze. Serves 6 to 8.

Vanilla Custard Filling

1 3¾-ounce package instant vanilla pudding	1¾ cups milk
	½ teaspoon vanilla

Combine ingredients and beat slowly with rotary beater, 1 to 2 minutes until thickened; let stand 5 minutes until set. If you prefer a thicker filling reduce milk to 1½ cups.

Simple Chocolate Glaze

3 ounces chocolate bits
2 tablespoons half-and-half cream

Melt chocolate bits over, not in, boiling water. Blend with cream and spread at once.

Prepare Boston Cream Pie in advance, preferably early in the day.

ANOTHER WAY

Add 1 tablespoon cognac to the Vanilla Custard and you have Tipsy Cake.

QUICK ALTERNATE

Purchase a sponge cake and split it in half; fill and frost as for Boston Cream Pie.

► Shrimp Creole

Shrimp Creole in Cream Puff Shell
Olive Tossed Salad
Raspberried Strawberries

COOKING COUNTDOWN

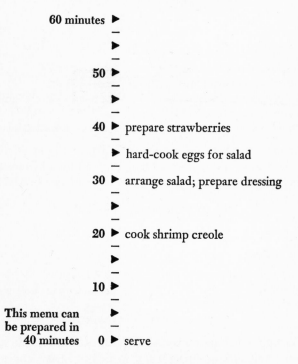

60 minutes ►
     –
     ►
     –
   50 ►
     –
     ►
     –
   40 ► prepare strawberries
     –
     ► hard-cook eggs for salad
     –
   30 ► arrange salad; prepare dressing
     –
     ►
     –
   20 ► cook shrimp creole
     –
     ►
     –
   10 ►
     –

This menu can ►
be prepared in –
40 minutes   0 ► serve

Must be prepared in advance:
Cream Puff Shell

SHRIMP CREOLE

1 pound cooked shrimp, shelled and deveined, or 2 7-ounce cans shrimp	Creole Sauce Cream Puff Shell or 2 cups cooked rice

If using canned shrimp, rinse in cold water and drain. Combine shrimp with Creole Sauce, bring to boiling, then simmer 5 minutes until well heated. Serve in Cream Puff Shell or over mounds of rice. Serves 4.

Creole Sauce

1 tablespoon butter or margarine	1 teaspoon sugar
½ cup frozen chopped onions	½ teaspoon salt
1 green pepper, seeded and diced	⅛ teaspoon coarsely ground pepper
1 1-pound can stewed tomatoes	per
1 tablespoon flour	⅛ teaspoon dried basil (optional)

Heat butter in skillet, add onions and green pepper stirring until bubbly, add stewed tomatoes stirring constantly, add remaining ingredients and cook about 10 minutes, until blended. Makes about 2 cups.

To boil shrimp

1 pound raw shrimp with shells, well washed	1 slice lemon
1 cup water	1 peppercorn or dash cayenne
	½ teaspoon salt
1 teaspoon caraway (optional)	

Drain shrimp; combine remaining ingredients in saucepan and bring to a boil. Add shrimp, bring water to boiling again; cover pan and reduce water to a simmer; cook 5 minutes. Remove shrimp and cool: shell, clean and devein; refrigerate. Shrimp now may be used in any recipe calling for cooked shelled shrimp.

There are 26 medium shrimp in 1 pound. There are 10 to 12 jumbo shrimp in 1 pound.

CREAM PUFF SHELL

Here is fun baking. The spectacular rise of the Cream Puff Shell belies the simple preparation. The shell will hold an entrée, an appetizer or a dessert preparation. The versatility of the basic cream puff batter adjusts to many forms from the tiny choux to the larger cream puffs as delineated, following the recipe.

Cream Puff Paste

1 cup boiling water   ¼ teaspoon salt
½ cup butter (¼ pound)   1 cup all-purpose flour
                4 eggs

Combine water, butter and salt in medium-sized saucepan; bring to boiling, stirring until butter is melted. Reduce heat and add flour all at once, stirring vigorously with wooden spatula or spoon until mixture forms a ball, pulling away from sides of pan. Remove from heat and add eggs one at a time, again mixing well until each egg is absorbed. Beat until smooth and dough is satiny. Use batter as directed in your recipe; one of the following will fit the need.

Any recipes made with Cream Puff Paste keep very well: store in plastic bag or airtight containers. They will remain crisp for several days.

Cream Puff Shell

Spread cream puff paste in well-greased 9-inch pie pan, smoothing the dough to an even covering on the bottom and building it well up around the rim. Bake in preheated 400° oven 50 minutes or until crisp and lightly browned. Do not peek until the 40 minutes are up, then allow to remain, if necessary. Makes 1 shell and will serve 4 to 6.

The versatile shell may be used for the following:

1. For entrée, fill with Shrimp Creole or other creamed dish.

2. For appetizer, fill with any of the dips in the appetizer section or with salads such as seafood or poultry; for the small shells the ingredients should be finely chopped.

3. For dessert, fill with scoops of ice cream and sauce or with any pie filling such as lemon, other custards or fruit filling. Use 2 cups of any filling.

Large Puffs

Drop cream puff paste from tablespoon making 12 large puffs or 16 medium size. Bake in preheated 400° oven 10 minutes; reduce heat to 350° and bake 25 minutes additional. Remove from oven; turn off oven heat. Cut a slit through side of each puff and return to oven with door ajar and allow to remain for 10 minutes to dry very well. Remove and cool.

For entrée fill with sauced poultry, meat or fish.

For dessert, fill with sweetened whipped cream, custard or ice cream.

Petite Puffs

Drop rounded teaspoons of batter onto greased cooky sheets; bake in preheated 400° oven about 20 minutes until lightly browned. Makes 8 dozen.

For appetizer, fill with seafood, chicken salad or any of the suggested dips in the appetizer section.

For dessert, fill with custard or sweetened whipped cream or frozen dessert whip, defrosted.

OLIVE TOSSED SALAD

1 medium head iceberg lettuce	2 hard-cooked egg whites, sliced
1 cup salad olives, drained	in rings
Avocado Dressing	

Remove core and outside bruised leaves of lettuce; soak in water 30 minutes, drain. Insert fingers in base of head (where core was removed), spread apart and separate leaves easily. Place in Turkish towel in refrigerator to crisp. To serve, tear lettuce into bite-sized pieces, drop into large bowl and sprinkle with olives. Arrange egg white rings over top. Pour sufficient Avocado Dressing over salad to moisten all ingredients; toss lightly and well. Serves 4 to 6.

Avocado Dressing

1 ripe avocado, mashed   2 hard-cooked egg yolks, sieved
                    1 cup French dressing

Combine ingredients and blend until smooth; refrigerate.

RASPBERRIED STRAWBERRIES

Delicious and eye-appealing, this simple dish is a perfect finale for a
party. It is a year-round recipe, though far less expensive when
berries are in season. It can be expanded for a group and reduced for
a small number. As you can see, I like it very much.

1 quart strawberries   1 tablespoon cornstarch
1 10-ounce package frozen rasp-   1 tablespoon kirsch (optional)
  berries, defrosted, drained (re-   whipped cream or ice cream balls
  serve juice)

Wash, hull and dry strawberries with paper toweling and place in
glass (preferably) serving bowl; refrigerate. Pour about ¼ cup raspberry juice into saucepan and mix with cornstarch to make a paste.
Add remaining juice and cook, stirring, until clear, about 5 minutes.
Add raspberries and bring to boiling. Cool and add kirsch then pour
over strawberries; refrigerate until chilled, no longer than 1 hour.
Serve with whipped cream. Macaroons, purchased at the store, are
a very good accompaniment. Serves 6 to 8.

For a truly elaborate dessert, serve a separate bowl of ice cream
balls and use the berries as sauce. Just yummy, either way.

The balls may be made in advance; each wrapped in wax paper
and ready in the freezer. Use vanilla or an assortment of flavors.
This will serve 10 if you use 1½ quarts ice cream.

▶ Skillet Shrimp

Wine Sauced Shrimp   *Spaghettini*
Dilled Green Beans
Date Mélange or *Date Nut Roll*

COOKING COUNTDOWN

60 minutes ▶ prepare and bake date mélange
—
▶
—
50 ▶
—
▶
—
40 ▶
—
▶
—
30 ▶ shell and devein shrimp
—
▶
—
20 ▶ cook spaghettini
—
▶ assemble dilled green beans
—
10 ▶ prepare shrimp

This menu can be —
prepared in 30 minutes ▶
if Quick Alternate —
dessert is used   0 ▶ serve

WINE SAUCED SHRIMP

This is a wonderful dish for table service in an electric skillet.

¼ cup butter
1½ pounds shrimp, raw, shelled
  and deveined
1 teaspoon salt
2 tablespoons brandy
¼ cup finely chopped onion, fresh
  or frozen

½ teaspoon rosemary
1 bay leaf
⅔ cup dry white wine
1 tablespoon tomato paste
½ cup heavy or sour cream
Spaghettini

If using frozen shrimp, defrost in refrigerator. Heat butter in skillet and add shrimp; sauté 1 minute on each side until pink. Sprinkle with salt and brandy. Set aflame and allow to stand until flames die; add onion, rosemary, bay leaf, wine and tomato paste, and cook over low heat 5 minutes. Bring to a boil, cooking for 1 minute more. Add heavy cream to sauce, blend well and heat quickly. Serve over buttered Spaghettini. Serves 6.

Spaghettini

1 8-ounce package spaghettini
2 tablespoons butter

Cook spaghettini according to package directions; rinse in hot water; drain and toss with butter.

DILLED GREEN BEANS

Chill a 1-pound can of dilled green beans; toss with 2 tablespoons chopped pimiento. Serve in lettuce cups.

DATE MÉLANGE

1 cup coarsely chopped walnuts
  (1 6-ounce package)
1 cup coarsely chopped pitted
  dates

1 cup sugar
4 teaspoons flour
2 eggs, well beaten

Topping: ½ cup prepared whipped topping, lemon sherbet or whipped cream

Combine all ingredients; pour into well-greased 9-inch round cake pan. Bake in preheated 350° oven 45 minutes. Cool, cut in wedges and serve, topped with a dollop of cream or lemon sherbet. Serves 6.

QUICK ALTERNATE

Date Nut Roll

Slice an 8-ounce can date nut roll into 6 pieces. Serve with butterscotch sundae sauce; top with chopped nuts.

► Shrimp Supper Casserole

Harvard Beet Borscht
Shrimp Supper Casserole
Apple Ginger Slices

COOKING COUNTDOWN

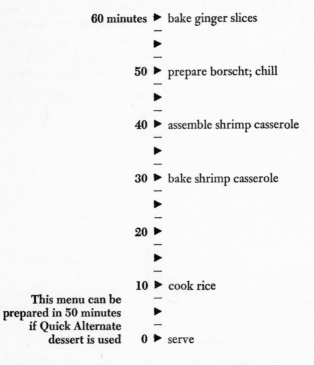

60 minutes ► bake ginger slices
—
►
—
50 ► prepare borscht; chill
—
►
—
40 ► assemble shrimp casserole
—
►
—
30 ► bake shrimp casserole
—
►
—
20 ►
—
►
—
10 ► cook rice

This menu can be
prepared in 50 minutes —
if Quick Alternate ►
dessert is used —
0 ► serve

May be prepared in advance:
Harvard Beet Borscht

HARVARD BEET BORSCHT

An ingenious cook, an artist of renown, created this derivative of a traditional Russian dish. This is a borscht with body.

1 1-quart bottle beet borscht
1 1-pound jar Harvard beets
1 onion, cut crisscross at stem end
2 tablespoons lemon juice

½ teaspoon salt
½ cup sour cream
snipped chives, fresh or frozen (optional)

Pour borscht into saucepan. Place Harvard beets in blender. Give it a quick whirl, switching speed on and off to mash well. Stir into borscht in saucepan; add onion and simmer 5 minutes. Add lemon juice and salt. If a more tart flavor is desired, add lemon juice to taste. Cool. Refrigerate until chilled. Serve in bowls topped with sour cream and sprinkled with chopped chives. Serves 6 to 8. Makes 6 cups.

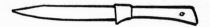

SHRIMP SUPPER CASSEROLE

2 pounds cooked medium-size shrimp, cleaned and deveined
1 15-ounce can artichoke hearts, drained
½ cup sliced pimiento olives
½ cup prepared croutons
1 4-ounce can sliced mushrooms with liquid

1 cup mayonnaise
½ cup sour cream
½ teaspoon salt
1 tablespoon Worcestershire
¼ cup sherry
1 tablespoon seafood seasoning
about 1¼ cups grated Parmesan cheese

Accompaniment: 3 cups cooked rice

Combine shrimps, artichokes, olives, croutons and mushrooms. Combine remaining ingredients except cheese. Toss two mixtures together and arrange in well-greased 6-cup casserole; sprinkle with grated cheese. Bake in preheated 350° oven 30 minutes. Serve with rice. Serves 6 to 8.

OTHER WAYS

1. Substitute scallops for shrimps; if large, cut in halves.

2. Omit mayonnaise and sour cream; substitute one 10-ounce can cream of mushroom soup and ⅓ cup half-and-half cream.

APPLE GINGER SLICES

1 1-pound 2½-ounce package gingerbread mix	⅛ teaspoon powdered nutmeg
	¼ cup sugar
2 cans prepared apple pie filling	¾ cup water
1 teaspoon cinnamon	¼ cup lemon juice
2 tablespoons butter	

Butter a 9 x 13-inch baking pan. Spread ½ package of gingerbread mix evenly in pan and cover with apple pie filling. Sprinkle with cinnamon, nutmeg and sugar. Spread second half of mix over apples. Combine water and lemon juice, pour over cake as evenly as possible. Dot with butter. Bake in preheated 375° oven 50 to 55 minutes. Serve warm or cold. Serves 12.

QUICK ALTERNATE

Serve 2 1-pound jars applesauce spiked with 1 teaspoon cinnamon. Add a plate of gingersnaps.

▶ Lobster Party Supper

Lobster Thermidor
Shoestring Potatoes   Molded Cucumber
Double Orange Sherbet   Fuji Mounds

COOKING COUNTDOWN

60 minutes ▶ make Fuji Mounds; refrigerate
—
▶
—
50 ▶ cook lobster, prepare thermidor mixture,
—   fill shells
▶
—
40 ▶
—
▶
—
30 ▶ prepare molded cucumber
—
▶
—
20 ▶
—
▶ heat potatoes
—
10 ▶ heat lobster thermidor
—
▶
—
0 ▶ serve

LOBSTER THERMIDOR

6 8-ounce frozen lobster tails	¼ cup dry white wine
2½ cups Béchamel Sauce	1 teaspoon dry mustard
1 tablespoon Worcestershire	½ pound mushrooms, sliced and
3 green onions, thinly sliced	sautéed
(optional)	½ cup grated Parmesan cheese

Cook lobster tails according to package directions; cut bottom membrane with scissors; remove meat from shells. Slice lobster into large-size pieces; combine with 1½ cups Béchamel Sauce, Worcestershire, onions, wine, mustard and mushrooms. Mix well and pile into lobster shells or scallop shells; cover with remaining sauce and sprinkle each with 1 tablespoon grated cheese. Place under broiler 6 inches from heat to brown and heat thoroughly, for 5 to 8 minutes. Serve at once. Serves 6.

Scallop shells are available in most houseware departments and are attractive for serving many seafood dishes.

Quick Béchamel Sauce

¼ cup chopped onion	1 teaspoon Worcestershire
1 tablespoon butter	¼ cup cream
2 10-ounce cans cream of chicken soup	dash cayenne

Sauté onions in butter. Add remaining ingredients and blend well.

Béchamel Sauce
If you wish more classic sauce

¼ cup butter	1 chicken bouillon cube
½ small onion, chopped	½ teaspoon salt
¼ cup flour	dash cayenne
2 cups milk	3 egg yolks, slightly beaten
½ cup light cream	

Place butter in skillet; add onion and sauté until transparent but not brown. Blend in flour and add milk gradually, then bouillon cube, salt and cayenne; bring to boil, stirring constantly. Stir a small amount into egg yolks, and return to sauce mixture. Add cream and blend. Makes 2½ cups.

SHOESTRING POTATOES

Canned shoestring potatoes are a crisp accompaniment for Lobster Thermidor. Spread the contents of a 4-ounce can on a cooky sheet and heat for 10 minutes in a preheated 375° oven. Shake cooky sheet to prevent possible overbrowning.

MOLDED CUCUMBER

1 cup finely diced peeled cucumber
1 tablespoon finely chopped green pepper
¼ teaspoon onion powder

2 cups cold water
1 tablespoon white vinegar
1 package instant lime-flavor gelatin
lettuce cups

Combine cucumber, green pepper and onion powder. Pour cold water and white vinegar into bowl and add instant lime-flavor gelatin; stir for ½ minute. Add vegetable mixture and continue stirring until slightly thickened. Immediately pour into 6 individual molds and chill 15 minutes. Unmold on lettuce cups. Serves 6.

ANOTHER WAY

May be poured into one 1-quart mold; allow 30 minutes to set.

DOUBLE ORANGE SHERBET

2 pints orange sherbet
1 cup orange juice

2 tablespoons anise- or orange-flavored liqueur

Scoop sherbet into 6 dessert glasses or dishes. Spoon about 2 tablespoons orange juice and 2 teaspoons liqueur over each serving. Serve with Fuji Mounds (page 164). Serves 6.

▶ Seafood Luncheon

Gaytown Seafood Bowl
Onion Monkey Bread
Orange Susie Crêpes or *Pears Grenadine*

COOKING COUNTDOWN

60 minutes ▶ cook seafood and eggs; refrigerate
—
▶
—
50 ▶ bake onion monkey bread
—
▶
—
40 ▶ make crêpes; combine ingredients for
—   orange sauce and filling
▶
—
30 ▶
—
▶
—
20 ▶
—
▶ prepare sauce
—
10 ▶ toss and arrange seafood on lettuce
—
▶
—
0 ▶ serve

GAYTOWN SEAFOOD BOWL

May be an appetizer, a first course or a luncheon entrée.

1 pound shrimp, cooked, or 2 8-ounce cans
1 8-ounce can crabmeat
1 8-ounce package lobster tails, cooked
2 heads Boston lettuce
Gaytown Sauce

Clean fresh shrimp, or if using canned, allow to soak in cold water 5 minutes, then drain. Remove membrane from crabmeat; drain. Cook lobster tails according to package directions; remove from shells and slice ¼ inch thick. Chill seafood and toss with Gaytown Sauce. Arrange seafood on lettuce leaves in shallow bowl. Serve with assorted crackers. Serves 6 to 8.

Gaytown Sauce

2 hard-cooked eggs, sieved
½ small onion, grated
2 cloves garlic, minced
½ teaspoon salt
¼ cup chili sauce
⅓ cup sour cream
1 cup mayonnaise

Combine and blend all ingredients.

ONION MONKEY BREAD

In contrast to the original recipes, this one uses refrigerated biscuits as a base.

¼ cup butter or margarine
4 teaspoons sesame seed or poppy seed
1 tablespoon instant minced onion or 2 tablespoons coarsely grated onion
2 packages (12 rolls each) refrigerated butterflake rolls

Heat butter in skillet; add sesame seed or poppy seed and minced onion, blending well. Separate each roll into 3 or 4 pieces and dip in butter mixture, coating both sides. Place on end in 8 x 5-inch loaf pan in two parallel rows. Place in 350° preheated oven and bake 25 to 30 minutes or until golden. Serve warm, reheating if made in advance. Makes one lovely loaf.

ORANGE SUSIE CRÊPES

2 eggs, beaten
1½ cups light cream or milk
¼ cup frozen orange juice concentrate, defrosted

1½ cups pancake mix
2 tablespoons melted butter
Orange Cream Filling
Orange Sauce

Combine eggs, cream, orange juice concentrate, pancake mix and and butter; beat until smooth. Do not overbeat. Pour 3 tablespoons batter on lightly greased 6 or 7-inch skillet, turning pan quickly to cover bottom evenly. Bake until browned, turn and brown reverse side. Continue to bake, stacking cakes until all batter is used. Keep them in a warm place. (For easy pouring, use a ¼-cup measure and fill ¾ full for each pancake.) Makes 18.

Fill each crêpe with 2 tablespoons Orange Cream Filling and roll tubelike. Place them in a casserole or ovenware platter and set in a low oven to keep warm. Serve 2 for each, as they are filling. Serve with hot Orange Sauce.

Orange Cream Filling

3 3-ounce packages cream cheese, softened

1 cup orange marmalade

Combine and cream until smooth. Makes 2 cups.

Orange Sauce

1 can frozen orange juice concentrate, *less amount used in Orange Susie Crêpes*
¾ cup sugar

2 tablespoons butter
2 tablespoons orange liqueur (optional)

Combine all ingredients except liqueur and heat to boiling while stirring; blend in orange liqueur. Makes about 1½ cups.

QUICK ALTERNATE

Pears Grenadine

1 tablespoon grenadine
1 1-pound can pears, drained and chilled

Add grenadine to drained pear syrup. Arrange pears in dessert bowl, sauce with syrup. Serves 6.

► Scallops New Bedford

Scallops New Bedford   Cabbage Slaw Mold
Pie Pastry in the Pan
Sour Lemon Pie Filling or Candy Bar Pie

COOKING COUNTDOWN

60 minutes ► bake pie crust

     ►

50 ► cook rice; keep warm

     ►

40 ► make lemon pie filling

     ► fill pie; chill

30 ►

     ► heat butter for scallops

20 ► thread skewers with scallops and
        vegetables
     ►

10 ► broil scallops

     ►

0 ► serve

Must be prepared in advance:
Cabbage Slaw Mold

SCALLOPS NEW BEDFORD

From the Atlantic seaboard come the scallops and the accompanying recipe. Use them as an appetizer on smaller skewers or on the 7-inch length for an entrée, as this menu suggests.

2 12-ounce packages frozen breaded raw scallops, defrosted

36 cherry tomatoes, or 6 medium tomatoes cut in sixths

24 1-inch squares of green pepper (about 2 peppers)

12 mushrooms (optional)

New Bedford Butter

3 cups cooked rice

Defrost scallops in refrigerator overnight or at room temperature about 1 hour. Thread on 7-inch skewers, alternating 4 scallops with 3 tomatoes and 2 green pepper squares. Cap each skewer with a whole mushroom. Place in pan or on broiler rack and brush with New Bedford Butter. Broil 3 minutes on one side, turn and brush reverse side; broil 3 more minutes. Serve 2 skewers on a mound of rice; pour butter sauce over. (Add pan drippings to lemon butter if any have accumulated.) You can push the skewered food onto the rice or have your guests perform the rite. Serves 6.

If you are unable to purchase breaded scallops, dip the defrosted raw scallops in ½ cup salad or peanut oil then roll in ½ cup fine dry cracker crumbs. Thread and broil as above.

New Bedford Butter

Delicious on fish or vegetables of most any variety.

½ cup butter

2 tablespoons lemon juice

½ teaspoon dill weed

½ teaspoon salt

½ teaspoon paprika

½ teaspoon garlic powder

¼ teaspoon coarsely ground pepper

Combine all ingredients in saucepan; heat until butter is melted. Makes about ½ cup.

ANOTHER WAY

With this recipe you can make a delicious appetizer using miniature frozen deviled crab, defrosted. If available they are packed in 7-ounce containers and make 6 small skewers and are wonderful hors d'oeuvres. Use ½ the New Bedford Butter recipe and 2 tomatoes for each. Try the breaded shrimp and broil them according to package directions, skewered as for scallops.

CABBAGE SLAW MOLD

2 packages lemon-flavored gelatin
1 cup boiling water
½ cup cold water
¼ cup cider vinegar
1 package slaw or 1 medium cabbage head, cut fine (4 cups)
3 tablespoons minced pimiento

3 tablespoons minced green pepper
½ cup sweet pickle relish
¼ teaspoon celery seed
1 head leaf lettuce
2 tomatoes, sliced
3 hard-cooked eggs, quartered

Garnish: paprika

Dissolve gelatin in boiling water, add cold water and vinegar; chill until of jelly-like consistency. Combine remaining ingredients and add to gelatin; blend well. Pour into greased 6-cup mold and refrigerate until firm. Unmold on leaf lettuce; border with overlapping tomato slices interspersed with quartered eggs. Be sure to dust eggs with paprika lest they look bare. Serves 8 to 10.

QUICK ALTERNATE

Simple celery cabbage (page 297)

PIE PASTRY IN THE PAN

A one-maneuver recipe; result, one crisp crust.

1½ cups flour
1 teaspoon sugar
½ teaspoon salt

7 tablespoons salad oil
2 tablespoons cold milk or water

Sift flour, sugar and salt into 9-inch pie pan; mix milk with oil (in measuring cup) and pour over dry ingredients in pan. Mix well, then press firmly onto bottom and sides of pan. Bake in preheated 425° oven 12 to 15 minutes until evenly browned. Cool and fill with desired recipe. Serves 6 to 8.

If you wish an even quicker format, use a prepared graham cracker or cooky crust, available in the markets. Have one on hand.

SOUR LEMON PIE FILLING

This is a perfect filling for Pastry in the Pan.

1 3¾-ounce package lemon-flavored whipped dessert mix
2 tablespoons lemon juice
dash salt

1 teaspoon grated lemon peel (optional)
2 tablespoons sugar
1 cup sour cream

Prepare the dessert mix according to package directions, substituting 2 tablespoons lemon juice for 2 tablespoons of water. When sufficiently thick quickly beat in salt, sugar and lemon peel; fold in sour cream; pour into prepared pie shell. Chill. Serves 6 to 8.

CANDY BAR PIE

Another delicious "quickie."

6 1⅝-ounce chocolate almond bars
18 large marshmallows

¼ cup milk
prepared 9-inch pie shell
1 cup whipping cream, whipped

Combine candy bars, marshmallows and milk in top of double boiler over hot, but not boiling, water. Stir occasionally until melted and smooth. Cool slightly and pour into prepared pie shell. Chill in refrigerator. Serve bordered with whipped cream. Serves 6 to 8.

► Bundled Fish Fillets

Bundled Fish Fillets   Sesame Potatoes
Green Peppers and Water Chestnuts
Orange Honey Glazed Bananas   Jelly Dotted Cookies

COOKING COUNTDOWN

60 minutes ►
—
►
—
50 ►
—
►
—
40 ► prepare fish
—
►
—
30 ► cook fish; keep hot to serve
—
►
—
20 ► prepare green peppers and water
—   chestnuts
►
—
10 ► cook potatoes; melt butter
—
This menu can   ► bake bananas
be prepared in   —
40 minutes   0 ► serve

Must be prepared in advance:
Cookies

BUNDLED FISH FILLETS

1 7½-ounce can shrimp, drained
1 pound fish fillets, fresh or frozen, sole, pike, flounder
1½ teaspoons salt
¼ teaspoon coarsely ground pepper
2 tablespoons butter or margarine
¼ cup chopped onion, fresh or frozen

1 tablespoon lemon juice
1 cup boiling water or 1 cup white wine
¼ teaspoon garlic flakes
2 tablespoons parsley or parsley flakes
½ cup half-and-half cream

Garnish: lemon slices

Drain shrimp and rinse in cold water; drain again. Defrost frozen fish, if used. Dry fish with paper toweling. Cut fish into 6 even pieces; split the thick pieces in half, if necessary. Sprinkle with 1 teaspoon salt and pepper. Place 1 shrimp on each fillet and roll into a cylinder. Tie fillet with string to hold the roll together. Heat butter in skillet and add fillets. Brown on one side, turn over, add onions and brown reverse side. This will take about 10 minutes. Pour lemon juice over fillets and add water. Sprinkle with garlic, parsley flakes and remaining ½ teaspoon salt. Simmer slowly about 10 minutes, basting with pan juices until fish flakes easily when tested with a fork. Remove string and place fillets on platter. Add cream and remaining shrimp to pan; stir to blend evenly. Heat well. Pour shrimp over fish and garnish with lemon slices. Serves 3 to 4. Recipe may be doubled using same proportions and will serve 6 generously.

SESAME POTATOES

12 frozen new potatoes

2 tablespoons melted butter or margarine
1 tablespoon toasted sesame seeds

Cook potatoes according to package directions (in salted water 10 to 12 minutes); drain. Toss with butter and sesame seeds and serve piping hot. Serves 4.

ANOTHER WAY

Omit sesame seeds and toss with snipped parsley and/or paprika.

GREEN PEPPERS AND WATER CHESTNUTS

2 tablespoons vegetable oil
1 tablespoon butter or margarine
3 medium-size green peppers, cut into strips ½ inch wide and 2 inches long

1 4-ounce can water chestnuts, drained and sliced thin
1 teaspoon salt
¼ teaspoon black pepper

Heat oil and butter in skillet until very hot. Add green pepper strips and sauté quickly, stirring frequently to prevent sticking, about 5 minutes. Add water chestnuts and toss with peppers; add salt and pepper. Sautéed green pepper is a pleasant change from raw. In this recipe, the pepper retains its bright green color and crunchiness. Serves 6.

ORANGE HONEY GLAZED BANANAS

4 medium-sized, firm bananas, peeled
3 tablespoons honey
3 tablespoons orange juice

2 tablespoons melted butter or margarine
1 teaspoon grated orange peel, fresh or dried

Cut bananas in halves lengthwise and place cut side down, in 8 x 8-inch baking pan. Combine remaining ingredients and pour over bananas, coating evenly. Bake in 450° preheated oven for 10 minutes. Arrange spokelike on serving platter; pour pan syrup over bananas. Serves 4 to 6.

OTHER WAYS

1. Heat 2 tablespoons cognac; pour over bananas on platter and ignite.

2. Add 1 cup heated drained bing cherries and 2 tablespoons cognac to bananas on platter; flame.

JELLY DOTTED COOKIES

1 1-pound roll refrigerated sugar cooky dough	2 cups chopped walnuts or pecans
¼ cup melted butter	¼ cup black or red raspberry jam or jelly

Cut dough in ¾-inch slices and cut each slice in fourths. Roll each piece into a smooth ball; dip in butter, then roll in nuts, covering well. Place on ungreased cooky sheet, well separated, as cookies spread. Bake in 375° oven, 10 to 12 minutes or until lightly browned. Remove from oven and immediately make an indentation in center of each cooky with finger or with ¼ teaspoon measure; now fill each indentation with ¼ teaspoon jam. Makes 4 dozen.

Store in airtight container; they keep well.

ANOTHER WAY

Use another jam or jelly of your choice; make a variety of colors; center some with whole pecans. Makes a pretty platter.

▶ Whitefish Amandine

Whitefish Amandine
Pink Pears   Green Beans Amelia
Apricot Nectar Cake or *Glazed Pound Cake*

COOKING COUNTDOWN

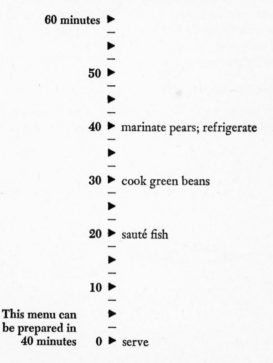

60 minutes ▶
—
▶
—
50 ▶
—
▶
—
40 ▶ marinate pears; refrigerate
—
▶
—
30 ▶ cook green beans
—
▶
20 ▶ sauté fish
—
▶
—
10 ▶
—
This menu can ▶
be prepared in —
40 minutes   0 ▶ serve

Must be prepared in advance:
Apricot Nectar cake

WHITEFISH AMANDINE

2 pounds whitefish, sole or other
    fish fillets, fresh or frozen
2 tablespoons lemon juice
2 teaspoons salt
⅛ teaspoon white pepper

½ cup flour
2 tablespoons vegetable shorten-
    ing
2 tablespoons butter
½ cup slivered almonds

2 or 3 drops Tabasco

Garnish: parsley and orange wedges

Defrost fish if frozen and dry with paper toweling. Sprinkle with lemon juice, salt and pepper. Dip in flour, coating evenly. Heat vegetable shortening and 1 tablespoon butter in skillet and add fish; sauté over moderate heat until brown; turn and brown reverse side, about 5 or 6 minutes on each side. Remove to heated platter; add second tablespoon butter to skillet; heat and add almonds and Tabasco, tossing until lightly browned. Pour over fish and garnish with parsley sprigs and orange wedges. Serves 6.

PINK PEARS

1 1-pound can pear halves
2 tablespoons grenadine
¼ teaspoon cinnamon

Drain pears, reserving syrup; measure ½ cup into a bowl; add grenadine and cinnamon, stirring until blended. Place pears in syrup and chill a minimum of 30 minutes. Serve in pretty compotes or on lettuce leaves. Serves 6.

If you like bright pears, add a few drops of red vegetable coloring.

GREEN BEANS AMELIA

A trip to Mississippi gave me this souvenir, a green bean variation.

3 tablespoons salad oil
1 medium onion, coarsely
    chopped
2 1-pound cans whole green
    beans, drained

1 8-ounce can tomato sauce
1 tablespoon lemon juice
2 tablespoons sugar
1 teaspoon salt
⅛ teaspoon freshly ground pepper

Heat oil in saucepan and add onion, browning until golden in color. Add beans and cook 5 minutes. Blend in remaining ingredients and simmer over low heat 20 minutes. Sauce will cook down and beans will be glazed. Serves 6.

APRICOT NECTAR CAKE

This imposing cake is prepared in a minimum of time. Its basis is a cake mix with slight change in method. It has versatility and may be served dusted with confectioners' sugar, with a sauce, or as shortcake. It freezes well and is fine to have on hand.

4 egg yolks	1 1-pound 3-ounce package lemon
¾ cup apricot nectar	cake mix (not chiffon)
¾ cup salad oil	4 egg whites, stiffly beaten
2 teaspoons lemon extract	Apricot Lemon Glaze

Combine yolks, apricot nectar, oil and extract in bowl of electric mixer; blend well. Add cake mix and combine at low speed. Scrape down beaters and sides of bowl with spatula and beat 2 minutes at high speed. Fold in beaten egg whites. Pour into greased and floured 10-inch tube pan and bake in preheated 350° oven 1 hour and 5 minutes. Cake will pull away from sides and will return to its form when pressed lightly with a finger. Let stand 10 minutes to cool; make holes in cake with long-pronged fork or ice pick, if you have one, and pour Apricot Lemon Glaze over cake while still in pan. Allow cake to cool, then remove from pan. Makes about 20 to 24 one-inch slices.

Apricot Lemon Glaze

1 cup confectioners' sugar, sifted   ½ cup apricot nectar
2 tablespoons lemon juice

Combine ingredients to make a smooth sauce.

QUICK ALTERNATE

Purchase a sponge cake or one of pound cake texture; puncture it with a sharp fork and marinate with Apricot Lemon Glaze.

▶ Fiesta Fish Dinner

Tomato Frio   Pescado Mexicano
Glazed Onions   Caraway New Potatoes
Rum Fluff Custard

COOKING COUNTDOWN

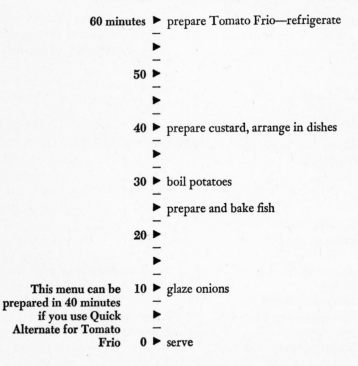

60 minutes ▶ prepare Tomato Frio—refrigerate
— ▶
50 ▶
— ▶
40 ▶ prepare custard, arrange in dishes
▶
—
30 ▶ boil potatoes
— ▶ prepare and bake fish
—
20 ▶
— ▶
—
This menu can be   10 ▶ glaze onions
prepared in 40 minutes   —
if you use Quick   ▶
Alternate for Tomato   —
Frio   0 ▶ serve

TOMATO FRIO

A chilled soup.

6 large tomatoes, peeled and finely chopped
1 large Bermuda onion, finely chopped
½ cup salad dressing or mayonnaise

2 tablespoons parsley, snipped
1 teaspoon freshly ground pepper
⅓ cup sour cream
¼ teaspoon curry powder

Combine tomatoes, onion, dressing, parsley and pepper; blend well and place in refrigerator to chill thoroughly. Combine sour cream and curry powder, and top each serving with a fluff of mixture. Serves 6.

QUICK ALTERNATE

Tomato Juice Cocktail

Substitute highly seasoned tomato juice; top with sour cream and curry powder.

PESCADO MEXICANO
(Baked Fish Steaks)

2 pounds frozen fish steaks, defrosted
2 tablespoons lime juice
2 tablespoons vegetable oil
1 teaspoon salt
½ teaspoon pepper

1 cup mayonnaise or salad dressing
24 pitted black olives, sliced
1 tablespoon parsley flakes
3 tablespoons cream
paprika

Wipe the fish with paper toweling; rub thoroughly with lime juice and oil and sprinkle with salt and pepper. Place in shallow baking dish and bake in preheated 350° oven 20 to 25 minutes. While baking, combine mayonnaise, olives, parsley and cream, blending to make smooth sauce. To serve, remove to heated platter and spread with mayonnaise sauce. Dust with paprika. Serve at once. Serves 6.

ANOTHER WAY

Melon and watercress are always appropriate garnishes for fish. Add them for a party look.

GLAZED ONIONS

2 tablespoons butter or margarine
½ cup maple-flavored syrup
1 teaspoon soy sauce

1 1-pound can whole onions, drained
1 teaspoon lemon juice

Heat butter in skillet; add syrup and soy sauce; bring to boiling and simmer 5 minutes while stirring. Add onions and lemon juice. Simmer very slowly, turning onions occasionally until richly glazed. Serves 4.

CARAWAY NEW POTATOES

2 pounds small, uniform-sized, new potatoes
2 tablespoons butter or margarine

1 tablespoon caraway seed, snipped parsley or chives
paprika

Scrub potatoes very well and pare a ¼-inch slice around each, forming a ring. Cook potatoes in boiling salted water 20 to 25 minutes, or until tender. Drain; shake in pan over heat for a minute to dry, then roll in butter and seeds; dust with paprika. Serves 6.

RUM FLUFF CUSTARD

1 3¾-ounce package instant vanilla pudding
2½ cups milk
1 egg white
dash salt

2 tablespoons sugar
2 tablespoons rum or sweet white wine
8 lady fingers
2 large bananas

Combine custard and milk and beat with rotary beater about 1 minute until blended. It will set in a very short time; meanwhile place egg white in mixing bowl and add salt; beat until soft peaks form; add sugar very gradually, beating until stiff and glossy. Fold into custard sauce until blended; add rum or wine. Place 4 halves of lady fingers upright in sherbets or dessert dishes; slice ½ banana into each dish and pour a generous amount of sauce over. Serves 4.

The sauce may be made in advance and chilled. Stir before serving.

ANOTHER WAY

Use a slice of angel food, sponge cake or cake shells as a base. Other fruits, such as sliced pineapple, peaches or berries, fresh or frozen, may be substituted.

► Friday Company

Fillets Elegante   Bourboned Squash
Bermuda Biscuits   Salad Athena
Spanish Romanoff Strawberries or
Strawberries with Sour Cream

COOKING COUNTDOWN

60 minutes ► bake squash
            —
            ► prepare Mushrooms Athena
            —
       50 ►
            —
            ►
            —
       40 ► bake fish
            —
            ►
            —
       30 ►
            —
            ►
            —
       20 ► bake biscuits
            —
            ►
            —
       10 ► arrange salad
            —
This menu can be   ►
prepared in 40 minutes   —
if you use Quick
Alternate for squash   0 ► serve

May be prepared in advance:
    Mushrooms Athena

Must be prepared in advance:
    Spanish Romanoff Strawberries

FILLETS ÉLÉGANTE

For more than fifty years, Louis Lurie, "Mr. San Francisco," has reserved a daily luncheon table at the famous Jack's Restaurant. A fascinating, ever changing group gather from far and near; recently, we sat at the round table with the charming Maurice Chevalier, who shares the same birthday with the ebullient Mr. Lurie. We raised our glasses in tribute, then with appreciative anticipation applied ourselves to the delicious food. Fish scored as the most popular entrée and this recipe is a streamlined version of a tantalizing dish served that day.

1 1-pound package frozen or fresh fish fillets	1 10-ounce can frozen cream of shrimp soup, thawed
freshly ground pepper	¼ cup grated Parmesan cheese
2 tablespoons butter or margarine	paprika and lemon wedges

Thaw fillets (sole, haddock, halibut or cod) enough to separate. Arrange in buttered shallow baking dish. Dash with pepper; dot with butter. Spread soup over fillets and sprinkle with cheese and paprika. Bake in preheated 400° oven 35 to 40 minutes. Serve with lemon wedges. Makes 4 servings.

BOURBONED SQUASH

The oven temperature accommodates 3 recipes; the fish, squash and biscuits.

1 acorn squash, cut in half	2 tablespoons granulated brown sugar
¼ teaspoon salt	
1 tablespoon butter	2 tablespoons bourbon or brandy

Place squash, cut side down, in shallow pan; add water to depth of ¼ inch. Place in preheated 400° oven and bake 30 minutes. Reverse with cut side up and sprinkle with salt, butter and sugar. Pour 1 tablespoon bourbon in each half and pierce squash lightly with tines of fork. Return to oven and bake an additional 20 to 30 minutes, or until tender. Serves 2. Increase recipe to whatever quantity needed.

ANOTHER WAY

For a Squash Supper, after 30 minutes of baking, remove squash from oven; fill each half with a frankfurter, diagonally sliced, ¼ inch thick. Return to oven for 20 to 30 minutes. Or, add two cooked pork sausages or ½ cup cooked sausage meat to each half.

QUICK ALTERNATE

Prepare 2 10-ounce packages frozen squash according to package directions, adding 2 tablespoons each of brown sugar and bourbon.

BERMUDA BISCUITS

1 8-ounce package refrigerated crescent rolls	1 tablespoon grated onion ¼ cup melted butter

Separate dough into crescents, then cut each piece in half, making two triangles. Brush each with combined onion and butter. Roll into crescent shape, rolling from wide end to point. Place on greased baking pan and place in preheated 400° oven. Bake 10 to 15 minutes or until golden brown. Makes 16 biscuits.

SALAD ATHENA

A delicious preparation to have on hand to go with greens as a salad or serve as a relish without embellishments.

Mushrooms Athena

1 pound mushrooms	¼ cup diced celery
½ cup olive oil or salad oil	½ teaspoon garlic powder
4 tablespoons lemon juice	1 medium carrot, thinly sliced
1 tablespoon onion flakes	1 teaspoon sugar
1 tablespoon parsley flakes	1 teaspoon oregano
1 tablespoon green pepper flakes (optional)	1 teaspoon salt
	dash of cayenne pepper

Accompaniments: 4 thick slices iceberg lettuce

Trim ends of mushroom stems; slice through the stems. Place remaining ingredients in saucepan and bring to boiling, for about 2 minutes. Place mushrooms in jar, pour seasoned sauce over them, cover tightly. Let stand until cool; refrigerate. Serve Mushrooms Athena over thick slices of iceberg lettuce. Serves 4 as a salad.

It is advisable to prepare mushrooms in advance; the flavor improves and they keep well.

ANOTHER WAY

May be served as a relish.

SPANISH ROMANOFF STRAWBERRIES

A freezer bonus.

2 cups sour cream	1 pint strawberries (hulled and
1 cup sugar	sliced)

1 tablespoon kirsch or Cointreau

Beat sour cream with sugar till blended; fold in berries and kirsch; pour into 5-cup mold; place in freezer. To serve, remove ½ hour in advance to soften slightly. Serves 6 to 8.

May be prepared several days in advance.

QUICK ALTERNATE

Serve 1 quart fresh, hulled strawberries with a topping of sour cream and brown sugar. Allow 2 tablespoons of cream and 1 tablespoon sugar for each guest. Will serve 6 to 8.

► Florentine Fillet and Fish Dinner

Fish Fillets Florentine   Crisp Potato Disk
Pickled Beets with Onion Rings
Lemon Angel Tarts or Lemon Cream Cups

COOKING COUNTDOWN

60 minutes ►
—
► combine beets and onions; refrigerate
—
50 ► cook spinach
—
► arrange and bake fish
—
40 ► grate potatoes
—
►
—
30 ► sauté potatoes
—
►
—
20 ► prepare lemon filling
—
►
—
This menu can   10 ► fill dessert shells
be prepared in   —
50 minutes   ►
if quick alternate   —
for beets is used   0 ► serve

Must be prepared in advance:
Meringue Shells

FISH FILLETS FLORENTINE

2 pounds fish fillets or halibut steak, fresh or frozen
2 10-ounce packages frozen spinach
2 teaspoons seasoned salt
2 teaspoons lemon juice
1 10-ounce can Cheddar cheese soup

2 teaspoons Worcestershire
½ teaspoon onion powder
2 tablespoons milk
2 tablespoons grated Parmesan cheese (optional)
paprika

Thaw fish if necessary; drain very well and dry with paper toweling. Cook spinach in ½ cup boiling water with ¼ teaspoon salt for 3 minutes, after it returns to boiling. Drain very thoroughly. Spread spinach evenly in a well-greased 9-inch shallow baking dish; sprinkle fish with seasoned salt and lemon juice; place on top of spinach. Combine cheese soup, Worcestershire, onion powder and milk, then pour over fish and spinach, spreading evenly. Bake in preheated 350° oven 25 to 30 minutes or until fish flakes easily when tested with a fork. (Just try it from the edge where it won't disturb the contour.) For a browned surface, sprinkle with the Parmesan cheese and place under broiler for a minute or two; watch closely. Add a sprinkling of paprika for color. Serves 4.

ANOTHER WAY

For Fish Fillets Divan, substitute one 10-ounce package frozen broccoli for the spinach.

PICKLED BEETS WITH ONION RINGS

1 1-pound jar sliced pickled beets
1 large onion, thinly sliced and separated into rings

lettuce

Toss beets and onions together and place in refrigerator to chill thoroughly. Serve in lettuce-lined bowl or on individual salad plates. Serves 4.

ANOTHER WAY

For additional flavor add a sliced lemon and/or 1 bay leaf and ½ teaspoon pickling spices.

QUICK ALTERNATE

Use a 1-pound jar sliced pickled beets with onion.

CRISP POTATO DISK

2 cups grated raw potatoes (2 potatoes)	½ teaspoon salt
1 tablespoon vegetable shortening	1 teaspoon snipped chives (optional)
2 tablespoons butter	

Pare and shred potatoes on large cutter of flat grater. Do not grate in advance as the potato discolors. Heat shortening in skillet until it sputters, tilting skillet to coat well; add potatoes and dot with butter. Cover until butter melts, then remove cover and reduce heat to moderate. Sprinkle with salt and chives; sauté about 15 minutes or until very brown and crisp. Turn over with broad spatula or pancake turner. If necessary cut "cake" in thirds and brown reverse side about 15 minutes. Serve piping hot. Serves 3.

Increase the quantities as needed. If you are "potato eaters," this will serve 2. Try 2 skillets for easier manipulation.

LEMON ANGEL TARTS

Have the shells on hand, stored in a tin can or frozen for use at a moment's notice. The Lemon Tart Filling, prepared with a mix, has the smoothness of any time-consuming recipe.

Meringue Shells

2 egg whites, at room temperature	1 teaspoon lemon juice
	⅛ teaspoon cream of tartar
dash salt	½ teaspoon vanilla
½ cup sugar	

Combine egg whites, salt and lemon juice in deep bowl (of electric mixer if you have one). Beat until frothy and add cream of tartar, then beat until stiff. Blend in vanilla and add sugar gradually, 1 tablespoon at a time, beating well after each addition. Test for sufficient beating by smoothing meringue between fingers; it should not be grainy. Grease and flour a cooky sheet and make 6 separated imprints by pressing rim of cup into flour. The circles make a pattern for meringues. Drop the beaten egg white mixture onto circles and shape by swirling an indentation in center of each one. Bake in preheated 225° oven for 1 hour; turn off heat and allow to stand in oven until cool. The meringues should be almost white and crisp. Makes 6.

Lemon Tart Filling

1 3¾-ounce package lemon-flavored whipped dessert mix
½ cup cold milk
2 tablespoons lemon juice
6 tablespoons cold water
½ cup sour cream
green sugar or 6 large strawberries

Combine dessert mix and milk; beat according to package directions. Add combined juice and water (which will make ½ cup liquid); beat until stiff. Fold in sour cream.

To assemble tarts

Pile the lemon filling in the meringue shells. Sprinkle with green sugar or top with strawberry. Serves 6. Recipe may be doubled.

ANOTHER WAY

Lemon Angel Pie

Line a 9-inch pie pan with meringue, shaping it to form a deep shell, higher at rim. Bake as directed for Meringue Shells; cool and fill with Lemon Tart Filling. Refrigerate until chilled. Do not chill more than 1 hour for a crisp crust. For a tortelike shell, refrigerate several hours or overnight.

QUICK ALTERNATE

Lemon Cream Cups

Serve Lemon Tart Filling in cooky-lined sherbets or in sponge cake shells.

▶ Flounder Dinner for Company

Variegated Green Salad   *Fillet of Flounder Guyenne*
Italian Broad Beans Buttered   *Rice Amandine*
A Cherry Jubilee

COOKING COUNTDOWN

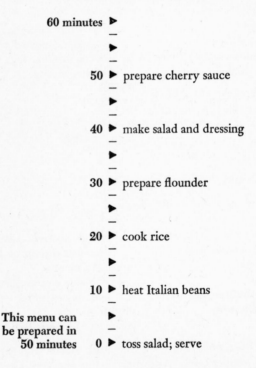

60 minutes ▶
    —
    ▶
    —
50 ▶ prepare cherry sauce
    —
    ▶
    —
40 ▶ make salad and dressing
    —
    ▶
    —
30 ▶ prepare flounder
    —
    ▶
    —
20 ▶ cook rice
    —
    ▶
    —
10 ▶ heat Italian beans
    —

**This menu can
be prepared in
50 minutes**   ▶
    —
0 ▶ toss salad; serve

VARIEGATED GREEN SALAD

4 heads Bibb lettuce, separated
1 14-ounce can artichoke hearts, drained
1 cucumber, diced

3 green onions, thinly sliced
Anchovy Dressing or prepared oil and vinegar dressing

Toss all ingredients together in large bowl; add sufficient dressing for your taste and blend well while tossing. Serves 6.

Anchovy Dressing

½ teaspoon salt
½ teaspoon dry mustard
1 teaspoon Worcestershire
2 tablespoons anchovy paste
½ cup sour cream

3 tablespoons tarragon vinegar
3 tablespoons minced chives
⅓ cup chopped parsley
1 cup mayonnaise

Blend all ingredients together thoroughly.

FILLET OF FLOUNDER GUYENNE

An import-copy of an Air France original.

1½ pounds flounder or sole fillets
¼ pound or 1 4-ounce can mushrooms, drained
1 teaspoon salt
⅛ teaspoon white pepper
1 cup dry white wine
12 oysters

½ pound cooked, cleaned and deveined shrimp or 1 7-ounce can shrimp
1 10-ounce can mushroom soup
2 tablespoons butter
snipped parsley
lemon wedges, paprika

Place fillets in buttered shallow baking dish. (Cook and serve ware is wonderfully convenient.) Add mushrooms and sprinkle with salt and pepper; pour in wine and cover pan or seal with aluminum foil. Place in preheated 350° oven and bake 10 minutes or until fish flakes easily when tested with a fork. Remove from oven. Add shrimp; if canned are used, rinse in cold water and let stand 5 minutes; drain. Poach oysters in their own liquor for 5 minutes, then drain and add to fish. Empty mushroom soup into pot in which oysters were cooked (don't dirty another). Dilute with ½ cup stock in which fish was baked; add butter. Heat and pour over fish. If your cooking ware permits, reheat over direct heat or spread with ¼ cup bread crumbs, dotted with a tablespoon of butter, and run the fillets under the broiler for 3 or 4 minutes until heated and browned. Sprinkle with snipped parsley and garnish with lemon wedges dipped in paprika. Serves 6.

ANOTHER WAY

A cover of whipped cream is a beautiful broiled brown topping; make a lattice of the cream from a pressurized can. Sour cream is also good, but allow it only to become shiny.

ITALIAN BROAD BEANS BUTTERED

2 10-ounce packages frozen Italian broad beans
¼ teaspoon freshly ground pepper

2 tablespoons butter
½ teaspoon salt

Place frozen beans in saucepan with butter. Cover tightly and heat until defrosted. Simmer 3 minutes and serve dusted with salt and pepper. Serves 6.

RICE AMANDINE

2 chicken bouillon cubes
2 cups water

2 cups precooked rice
¼ cup slivered almonds
2 tablespoons butter

Add bouillon cubes to water in saucepan and bring to boiling; allow bouillon cubes to dissolve, mashing them with a fork to hurry them along. Add rice, remove from heat and cover. Add almonds to melted butter in skillet and sauté until lightly browned. Toss with rice. Serves 6.

A CHERRY JUBILEE

Simple glamour!

1 1-pound can pitted bing cherries	½ teaspoon lemon juice
1 tablespoon cornstarch	spiral strip of orange peel (optional)
1 tablespoon sugar	1 quart vanilla ice cream
syrup from cherries	¼ cup brandy, warmed

Drain cherries, reserving syrup; combine cornstarch and sugar in saucepan; add syrup, blending well, and then add lemon juice and orange peel. Simmer until thickened and clear, about 5 minutes; remove peel; add cherries. Scoop ice cream into sherbets or dessert dishes; pour hot cherry sauce into serving bowl and pour brandy over immediately. Ignite and pour flaming over ice cream. Serves 6.

ANOTHER WAY

For assurance of the glamour flame, warm the brandy in a small ladle, ignite and then pour over cherries. The children may share this fun; serve them the sauce before adding brandy.

► Tropical Fillet of Sole

Sole Fillets à la Jane
Macedoine of Vegetables
Coconut Custard Pie or *Coconut Custard Cup*

COOKING COUNTDOWN

60 minutes ► chill vegetables
—
►
—
50 ► prepare custard filling
—
►
—
40 ► fill pie shell; refrigerate
—
► arrange fish in pan
—
30 ► bake fish
—
►
—
20 ►
—
►
—
This menu can be —
prepared in 35 minutes 10 ► assemble vegetables — dressing
if you chill vegetables —
in advance and use ►
Quick Alternate for —
Coconut Custard Pie 0 ► serve

Must be prepared in advance:
Baked Pie Shell
May be prepared in advance:
Macedoine of Vegetables

SOLE FILLETS À LA JANE

Subtly unusual flavor with a gourmet air; for family or party fare.

2 pounds fresh or frozen sole fillets
3 tablespoons melted butter or margarine
3 tablespoons lemon juice
1½ teaspoons salt
½ teaspoon paprika
⅛ teaspoon white pepper
3 or 4 bananas, halved lengthwise

Garnish: lemon wedges, paprika, parsley clusters

Use fresh sole if possible. Defrost fish if frozen; wash, then dry with paper toweling. Place in well-greased 13 x 9-inch baking dish in one layer. Combine butter, lemon juice, salt, paprika and pepper. Pour ¼ cup of mixture over fish; top with layer of bananas, cut side down. Pour remaining butter mixture over bananas. Place in preheated 350° oven and bake 25 to 30 minutes or until fish flakes when tested with fork. Baste once with pan drippings while baking. Remove carefully to platter and dust with paprika; place lemon wedges on parsley, at intervals around platter. Serves 6.

MACEDOINE OF VEGETABLES

1 10-ounce package frozen mixed vegetables or 1 1-pound can mixed vegetables, drained
¼ cup salad dressing or mayonnaise
¼ cup creamy French dressing
½ teaspoon snipped fresh dill or dill weed
4 large pimiento-stuffed olives, halved lengthwise
1 6-ounce can artichoke hearts, drained and halved
4 lettuce cups

Prepare vegetables according to package directions, cooking only 5 minutes after they come to a boil. Drain and chill. Combine French dressing, mayonnaise and dill; toss with vegetables until well blended. Serve in lettuce cups on individual plates and garnish with olives and artichoke hearts. Serves 4.

This delicious salad is a great way to use leftover vegetables. Add any firm-textured variety you may have on hand. To increase the quantity, add a small can of a vegetable of your preference and, if necessary, increase the dressing according to the proportions in the recipe.

COCONUT CUSTARD PIE

1 9-inch baked pie shell (see Pie Pastry in the Pan, page 335)

Coconut Custard Filling

1 2¾-ounce package egg custard	1 3½-ounce can flaky coconut
1 egg yolk	(1⅓ cups)
½ teaspoon almond extract	

Topping: Toasted Coconut, nutmeg (optional)

Prepare pie shell from pie crust mix, frozen prepared crust, or your favorite recipe. Prepare the custard according to package directions, using method as directed with 1 added egg yolk; add flavoring extract. Cool 15 minutes and fold in 1 cup of the coconut; pour into cooled pie shell. Chill in refrigerator about 30 minutes until set. To serve, sprinkle with remaining ⅓ cup Toasted Coconut; sprinkle with nutmeg, if desired. Serves 6 to 8.

May be prepared early in the day.

Toasted Coconut

Spread coconut on sheet of foil or baking dish and place in preheated 350° oven for about 10 minutes. Watch carefully as it browns quickly; stir to brown evenly.

May be prepared early in the day.

QUICK ALTERNATE

Coconut Custard Cup

Prepare Coconut Custard Filling as for Coconut Custard Pie. Pour into prepared crust purchased at the market or serve in dessert dishes with a cooky as an accompaniment.

► Fish with Grapes

Fillet of Turbot Véronique   Spinach Soufflé
Taste and Tell Cole Slaw
Jelled Fruit

COOKING COUNTDOWN

60 minutes ► bake spinach soufflé

► prepare cole slaw; refrigerate

50 ►

►

40 ► poach fish

►

30 ► prepare jelled fruit

►

20 ►

►

10 ►

► broil fish

0 ► serve

May be prepared in advance:
Taste and Tell Cole Slaw

FILLET OF TURBOT VÉRONIQUE

This entrée can be served with pride to guests. I suggest Quiche Lorraine (page 420) as a compatible appetizer.

2 pounds turbot or sole fillets	salt and pepper
Wine Court Bouillon	¼ cup slivered almonds
2 tablespoons butter	1 1-pound can white grapes,
1 tablespoon flour	drained, or 1 cup seeded or
1 cup fish bouillon (in which fish is poached)	seedless fresh grapes

Cut fillets in serving-sized pieces and place in saucepan with Wine Court Bouillon; bring to boil, then reduce heat to a simmer and cook about 15 minutes or until fish flakes easily with a fork. Test carefully, so that you do not tear fish. Remove with slotted spoon to large, shallow, generously buttered, ovenproof dish; place in single layer and keep warm. Heat butter in skillet and add flour, stirring until smooth and thickened; add strained bouillon, blending well until heated and smooth. Adjust seasonings, adding more salt and pepper if necessary, then pour over fish, evenly. Sprinkle with almonds, and distribute grapes over sauce; place under broiler, about 6 inches from heat until bubbly and golden brown. Serves 6.

For a special "look," pipe with ½ cup heavy cream, whipped, then broil. To make a perfect line, use a pastry tube to pipe the cream. For this fish recipe, lines made by dropping the cream from a spoon, will be most attractive.

Wine Court Bouillon

1 cup dry white wine	2 stalks celery with leaves
2 cups water	1 bay leaf
1 whole onion	3 sprigs parsley
4 cloves	1 carrot
2 teaspoons salt	¼ teaspoon dried thyme

Combine all ingredients in a large saucepan; bring to a boil and simmer 5 minutes. Strain. Any excess bouillon may be frozen. Use it for your next poached fish recipe or as a base for chowders.

SPINACH SOUFFLÉ

The frozen Spinach Soufflé is delicious. Prepare two 10-ounce packages according to directions.

TASTE AND TELL COLE SLAW

As one of the judges at a "Taste and Tell" community luncheon, I gave my vote to this recipe in the salad category. The combination is unusually good.

2½ tablespoons sugar	1 teaspoon salt
1½ tablespoons wine vinegar	3 cups shredded cabbage
1½ tablespoons white vinegar	½ cup snipped parsley
2 tablespoons salad oil	½ cup thinly sliced green onions

Combine sugar, vinegars, oil and salt in large bowl; mix until well blended. Add cabbage, parsley, and green onion and toss lightly until vegetables are well and evenly coated. Refrigerate and let stand until chilled. If possible allow salad to marinate 2 to 3 hours, and if it simplifies planning, it can stand overnight. It keeps well. Serves 6.

Snipped Parsley

Here's a great way to snip parsley. Place your parsley, without stems, in a measuring cup; with scissors, snip quickly until cut to desired fineness. Also cut the amount needed by observing the quantity in the cup. I like a Pyrex cup as it is easier to measure with a "see-through" container.

JELLED FRUIT

The attractive gelatin mold, needing chilling time to set, has been on the advance preparation list. A new product, an almost instant gelatin, permits inclusion of some jelled molds such as this one.

1 3-ounce package instant cran-   2 cups cold water
berry-orange-flavored gelatin   1 banana, sliced

Have banana sliced; combine gelatin and water in bowl; stir for ½ minute. Add banana and continue stirring until slightly thickened. Pour into 4 or 5 dessert dishes and refrigerate until set, for about 15 minutes. Serves 4 to 5.

May be prepared in advance.

OTHER WAYS

1. ½ cup grapes may be added.

2. 1 cup well-drained fruit cocktail may be substituted.

3. Use other gelatin flavors of your choice.

4. May be served in 1-quart mold; allow 30 minutes to set.

Check package directions for those ingredients which may or may not be included.

► The Smelts Are Running

Smelts
Kidney Bean Salad   Bacon Rice
Dobosch Torte or *Chocolate Filled Crescents*

COOKING COUNTDOWN

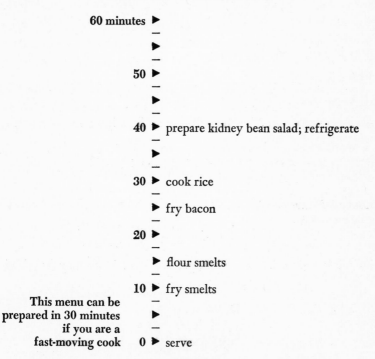

60 minutes ►
—
►
—
50 ►
—
►
—
40 ► prepare kidney bean salad; refrigerate
—
►
—
30 ► cook rice
—
► fry bacon
—
20 ►
—
► flour smelts
—
10 ► fry smelts
—
►
—
0 ► serve

This menu can be
prepared in 30 minutes
if you are a
fast-moving cook

Must be prepared in advance:
Dobosch Torte

SMELTS

In the Midwest, when the gleaming lamps of the smelt fishermen form patterns in the night, it's a sure sign that spring has arrived. The fish they catch are delicious (you even eat the bones), and their seasonal bargain price makes smelts doubly attractive.

2 pounds smelts, headless and dressed	½ cup Seasoned Flour ½ cup salad oil

Pour the flour into a paper bag; drop in the smelts a few at a time. Close the bag and shake so that smelts are completely coated. Heat the oil and add smelts in one layer. Sauté at moderately high heat for about 3 minutes on each side or until nicely browned. Serves 4 to 6.

As has so often been said, it's hard to estimate another's appetite. Devotees of smelts are voracious, in which case you will need an added pound or two. To help you plan, here is an estimate of the number per pound:

Small (generally referred to as #1 size) — 18 to 22 per pound
Jumbos — 10 to 12 per pound

Seasoned Flour

½ cup flour	1 teaspoon paprika
1 tablespoon salt	½ teaspoon pepper

Mix and blend well. Celery salt, garlic salt, or herbs may be added.

KIDNEY BEAN SALAD

1 1-pound can kidney beans, drained	¼ teaspoon pepper
1 large onion, sliced in rings	2 tablespoons salad oil
3 tablespoons sweet relish	2 tablespoons sugar
½ teaspoon salt	2 tablespoons vinegar
	2 tablespoons water

Combine kidney beans, onions, relish, salt and pepper. Place oil, sugar, vinegar and water in a small saucepan. Heat to boiling point and pour over beans. Toss lightly and place in refrigerator to chill thoroughly. Serves 4.

BACON RICE

1 cup uncooked long-grain rice
2 cups beef broth or 1 10-ounce can plus ¾ cup water

3 green onions, finely sliced
4 slices cooked, crumbled bacon

Combine rice, broth and onions in saucepan. Bring to boiling, cover and reduce to a simmer. Cook 30 minutes or until water is absorbed. Turn into serving bowl and sprinkle with crumbled bacon. Serves 4 to 6.

DOBOSCH TORTE

A delightfully quick modern method for a famous traditional torte.

1 2-pound prepared pound cake or
1 Confection Pound Cake
  (page 290)

Chocolate Butter Cream

Slice cake into 7 layers with sharp knife, keeping them in same order in which they were cut. Frost layers with Chocolate Butter Cream, return them to original shape, and frost top and sides of cake. Refrigerate overnight if possible. Cake will keep for 10 days in refrigerator and freezes well for a length of time. Serves 10. As it is very rich, thin slices are sufficient.

Chocolate Butter Cream

1 6-ounce package semi-sweet chocolate pieces
¼ cup boiling water
2 tablespoons confectioners' sugar
3 egg yolks

½ cup butter, firm and thinly sliced
1 teaspoon vanilla or 1 tablespoon dark rum

Electric mixer method

Melt chocolate with boiling water. With electric mixer, beat in sugar, then eggs, butter and vanilla or rum. Beat until very smooth.

Blender method

Place chocolate pieces in blender and whirl at high speed for 7 seconds. Turn off motor and scrape down sides of container with rubber spatula. Add sugar, egg yolks, butter and vanilla and blend for ½ minute. Butter cream should be very smooth.

QUICK ALTERNATE

Chocolate Filled Crescents

Delectable! In both taste and ease.

1 8-ounce package refrigerated crescent rolls (8 biscuits)
2 1¾-ounce milk chocolate bars (in sections)
1 tablespoon cream
1 tablespoon coarse sugar (approximately)

Remove dough from package and separate triangles. Place 3 sections of chocolate in the middle of each and fold together, sealing tightly. Brush with cream and sprinkle with coarse sugar. Bake 12 to 15 minutes in preheated 400° oven until lightly browned. Serve very hot while chocolate is lusciously melted. Makes 8.

Coarse Sugar

Coarse Sugar is available in most markets. It can be made easily at home. Crush 4 or 5 sugar cubes with a rolling pin to the consistency of commercial sugar.

Variety Is the Spice

IN CONTRAST TO the menu arrangement of preceding chapters, this section is a colorful collection of composite recipes, in most part complete three-course meals. They need no menus, for merely adding desert and/or salad will suffice for hearty dining.

Some are the simple dinner-in-a-dish kind, prepared with a fresh start or from leftovers. The soufflé recipes stress lightness, an airy approach and high-rise appeal. Among them are a few declassified favorites of mine that contain an element of surprise and will assure ample dining. The chowders, which we seem so often to enjoy, afford hearty fare, and recipes using the quickly prepared standby ground beef are included as another easily assembled dish.

Others comprise combinations of canned prepared foods with seasonings and other personalizing touches added. Originally, these were created for the sportsman, some having been recruited from the galley of a private yacht and cut down to average-size servings. The recipes are equally good for landlubbers staying at home. Or the recipes may be prepared at home and reheated at the campsite. An alternate plan is to carry the cans to your camp and then prepare the dishes on the spot.

In these last pages I have also deviated from the previous format to add a few non-regimented ideas, some old, others of recent innovation.

Dinner-in-a-Dish

CHICKEN TETRAZZINI CASSEROLE

Cooking time: 45 minutes

1 8-ounce package spaghetti, cooked	½ cup water
1 cup sour cream	¼ teaspoon salt
2 10½-ounce cans cream of celery soup	¼ teaspoon celery salt
	dash Tabasco
½ pound fresh mushrooms, sliced and sautéed or 1 4-ounce can mushroom stems and pieces, drained	¼ pound Cheddar or American cheese, shredded
	2 tablespoons sherry
	3 cups diced cooked chicken

Topping: 2 tablespoons bread crumbs and 2 tablespoons butter

When cooking spaghetti add 1 tablespoon salad oil or butter to water; it helps prevent sticking; drain. Combine and toss remaining ingredients with spaghetti. Pour into well-greased 2-quart casserole; top with bread crumbs and dot with butter. Bake in preheated 375° oven 35 minutes until heated through and browned. Serves 6 to 8.

Serve with a 1-pound can mixed fruits, drained, then marinated with 2 tablespoons kirsch.

To sauté mushrooms

Heat 2 tablespoons butter in skillet, add mushrooms and sauté gently about 5 minutes, tossing to cook evenly.

To steam mushrooms

Add ¼ cup water and 2 tablespoons butter; cover and cook 5 minutes. Mushrooms will be soft and juicy.

DRUMSTICK MOLE
(Chicken Chili)

Cooking time: 25 minutes

A Mexican suggestion made with U.S. shortcut speed, by using canned chili. Great for a crowd. It freezes well — make several batches in advance, freeze for the special date. Budgetwise, it's a gem.

2 tablespoons salad or peanut oil
⅓ cup diced green pepper
⅓ cup chopped onion
1 medium clove garlic, minced
1 1-pound can chili with meat and beans
1 tablespoon unsweetened cocoa or 2 teaspoons grated unsweetened chocolate

⅛ teaspoon cinnamon
dash of ground cloves
2 pounds cooked chicken legs (about 8) or other parts of cooked young chicken
½ cup water or broth

Heat oil in skillet and add green pepper, onion and garlic, sauté 5 minutes. Blend in chili, cocoa, cinnamon and cloves; heat. Add chicken and water or broth, cover and simmer 20 minutes; moving chicken pieces once or twice to avoid sticking. Serve from tableware skillet or remove to platter. Serves 4.

With this substantial dish, add a simple tossed salad and Golden Broiled Oranges (page 76).

To cook chicken

1 teaspoon seasoned salt
½ teaspoon onion powder

2 tablespoons vegetable oil
½ cup water

Dry chicken pieces with paper toweling and sprinkle with seasoned salt and onion powder. Heat oil in large skillet; add chicken and sauté until lightly browned on both sides, about 10 minutes. Pour water in bottom of pan; cover and simmer 30 minutes or until tender.

ANOTHER WAY

Franks in Chili

Substitute 1 pound frankfurters for chicken in the pepped-up chili mixture, and serve on buns if you wish.

CHICKEN AND NOODLES DIVAN *Cooking time: 40 minutes*

2 cups diced, cooked chicken
1 10-ounce package frozen broccoli
4 tablespoons butter
1 cup sliced mushrooms
1 5¾-ounce package noodles and cheese sauce mix
¾ cup half-and-half cream or milk
2 tablespoons dry sherry
2 tablespoons Parmesan cheese

Cut the chicken in rather large pieces; cook the broccoli 2 minutes less than package directions, reserving ¼ cup of liquid in which it was cooked; set drained broccoli aside. Heat 2 tablespoons butter in skillet and add mushrooms; sauté 5 minutes; add chicken. Cook noodles according to package directions; drain well. Turn into skillet in which mushrooms were sautéed and toss with cheese sauce mix, remaining 2 tablespoons butter, broccoli liquid and ½ cup cream; add chicken and mushrooms. Grease a 6-cup casserole very well and arrange broccoli in even layer in casserole. Top with chicken mixture; pour remaining ¼ cup cream and sherry around edge of mixture; sprinkle with Parmesan cheese and bake in preheated 350° oven 25 to 30 minutes. For a crisp crust, place under broiler 2 or 3 minutes. Serves 4 to 6.

This is a great dish for using leftover chicken.

The casserole may be prepared in advance, refrigerated; add remaining ¼ cup of cream, 2 tablespoons sherry and sprinkle with Parmesan cheese just before baking.

Serve with dishes of ice cream sauced with bing cherries. They may be flamed. Pour brandy into small ladle and warm over heat; light a match to the brandy but hold your head high and away.

COUNTRY HAM CASSEROLE   *Cooking time: 45 minutes*

Loaded with flavor and calories, the casserole requires a minimum of effort.

1 8-ounce package medium green or egg noodles
2 cups diced, cooked ham
2 cups sour cream
1 cup grated cheese, Cheddar or Parmesan

Cook noodles in boiling salted water (½ teaspoon salt per cup of water) for 10 minutes; drain. Combine with remaining ingredients and turn into greased 6-cup baking dish. Cover totally with cover or foil; bake in preheated 375° oven 30 to 35 minutes until bubbly and hot. Serves 6.

Serve with a 1-pound can of applesauce, mixed with ½ teaspoon cinnamon and 1 teaspoon lemon juice.

OTHER WAYS

1. Substitute ½ pound medium-sized sautéed mushrooms (page 372) for ham. Serve as an accompaniment or as an entrée with a salad.

2. Bake the noodles without either ham or mushrooms for a still delicious accompaniment. It is a very favorite pasta.

POACHED CHICKEN AND VEGETABLES
Cooking time: 35 minutes

1½ pound bag frozen mixed vegetables or 3 cups raw vegetables, thinly sliced
1 leek or onion, thinly sliced
1 bay leaf (optional)
1 13¾-ounce can chicken broth
1 3-pound young fryer or pieces of your choice
1 cup white wine or vermouth
Steamed Dumplings

Place frozen vegetables and leek in large saucepan. Add chicken broth and bay leaf, bring to boiling and simmer about 5 minutes until vegetables are defrosted. Place chicken pieces in flat layer on vegetables; add wine; again bring to boiling, cover and simmer 30

minutes or until chicken is tender. Serve with Steamed Dumplings.
Serves 4.

For dessert, add a no-bake chocolate pie — a complete packaged
pie mix, including crust.

ANOTHER WAY

Chicken may be served with noodles, rice, or Spaetzle (page 98).

STEAMED DUMPLINGS

1½ cups flour
½ teaspoon salt
2 teaspoons baking powder
1 tablespoon butter or vegetable
  oil

⅔ cup milk
1 tablespoon snipped fresh parsley or parsley flakes (optional)

Combine dry ingredients; mix butter with milk and stir into dry
mixture, making a soft dough. Drop from tablespoon onto chicken
the last 15 minutes of cooking time, cover tightly and cook without
peeking.

FRANKFURTER DINNER POT   *Cooking time: 20 minutes*

2 tablespoons butter
1 pound frankfurters, cut diago-
  onally in 1-inch slices
1 tablespoon flour, instantized or
  all-purpose
1 ⅝-ounce package dry onion
  soup mix
½ teaspoon celery seed

1 cup water
2 tablespoons vinegar
1 tablespoon brown sugar
dash pepper
1 cup sour cream
4 cups cooked, sliced potatoes
1 tablespoon chopped parsley

Heat butter, add frankfurters and sauté until browned, about 5 minutes. Remove from heat and blend in flour and onion soup mix.
Stir in water, vinegar, sugar and pepper. Return to heat and cook,
stirring until thickened. Cover; simmer 10 minutes; stir in sour
cream and add potatoes, parsley and celery seed. Heat but do not
boil. Serves 4 to 6.

Vegetable Cole Slaw (page 224) and Apple Ginger Slices (page 326) go well with this dish.

EGGPLANT CASSEROLE   *Cooking time: 40 minutes*

My niece, Mimi Wartell, a superb cook, was a finalist in a national baking contest. This is one of her favorite recipes, a fine preparation. Double it for buffet service.

1 medium-size eggplant	¼ cup flour
1 tablespoon salt	2 tomatoes, cut in sixths, peeled,
2 pounds ground beef or lamb	seeded, and chopped
¼ teaspoon thyme	1 8-ounce can tomato sauce
⅛ teaspoon white pepper	1 teaspoon oregano
1 teaspoon salt	½ cup grated Parmesan or Romano cheese
½ cup vegetable oil	

paprika

Cut eggplant in ½-inch slices; do not peel. Sprinkle with 1 tablespoon salt and set aside for 1 hour. Meanwhile, season ground meat with thyme, salt and pepper; form into 8 thin patties. Heat ¼ cup oil in skillet and sauté patties about 2 minutes on each side until lightly browned. Remove from pan and set aside. Heat remaining oil in skillet; dip eggplant slices in flour and sauté lightly on each side. Drain on paper toweling. Grease a 12 x 8-inch baking dish and arrange 4 patties in one layer; next layer one half of the eggplant slices; cover with one half the tomatoes, tomato sauce, oregano and cheese. Repeat the layers, with cheese the topping. Bake uncovered in preheated 350° oven 30 minutes or until set and lightly browned. Dust with paprika. Serves 6 to 8.

The casserole may be assembled and baked the previous day; reheat to serve. The flavor improves with advanced preparation.

The dish is complete except for dessert. Serve Jelled Fruit (page 366).

ANOTHER WAY

Substitute 2 cups cooked ground leftover beef or lamb for the freshly ground.

HAMBURGER MACARONI BEEF PIE

Cooking time: 45 minutes

1 10½-ounce can cream of celery soup
¼ cup milk
¾ cup grated Parmesan cheese
1 egg, beaten
2 tablespoons vegetable oil
1 cup chopped onion
1 pound ground beef

1 8-ounce can tomatoes, drained and chopped
½ teaspoon cinnamon
½ teaspoon salt
⅛ teaspoon freshly ground black pepper
¼ cup dry red wine (optional)
1 pound macaroni, drained

Combine soup and milk in saucepan and blend in ¼ cup of cheese, stirring until melted. Stir small amount of hot sauce into egg, then return to saucepan. Heat oil in skillet, add onions and beef; cook over hot heat 5 minutes, stirring constantly. Add tomatoes, cinnamon, salt, pepper, wine and cheese; heat. Spread half of macaroni in well-greased 2-quart casserole, pour meat mixture over; cover with remaining macaroni and sprinkle with remaining Parmesan cheese. Bake in preheated 375° oven 30 to 35 minutes. To serve, cut into squares. Serves 6.

Add a dish of relishes and for dessert serve Mint Parfaits: layers of vanilla ice cream, layered alternately with mint jelly.

BEEF CHIPS AND NOODLES AU GRATIN

Cooking time: 30 minutes

1 8-ounce package medium noodles, cooked
2 5½-ounce jars dried beef, separated
2 cups shredded Cheddar or Swiss cheese (2 6-ounce packages)

2 1-ounce packages white sauce mix
½ cup soft bread crumbs
2 tablespoons butter or margarine, melted
4 slices Cheddar or Swiss cheese, cut in ½-inch strips

Drain noodles well and turn into greased 6-cup casserole. Spread with one half of beef and one half of cheese. Repeat the layers with remaining noodles, beef and cheese. Prepare white sauce mix according to package directions and pour over layers. Toss bread crumbs with butter and sprinkle over casserole. Arrange cheese strips in lattice fashion over top of casserole. Bake uncovered in preheated 400° oven 20 minutes until bubbly hot. Serves 6.

Salt is not added as dried beef adds a sufficient amount in its saltiness. If you have any doubts, taste before baking and allow for extra flavor when completed.

For dessert serve Frosted Date and Nut Cake. Remove cake from can; slice and place on dessert plates. "Frost" with whipped dessert topping mix.

BEEF À LA MIROTON
Cooking time: 20 minutes

This stew has a long French history and is one of those few recipes really designed for leftovers.

3 cups sliced cooked potatoes, about 4 raw potatoes or 2 1-pound cans sliced potatoes, drained	1 10½-ounce can onion soup
	1 tablespoon flour
	1 tablespoon parsley flakes
	1 teaspoon Worcestershire
2 cups sliced beef, in 1 x 2-inch strips (firmly packed)	2 tablespoons bread crumbs
	2 tablespoons butter or margarine

Cook potatoes, if using raw; drain and arrange in overlapping layers in well-greased 6-cup casserole. Top with beef strips. Make a paste of 2 tablespoons soup and the flour, then add to remaining soup with parsley flakes and Worcestershire; blend well. Pour evenly over contents of casserole. Sprinkle with bread crumbs and dot with butter; bake in preheated 400° oven 15 to 20 minutes until very hot. If crumbs need more browning, place under broiler for 1 or 2 minutes. Serves 4.

Rosy Fruit Compote (page 84) makes an excellent accompaniment. For dessert serve Candy Bar Pie (page 336).

GREEN PEPPER BEEF AND TOMATOES
Cooking time: 15 minutes

Here is a superb dish, either with leftovers or a fresh start.

2 cups cooked beef or other meat, cut in ½-inch strips
¼ cup soy sauce
2 tablespoons vegetable oil
¼ cup chopped onions, fresh or frozen
1 cup sliced celery
1 cup sliced green pepper, in ½-inch strips

½ cup hot water
1 beef bouillon cube
1 tablespoon cornstarch
¼ teaspoon dry ginger or 1 teaspoon slivered ginger root
2 tomatoes cut in ½-inch wedges, or 1 1-pound can tomato wedges, drained

Accompaniment: Chinese noodles or fluffy rice

Add meat to soy sauce and set aside. Heat oil in saucepan and add onion, celery and green pepper; sauté about 5 minutes until onion is tender; add meat with soy sauce and toss lightly. Dissolve bouillon cube in water, add cornstarch and ginger stirring until it is dissolved. Add to meat mixture; simmer for 5 minutes, stirring until sauce is thickened and clear. Add tomatoes and simmer 5 minutes until well heated. Serve with Chinese noodles or fluffy rice. Serves 4.

Lettuce wedges with French Dressing (page 247) and Cherry Swirl (page 311) would be good with this.

ANOTHER WAY

May be prepared with 1 pound thinly sliced beef tenderloin.

BETE'S SPAGHETTI DINNER   *Cooking time: 50 minutes*

2 tablespoons butter or margarine
1 cup chopped onions
1 pound ground beef
⅓ cup chopped green pepper
1 4-ounce can mushroom stems and pieces

1 4-ounce jar stuffed olives, sliced, or ½ cup salad olives, sliced
1 1-pound can tomatoes
1 teaspoon salt
1 8-ounce package spaghetti, cooked

½ pound American cheese, cubed

Heat butter; add onions and sauté until lightly browned. Add meat, stirring until browned and pink has disappeared. Fold in remaining ingredients, blending well with spaghetti. Turn into well-greased 6-cup casserole and bake in preheated 375° oven 40 minutes. Serves 6.

Prepare casserole in advance; refrigerate. Bake before serving or bake and reheat to serve.

May be prepared with 2 cups ground leftover beef.

Serve with crisp zucchini strips.

For dessert prepare a package of instant butterscotch pudding and top with cream from a pressurized can.

PILAF HASH   *Cooking time: 40 minutes*

2 tablespoons vegetable shortening
½ cup coarsely chopped onion, fresh or frozen
½ cup raw long-grained rice
1 8-ounce can tomatoes
½ cup water
1 10½-ounce can brown gravy
1 tablespoon prepared horseradish
½ teaspoon salt
⅛ teaspoon coarsely ground pepper
¼ teaspoon garlic powder (optional)
2 cups diced, cooked meat

Heat shortening in saucepan (one with cover). Add onion and rice; sauté until brown, turning frequently. Add tomatoes and water; mix thoroughly. Bring to boiling and cover tightly; reduce to low heat; cook 25 minutes or until liquid is absorbed and rice is tender. Add gravy, horseradish, seasonings and meat; cook 5 minutes until blended. Serve very hot. Serves 4.

Fruit and cheese complete the menu (page 45).

OTHER WAYS

1. If convenient, serve the Pilaf from an electric skillet or cook-serve ware. Either has apt informality and assures a piping hot Pilaf.

2. Substitute for the can of gravy, one 1-ounce package brown gravy mix cooked according to package directions or 1¼ cups of leftover gravy.

SYRIAN LAMB PILAF

Cooking time: 30 minutes

1 pound ground lamb, leftovers or freshly ground
½ teaspoon salt
¼ teaspoon pepper
2 tablespoons vegetable shortening
1 cup chopped onion
2 cloves garlic, minced or pressed
1 cup wheat pilaf (bulgur) or rice

1 1-pound can tomatoes
½ cup beef stock
1 teaspoon salt
¼ teaspoon pepper
1 cup yogurt
1 tablespoon chopped fresh dill, or dry dill weed
parsley

Season lamb with salt and pepper. Shape into 1½-inch balls. Brown lamb balls in shortening in skillet on all sides; drain all but 2 tablespoons fat. Brown onions and garlic in skillet with lamb, about 5 minutes. Stir in wheat pilaf, tomatoes, beef stock, salt and pepper. Cover and simmer 20 minutes. Serve topped with yogurt, dill and parsley. Serves 4.

This recipe adapts very well to any leftover cooked meat or poultry. Use 2 cups of coarsely chopped cooked meat instead of ground lamb balls and brown quickly in 2 tablespoons butter, then proceed with recipe.

Relishes and Minted Pears (page 244) would be very good with this.

NOODLE OYSTER SCALLOP

Cooking time: 40 minutes

2 5¾-ounce packages noodles with cheese sauce mix
1⅓ cups milk
1 tablespoon onion flakes

1 10-ounce can mushroom soup
1 pint oysters with liquor
½ cup cornflakes, crushed coarsely

Cook noodles; drain and return to saucepan; add cheese sauce mix with milk and heat until blended. Stir in onion flakes and soup. Check oysters to remove any shell; drain oyster liquor into noodle mixture. Layer noodles and oysters alternately in well-greased 6-cup casserole and bake 25 minutes in 350° oven; sprinkle with cornflake crumbs and bake an additional 5 minutes until cornflakes are toasted. Serves 4 to 6.

Add lettuce wedges with Lorenzo Dressing (page 407) and serve slices of pound cake, topped with chilled drained fruit cocktail.

PAELLA   *Cooking time: 60 minutes*

Even in its home locale, Paella has many variations. In its travels from Spain to local kitchens, it dropped many possible ingredients, but has emerged with an easy method and good results.

1 3-pound fryer, disjointed	1 clove garlic, minced
2 chicken breasts, boned and cut in 8 pieces	(optional)
	2¼ cups long-grained rice
¼ cup vegetable oil	2 13-ounce cans chicken broth
1 tablespoon salt	¼ teaspoon saffron, shredded
¼ teaspoon pepper	2 pounds frozen, deveined and
1 medium onion, coarsely chopped	cleaned shrimp, defrosted

Dry chicken pieces with paper toweling; heat oil in large ovenware skillet and add chicken. Sprinkle with salt and pepper; sauté until well and evenly browned. Remove from skillet and set aside. To drippings in skillet add onion and garlic. (If necessary, add 2 tablespoons oil to drippings in pan.) Sauté until onions are soft and translucent for 8 minutes; do not brown. Add rice and brown slightly, stirring with onions and garlic. Add broth and saffron; bring to boiling and cook 5 minutes. Stir to mix flavors, then bury chicken in the rice, arranging nicely. Place in preheated 350° oven and bake 25 minutes. Add shrimp, arranging in the rice; return to oven and bake an additional 20 minutes. Serve from your skillet or transfer to casserole or platter. The dish is named for the Spanish utensil *Paellera*, a large, low-rimmed skillet, hence the "pot" service would be appropriate. Serves 6 to 8.

For dessert serve peeled and sliced oranges thickly covered with flaky coconut.

OTHER WAYS

1. Sliced Spanish sausage, diced ham, halved artichokes, frozen peas, pimiento and/or additional seafood may be added with the shrimps.

2. Paella may be made with cooked chicken. Have it on hand in anticipation of preparing Paella. Do not sauté cooked chicken; add to the rice before baking.

TUNA CHOW MEIN CASSEROLE   *Cooking time: 30 minutes*

Another full, flavorsome meal in one dish, a family standby.

1 7-ounce can tuna, drained and flaked
1 1-pound can Chinese vegetables, drained
1 4-ounce can mushroom stems and pieces

1 8-ounce can water chestnuts, drained and sliced
1 3-ounce can Chow Mein noodles
2 10½-ounce cans cream of mushroom soup

Combine tuna, vegetables, mushroom pieces, chestnuts and one half of noodles; add soup and mix lightly but well. Turn into well-greased 2-quart casserole. Sprinkle remaining noodles over top, spreading evenly. Bake in preheated 350° oven for 30 minutes. Serves 6 to 8.

For dessert serve unhulled strawberries around a mound of sugar. Just dip, bite, hull and eat.

ANOTHER WAY

Substitute 1 cup leftover diced poultry, meat or fish for tuna.

TUNA DIVAN   *Cooking time: 20 minutes*

Combining a vegetable with the main course makes menu planning easier and shortens cooking time. If you wish, add an appetizer to keep your guests occupied while you put the finishing touches on this meal.

1 10-ounce package frozen broccoli
1 7-ounce can tuna, drained
1 10-ounce can condensed cream
 of mushroom soup

½ cup milk
1 tablespoon snipped parsley
1 tablespoon sherry
2 hard-cooked eggs, sliced
½ cup crushed potato chips

½ cup grated cheese

Put broccoli in boiling salted water; return to boiling; cook 3 minutes. Drain and arrange in buttered 6-cup baking casserole. Flake tuna and spread over broccoli. Mix soup, milk, parsley, sherry and eggs; pour over tuna. Sprinkle with potato chips and cheese. Bake in preheated 450° oven 15 minutes. Serves 4.

Here is a pretty and refreshing relish dessert. Place halves of chilled pears on slices of chilled cranberry sauce. Garnish with red or green coarse decorating sugar.

OTHER WAYS

1. Substitute 4 to 6 large chicken slices for the tuna.

2. Use one 10-ounce package frozen chopped spinach instead of broccoli for Tuna Florentine.

HAM AND OLIVE BAKE   *Cooking time: 35 minutes*

Really a delicious combination; a standard recipe with a slight twist.

1 10-ounce can cream of Cheddar
 cheese soup
½ cup milk
2 cups cooked noodles, drained
2 cups diced leftover ham

2 tablespoons prepared horseradish
⅓ cup sliced pitted olives, ripe or
 stuffed green

Topping:

2 tablespoons dry bread crumbs, 1 tablespoon butter and 6 slices tomatoes (optional)

Combine all ingredients and spoon into greased 6-cup casserole. Top with a sprinkling of bread crumbs and dot with butter. Bake in preheated 375° oven 25 minutes or until lightly browned. Garnish with sliced tomatoes, if desired. Serves 6.

Third Hole Chocolate Cake (page 103) and ice cream would complete a luncheon.

ANOTHER WAY

Substitute 2 cups cooked rice for the noodles.

SCALLOPED POTATO HAM BAKE *Cooking time: 45 minutes*

This combination is so good, it must be included as a recipe.

| 1 5¾-ounce package prepared scalloped potatoes | 2 cups diced cooked ham or 6 frankfurters, cut in ½-inch slices |

Prepare potatoes according to package directions, adding ham or frankfurters in layers. Bake 45 minutes or as directed for scalloped potatoes. Serves 4 to 6.

Lemon Cake makes a good dessert. For 1 layer of bakery cake, prepare a package of instant lemon pudding, substituting a tablespoon of lemon juice for one of water. Spread over cake and garnish with swirls of whipped cream or frozen, whipped topping, defrosted.

Chowders—The Spooned Meal

There should be a chowder kettle in every kitchen. The vast recipe variety covers every palate. Make a double quantity; freeze half to have on hand for that frosty day. Here is a varied selection.

BRUNSWICK STEW
Cooking time: 20 minutes

One could say, "as American as Brunswick Stew." Brunswick County in both North Carolina and Virginia have claimed it, but the accepted title now goes to Virginia and the date of the creation is established as 1825. Used for large gatherings, political rallies and other vigorous events, the recipe and the occasions have modified through the years. The simplified recipe is positive evidence of change.

2 slices bacon	1 8-ounce can butter beans, drained
1 1-pound 3-ounce can chicken stew	1 8-ounce can niblet corn, drained (optional)
¼ cup chopped onion, fresh or frozen	1 10-ounce package refrigerated flaky biscuits
¼ teaspoon garlic flakes or powder	

Fry bacon in saucepan until crisp; remove from pan to paper toweling to drain. Drain off drippings, reserving 1 tablespoon in saucepan. Add onions and sauté until tender, about 5 minutes. Add remaining ingredients and simmer 5 minutes until flavors blend. Bake biscuits according to package directions and serve with stew or split biscuits in half and serve stew over them as for shortcake (another innovation). Serves 2 to 3.

Serve old-fashioned jellied Bismarcks for dessert.

ANOTHER WAY

Double or triple the recipe without worry.

CHICKEN IN THE POT PRONTO   *Cooking time: 40 minutes*

If Chicken in the Pot is your dish, please try this quick version. And if you are old enough, you will recall the days of yore when Mother cooked that "old hen" for hours on end to achieve a rich flavor. The chickens today are tender; the precooked soup a boon and the result merits comparison.

3 pounds chicken, disjointed parts of your selection
5 cups water
2 onions, quartered
2 carrots, cut in 1-inch slices
1 teaspoon celery salt
2 teaspoons salt

1 10-ounce package frozen peas or mixed frozen vegetables
1 1¾-ounce envelope chicken noodle soup mix
1 10-ounce can tomato soup (optional)
parsley flakes or snipped parsley

Combine chicken, water, onion, carrots, celery salt and salt in large saucepan. Bring to boiling, cover and reduce heat; simmer 30 minutes or until chicken is tender. Remove chicken and onion from broth; cut chicken from bone and return to broth. Bring broth to boiling; add vegetables and when it returns to boiling, add noodle soup mix and tomato soup, if desired. Boil 5 minutes additionally. Serve from tureen with a sprinkling of parsley flakes for topping. Serves 6.

Add a dish of Rosy Fruit Compote (page 84) and a simple dessert such as a prepared pudding and have a complete dinner.

ANOTHER WAY

Canton Chicken in the Pot is a delicious full meal.

Add one 1-pound 3-ounce can Chinese vegetables, drained, and 3 chicken bouillon cubes dissolved in a small amount of hot soup.

CHICKEN CORN POTAGE   *Cooking time: 10 minutes*

1 1-pound 3-ounce can chicken stew
1 7-ounce can whole kernel corn
1½ cups milk

1 8-ounce jar boned chicken
¼ teaspoon salt
½ teaspoon curry
1 teaspoon onion flakes

⅛ teaspoon thyme

Combine all ingredients in saucepan. Bring to a simmer and cook slowly for 10 minutes, stirring occasionally. Serves 4.

For dessert, fill a prepared graham cracker pie crust with a 3¾-ounce package of prepared instant coconut pudding mix. Chill.

ANOTHER WAY

This is a wonderful dish in which to use leftover poultry. If a thinner mixture is desired, add a chicken bouillon cube dissolved in ¾ cup water.

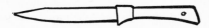

GARBURE AMÉRICAINE   *Cooking time: 50 minutes*

The French gave the base for a wonderful American Chowder dinner.

2 cups shredded cabbage, firmly packed
2 carrots, shredded
1 1⅜-ounce package dry onion soup mix
¼ teaspoon garlic powder
½ teaspoon celery salt
½ teaspoon salt
¼ teaspoon marjoram

½ pound Knockwurst or garlic frankfurters, cut in ¼-inch slices
4 cups water
2 1-pound cans pork and beans
2 tablespoons butter
2 tablespoons flour
2 tablespoons snipped parsley
croutons

In a large saucepan (10- or 12-cup) combine cabbage, carrots, soup mix, garlic powder, celery salt, salt, marjoram, sausage, water and beans. Bring to a boil; reduce heat and simmer ½ hour. Heat butter in small skillet and add flour, stirring until smooth and bubbly; pour in 1 cup of soup mixture and blend thoroughly. Return this mixture to soup and simmer an additional 20 minutes. Sprinkle with parsley and serve with croutons. Makes 2 quarts. Serves 10 to 12 as a first course. As an entrée, serves 6. Don't expect any leftovers.

To complete the menu have Spinach Salad and Confection Pound Cake for dessert.

INDIAN TRAIL CHOWDER   *Cooking time: 10 minutes*

1 15-ounce can beef meat balls
1 10-ounce can tomato soup
2 8-ounce cans lima beans, not drained
¾ cup water
2 teaspoons instant onion flakes

1 teaspoon vinegar
½ teaspoon sugar
½ teaspoon salt
⅛ teaspoon pepper
¼ cup instant prepared rice (optional)

Combine all ingredients, except rice, in saucepan and bring to boiling, stirring occasionally. Add rice and cook 5 minutes. Serves 4 to 6.

Follow this delicious meal-in-a-bowl with slices of quick Third Hole Chocolate Cake (page 103).

FRENCH ONION SOUP   *Cooking time: 45 minutes*

The two o'clock in the morning rendezvous at Les Halles, the former market place of Paris, is famed in song and story. Farmers and revelers joined in anticipation of the inimitably prepared and steaming onion soup. This is the recipe as it was given me.

2 cups thinly sliced yellow onions
¼ cup butter or margarine
½ teaspoon sugar
1 clove garlic, minced, or ¼ teaspoon garlic powder
1 teaspoon salt

6 cups beef broth or 3 10-ounce cans beef broth and 2¼ cups water
1 teaspoon Worcestershire
6 slices French bread or 3 halved hard rolls

¼ cup Parmesan cheese

Add onions to heated butter in saucepan and sprinkle with sugar. Cook slowly for 10 minutes, stirring frequently, until light golden but not brown. Add garlic, salt, broth and Worcestershire. Cover and simmer for 30 minutes. Sprinkle bread thickly with cheese and place under broiler for 3 to 5 minutes, until cheese is lightly browned. Serve piping hot soup in bowls, and top each serving with a slice of cheese-topped toast. Serves 6 to 8.

Add a bowl of citrus fruits and accompany it with rice pudding. The kind from a can is so quickly available and good.

OTHER WAYS

1. If you enjoy the extra heartiness of wine, add ½ cup of a dry red variety.

2. Chicken broth may be used; add dry white wine, if desired.

3. Serve with a bowl of cheese for those who like extra helpings.

CRAB BISQUE   *Cooking time: 15 minutes*

This combination has gourmet flavor.

1 7-ounce can king crabmeat	1½ cups water
½ cup dry sherry	⅛ teaspoon basil
1 10-ounce can green pea soup	⅛ teaspoon thyme
1 10-ounce can cream of tomato soup	½ cup whipped cream, from pressurized can (approximately)

Separate crabmeat, removing any connecting cartilage; place in bowl and cover with sherry. Combine with remaining ingredients in saucepan and bring to boiling; cover and reduce heat; simmer 10 minutes. Pour into bowls and serve topped with whipped cream; sprinkle lightly with salt. Serves 4 to 6.

Add Chef's Salad (page 408) and chilled apricots.

Improvisations—Quick and Delicious

Though the prepared food may be heated and eaten as it comes from the can, the added ingredients give the fillip of extraordinary preparation.

BEEF BALLS AND RAVIOLI   *Heating time: 5 minutes*

1 15½-ounce can beef ravioli in sauce
1 tablespoon parsley flakes
½ teaspoon instant minced onion flakes
½ teaspoon seasoned salt

1 15-ounce can beef balls in beef gravy
¼ teaspoon garlic powder (optional)
3 tablespoons grated Parmesan cheese

Spread ravioli and sauce evenly in ovenware skillet; sprinkle with parsley flakes, instant onion flakes and seasoned salt. Top with meat balls and gravy, sprinkle with garlic powder. Place on heat and simmer without stirring, about 5 minutes until hot. To serve, sprinkle with cheese and broil on rack 6 inches from heat until browned and bubbly hot. Serves 4.

Though assembling the skillet takes but a few minutes, it may be done in advance, ready to place under the broiler.

Serve with asparagus and Vinaigrette Dressing (page 301), crusty toasted bread, and chilled fruit, fresh or canned.

MEATBALLS BURGUNDY

Heating time: 15 minutes

2 tablespoons butter
½ cup chopped onions, fresh or frozen
1 1-pound jar cooked onions, drained
1 15-ounce can beef meatballs (about 10)

¼ teaspoon thyme
⅛ teaspoon garlic powder
1 4-ounce can mushroom pieces, drained
4 tablespoons dry red wine

Heat butter in saucepan; add onion and sauté until limp and slightly browned. Stir in cooked onions until coated with butter, then add meatballs with gravy, thyme, garlic powder and mushrooms; heat until bubbly. Blend in wine; heat well but do not boil. Serves 4.

Serve with instant mashed potatoes, a salad and French Chocolate Cream (page 284).

ANOTHER WAY

To make Beef Burgundy, substitute 2 cups cooked beef, diced, for the meatballs or one 1-pound 13-ounce can beef stew. Serves 4.

MEATBALLS STROGANOFF — AND ON

Heating time: 15 minutes

The "On" is for "on the table," in very few minutes.

1 medium onion, sliced in ¼-inch rings
2 tablespoons salad oil
1 15-ounce can meatballs (about 10)

⅛ teaspoon garlic powder
⅛ teaspoon thyme (optional)
2 tablespoons dry sherry
2 tablespoons sour cream
Spaetzle

Lightly brown onion in a skillet in salad oil; add meatballs, garlic powder and thyme; heat thoroughly. Add sherry and blend well, then add sour cream and heat but do not boil. Serve over Spaetzle. Serves 2 to 3.

We include a recipe for Spaetzle (page 98) but must add there is a very good prepared product which may be a whit quicker.

Complete the supper with a chocolate sundae and Fattening Cookies (page 269).

ANOTHER WAY

Rice or noodles are delicious with this excellent gravy.

CORNED BEEF HASH — IN A HURRY

Heating time: 30 minutes

The can of corned beef hash is a jewel in the pantry array. Add it to leftover ground meat as a stretcher. Slice and sauté it. Use it as a base in other simple combinations.

Baked Hash

1 15-ounce can corned beef hash
1 7-ounce can sliced pineapple, drained
¼ cup brown sugar
½ teaspoon dry mustard

Spread corned beef in greased 9-inch pie pan. Cover with pineapple slices and sprinkle with brown sugar and mustard. Bake 20 to 30 minutes in preheated 350° oven. Serves 2 to 3.

While you are enjoying the baked hash, bake a frozen fruit turnover.

Corned Beef Patties

1 15-ounce can corned beef hash
1 egg, slightly beaten
2 tablespoons chopped green pepper
2 tablespoons chopped onion, fresh or frozen
2 tablespoons butter or margarine
4 poached eggs (optional)

Combine corned beef hash, egg, green pepper and onion; mix well. Shape into 4 patties. Heat butter in skillet and add patties, sauté until browned, turning once to brown second side. Top each with poached or fried egg if desired. Makes 4 portions.

Bake a tube of refrigerated Danish rolls and eat them with lots of butter and the support of good coffee.

BEEF AND BEAN STEW FOR THE ROAD
Heating time: 10 minutes

1 1½-pound can beef stew
1 1-pound can butter beans with
   molasses

½ cup dry red wine
⅛ teaspoon garlic powder
1½ teaspoons chili powder
½ teaspoon salt

Combine all ingredients in saucepan; stove to table ware is good service for this homespun dish. Simmer 10 minutes until well blended and heated. Serves 4.

For dessert, fill prepared tart shells with canned blueberry pie filling. Dust with nutmeg.

FIRESIDE STEW
Heating time: 30 minutes

This recipe was originally assembled with the sportsman in mind. We think it's too good to confine it to the outdoors; give it woodsy atmosphere by serving it from the pot in front of your fireplace. Add a bowl of fruit, a platter of cheese and a jug of Chianti.

2 1½-pound cans beef stew
1 10-ounce package frozen mixed
   vegetables, thawed
1 8-ounce can tomato sauce
2 tablespoons instant minced onion

1 teaspoon chili powder
½ teaspoon oregano
½ teaspoon monosodium glutamate
2 cups prepared biscuit mix
¾ cup milk

Combine beef stew with vegetables, tomato sauce and seasonings in a large Dutch oven. Cover and heat thoroughly, stirring occasionally. While the stew is heating, combine biscuit mix and milk and stir with a fork until completely moistened. Spoon 8 portions of the dough onto the hot stew; cover and steam dumplings for 20 minutes or until done. Serves 4.

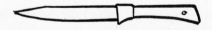

SPAGHETILI   *Heating time: 30 minutes*

Of all the chili combinations, this one takes top-billing. Quickly assembled, and even more quickly consumed. Bake it for home dinner, buffet or barbecue. On an outing, carry the cans with you and cook the dish on the spot. Increase the recipe to your needs; multiply by 4 and feed 20 hungry ones.

1 15½-ounce can spaghetti with tomato sauce
1 1-pound can kidney beans, drained
1 15-ounce can chili without beans
1 medium onion, thinly sliced in rings or ¼ cup onion flakes
⅓ cup grated Cheddar cheese
¼ cup dry bread crumbs
1 tablespoon butter or margarine

Grease a 2-quart casserole and layer one half each of spaghetti, beans, chili, onions and cheese. Repeat layers, topping with cheese and bread crumbs; dot with butter. Bake in preheated 375° oven 30 minutes. Serves 5.

Just add Crisp Spinach Salad (page 167), Ruth's Brownies (page 302), and/or fruit in season.

Homespun Meals

CHILI CON CARNE   *Cooking time: 40 minutes*

2 tablespoons shortening	1 teaspoon salt
1 onion, chopped	¼ teaspoon pepper
1 pound ground beef	¼ teaspoon garlic powder
2 1-pound cans tomatoes	1 teaspoon chili powder
3 1-pound cans red beans, drained	¼ teaspoon cumin (optional)

Heat shortening in saucepan; add onion and sauté lightly, then add meat. Cook separating meat until all pink disappears and beef is browned. Add tomatoes, cover and simmer slowly for 15 minutes; add beans and seasonings and simmer a minimum of 15 minutes until well blended and heated. Serves 6.

Special Note: This is Mary Ann's recipe for which we have shortened the cooking time to accommodate our hurried cooks. However, Mary Ann hopes you will cook it in advance, allowing a maximum of 2 hours to "marry" and mellow flavors.

Serve with hot cornmeal muffins made from a mix (the 8-ounce package, baked according to directions), a simple salad and Ginger Pie Apples (page 168) for dessert.

JUICY HAMBURGERS   *Cooking time: 20 minutes*

Burger Sauce

¼ cup melted butter	¼ teaspoon garlic powder or ½
½ cup chili sauce	clove garlic, minced
1 tablespoon Worcestershire	½ teaspoon sugar
1 teaspoon seasoning salt	

Accompaniment: 8 burger buns

Burger Patties

1½ pounds lean beef	⅛ teaspoon coarsely ground pep-
2 slices bread, crumbled	per
1 small onion, coarsely grated	1 egg
1 teaspoon salt	½ cup water

Combine Burger Sauce ingredients in saucepan and heat until well blended. Stir into Burger Patties ingredients and blend very well. Shape into 8 patties; place on rack and broil 6 minutes on each side or until of desired doneness. May be broiled on outdoor grill. Serve with desired "fixin's" or baste with additional Burger Sauce on the always available hamburger buns.

Serve with Red Cabbage and Apple Slaw (page 210) and Magic Lemon Pie (page 277).

OTHER WAYS FOR INDOOR COOKING

1. Roll patties in 2 cups coarsely crushed cornflakes, coating well. Sauté in 2 tablespoons butter or vegetable shortening.

2. Double Burger Sauce recipe, use half for Burger Patties ingredients and spoon half over cooked hamburgers (double juiciness).

SURPRISE BURGERS   *Cooking time: see chart below*

A little "something extra" has been added.

Burgers

2 pounds ground beef	¼ teaspoon garlic powder
1 teaspoon salt	⅛ teaspoon coarsely ground pep-
1 tablespoon Worcestershire	per

1 egg

Filling

6 slices American cheese	¼ cup sweet pickle relish
6 thin slices onion	¾ cup barbecue sauce, prepared
1 tablespoon mustard	or your recipe

Combine beef and remaining Burger ingredients, blending well. Divide into 12 pieces, flattening each into a 5-inch circle. On each of

6 patties, place a slice of cheese, top with a slice of onion and spread with mustard and sweet pickle relish. Cover the 6 patties with remaining 6 and press edges together to seal. Broil in oven or grill over barbecue coals until of desired doneness, basting with barbecue sauce. Serve with additional barbecue sauce. Serves 6.

Broiling time chart

Place 1 inch-thick hamburgers about 2 inches from heat.
For rare — broil 4 minutes on each side.
For medium — broil 6 minutes on each side.
For well done — broil 7 minutes on each side.

To barbecue — place over gray coals about 2 inches from heat. Use same timing.

Add shoestring potatoes from a sack, relishes and Cherry Cobbler.

BEEF RING ROMANOFF   *Cooking time: 45 minutes*

A party look to an old standby, rejuvenated and so very good. Add an appetizer and it is party fare.

2 pounds ground beef
1 1½-ounce envelope onion soup mix
½ cup dry cracker crumbs
½ cup chili sauce
½ cup water
1 teaspoon steak sauce
2 eggs
2 6-ounce packages prepared noodles with sour cream or
1 recipe Noodles Romanoff (page 84)

Combine all ingredients except the noodles and sauce mix. Stir meat mixture thoroughly, until very smooth. Turn into greased 6-cup ring mold and bake in preheated 375° oven 45 minutes. While beef is baking, prepare noodles according to package directions and let stand over low heat. Drain any liquid from beef ring and turn over on serving platter. Center with prepared noodles and border with Tangy Carrots (page 305). Serves 6 to 8.

For dessert, Cinnamon Chocolate Cream (page 273).

SPAGHETTI À LA LESTER   *Cooking time: 60 minutes*

The astute Marco Polo brought spaghetti from China. Italy adopted it as its very own; Thomas Jefferson brought it to the United States, and all who have savored this favorite recipe, affirm it may well go down in history.

2 tablespoons olive oil	1 teaspoon salt
2 onions, coarsely chopped	½ teaspoon freshly ground pepper
3 tablespoons parsley flakes	½ teaspoon oregano
2 cloves garlic, minced, or 2 teaspoons garlic powder	2 4-ounce cans mushroom stems and pieces, drained
2 pounds ground beef	1 1-pound package spaghetti, cooked and drained
2 6-ounce cans tomato paste	
2 1-pound cans tomatoes	

Heat oil in skillet; add onion and sauté until tender. Add parsley flakes, garlic and beef; sauté until meat is brown and has lost all semblance of pink. Stir in tomato paste and blend; add tomatoes and seasonings. Bring to boiling; reduce heat and cover; simmer 45 minutes. Add mushrooms last 20 minutes of cooking. Serve over cooked spaghetti to 6.

Cook spaghetti according to package directions. Add 1 tablespoon salad oil to boiling water to prevent sticking.

If you prefer a thinner sauce (or to stretch this amount) add tomato juice until of desired consistency.

Serving suggestion

Use twin containers, one for the spaghetti, the other for the sauce. This makes for a fine table service with the host as the star performer. The spaghetti can be served to each guest individually with the sauce spooned generously over each serving. It would be a lovely balance for the hostess to serve the salad from her end of the table. Add your good Chianti and Italian bread.

Have the sauce on hand. It improves as it stands and may be simmered another half hour when reheating.

Serve with Sauerkraut Slaw (page 96) and, for dessert, Meringue Spice Cake (page 260).

SPEEDY PIZZA   *Cooking time: 20 minutes*

¾ pound ground beef
1 cup biscuit mix
⅓ cup milk

1 8-ounce can pizza sauce
4 ounces (1 cup) grated Mozzarella or other cheese
¼ cup Parmesan cheese

Place beef in skillet and sauté until browned and all pink has disappeared. Prepare biscuit mix according to package directions for biscuits; roll out dough to 9-inch circle and place on flour-lined cooky sheet. Spread evenly with pizza sauce, drained browned beef; top with Mozzarella and Parmesan cheeses. Bake in preheated 425° oven for 12 minutes. Makes 4 servings.

For salad, a bowl of drained canned vegetables, marinated with French dressing.

For dessert, a 1-pound can lemon pudding, chilled, and cookies.

TAMALES NOGALES   *Cooking time: 25 minutes*

¼ cup chopped onion
2 tablespoons salad oil
1 pound ground beef
½ teaspoon garlic powder
1 tablespoon chili powder

¼ teaspoon cumin (optional)
1 10-ounce can tomato soup
½ cup sliced green olives
2 13½-ounce jars prepared tamales (about 12)

Sauté onion in oil until tender. Add meat and seasonings and cook until beef is nicely browned. Add soup and olives and blend well. Remove tamales from wrappers and place in a greased baking dish. Pour sauce over all and bake in a preheated 350° oven for 15 minutes or until hot and bubbly. Serves 4.

Serve with pickled beets; for dessert, chocolate cake.

Open and Closed Sandwiches

CHEF'S SPECIAL SANDWICH   *Cooking time: 10 minutes*

A fine menu selection for many occasions when simple glamour is needed. It smells, looks and tastes good.

1 10-ounce can cream of golden mushroom soup
¼ cup milk or half-and-half cream
1 tablespoon drained chopped pimiento
4 slices white bread toast, halved

4 slices cooked ham
4 large slices Swiss cheese
2 tablespoons dry sherry
⅓ cup grated Cheddar or Parmesan cheese
paprika

Combine soup, milk and pimiento in saucepan; heat slowly until blended and smooth. Keep the sauce hot. Place toast in 4 individual casseroles or 1 large shallow baking pan, lightly greased. Cover each slice with a slice of ham and a slice of cheese; add sherry to the sauce and pour an equal amount over each sandwich; sprinkle with grated cheese. Place in preheated 375° oven and bake 10 minutes until bubbly and slightly browned. Dust with paprika. Place under broiler for a minute or two if a browner topping is desired. Serves 4.

Serve chilled pineapple with chopped candied ginger as a dessert salad.

ANOTHER WAY

Add slices of cooked chicken or turkey. Omit ham if you wish.

FRENCH SANDWICH   *Cooking time: 10 minutes*

3 tablespoons softened butter
8 slices white bread
4 thin slices ham
½ cup (2 ounces) grated Cheddar cheese or 4 thin slices Swiss cheese

3 eggs, slightly beaten
3 tablespoons water
½ teaspoon salt

Butter 4 slices bread; cover each with a slice of ham and cheese; top with remaining 4 slices bread; pin together with toothpicks or tie with string. Combine eggs, water and salt; dip sandwiches in egg mixture until coated on both sides. Heat remaining butter in skillet and add sandwiches; sauté about 2 or 3 minutes on each side until lightly browned and cheese has melted; slice in halves. Serves 4.

These are quite rich; add a simple salad of sliced celery cabbage with light French dressing. For dessert, a package of frozen peaches, partially defrosted.

ANOTHER WAY

For delicious hors d'oeuvres, slice sandwiches in fourths with a very sharp knife.

REUBEN SANDWICH   *Cooking time: 5 minutes*

A sandwiched meal; the fame of this sandwich has spread to all corners, including ours. It is unusual, both in content and goodness. Plan a "Reuben" with the leftovers or buy 8 slices of corned beef from your market.

8 slices fresh dark rye bread
Thousand Island Dressing (page 171) or Mustard Mayonnaise
½ cup sauerkraut, drained (more, if desired)

8 slices corned beef
4 slices Swiss cheese
3 tablespoons softened butter

Spread 4 slices of bread with Mustard Mayonnaise or Thousand Island Dressing, top each of the 4 slices with 2 tablespoons sauerkraut; cover with 2 slices corned beef and 1 slice cheese and top with remaining slice of bread. Butter outside of each sandwich liberally. Place on broiler rack about 5 inches from heat for 5 minutes or until hot and bubbly. Serves 4.

For the menu add Golden Pears (page 127) and Topper Brownies (page 123).

Mustard Mayonnaise

¾ cup mayonnaise
2 teaspoons prepared mustard
2 tablespoons prepared horserad-
ish

½ teaspoon Worcestershire
1 tablespoon sweet pickle relish
dash cayenne

Combine all ingredients, blending well. Sufficient for 4 sandwiches.

Simple Mustard Mayonnaise

Subtly flavored and good.

2 teaspoons prepared Dijon type
mustard

½ cup mayonnaise
dash cayenne

Combine all ingredients, blending well. Makes about ⅓ cup.
   Double or triple either mayonnaise recipe as needed.

OTHER WAYS

1. The sandwich grill is a perfect appliance for the "closed" Reuben.

2. For an "open" Reuben, use only 4 slices of bread, arranged as for "closed" Reuben. Bread is bottom layer and cheese the top layer. Place 5 inches from broiler heat about 3 minutes until cheese is hot and partially melted.

REUBEN VARIATION

This sandwich is the cold version.
   For 1 sandwich, place 2 slices of rye bread on a plate; on one piece, place slices of corned beef and Swiss cheese and on the other, spread ¼ cup Vegetable Cole Slaw (page 224). Serve with Mustard Mayonnaise or Thousand Island Dressing. Garnish with sweet pickles, radishes, and/or olives.

   Serve cantaloupe à la mode to complete the luncheon.

ANOTHER WAY

The sandwich may grow in height if you want a more substantial arrangement. Add sliced tongue or sliced chicken, or double the quantity of whatever filling you use. It is a flexible sandwich one-meal dish.

WESTERN SANDWICH

Cooking time: 10 minutes

1 tablespoon butter	¼ cup milk
¼ cup diced onion	1¼ cups finely diced ham
¼ cup diced green pepper	¾ teaspoon salt, approximately
5 eggs	⅛ teaspoon pepper

Accompaniment: buttered toast

Heat butter in 10-inch skillet, add onion and green pepper; sauté slowly until onion is yellow. Beat eggs lightly with milk; stir in ham, salt and pepper. Pour into skillet with onion-pepper mixture; scramble gently over low heat, drawing mixture from edge of pan with tines of a fork so mixture may run to bottom of skillet. Cook just until set. Serve on slices of buttered toast. Serves 4 to 6.

For brunch add Apricot Coffee Cake Tivoli (page 154).

BARBECUE SANDWICH

Slice cooked beef, veal or pork very thin and place 3 or 4 pieces on a slice of fresh bread, for each sandwich. Cover thickly with hot Barbecue Sauce #34.

Serve with cole slaw and ready-made doughnuts.

Barbecue Sauce #34

This delicious sauce is fine flavor for barbecue or oven broiling; adjusts well to either meat, poultry, or fish, and is excellent for reheating leftovers. Make it in quantity to have on hand, as it keeps very well stored in refrigerator or freezer.

3 tablespoons butter	2 teaspoons dry mustard
½ cup chopped onion, fresh or frozen	2 tablespoons Worcestershire
1 cup chili sauce	3 tablespoons brown sugar
¼ teaspoon salt	½ cup water
	¼ cup white vinegar

Heat butter in saucepan, add onion and sauté about 5 minutes until soft and golden but not brown. Add remaining ingredients, bring to boiling then simmer 5 minutes. Makes about 2½ cups.

The Beautiful Salad

AVOCADO CRAB BOWL

4 cups salad greens, choice of Bibb, Boston romaine and/or iceberg

1 7-ounce can crabmeat or 1 10-ounce package frozen crabmeat, defrosted

3 tomatoes, cut in sixths

3 hard-cooked eggs, sliced

2 avocados, peeled and sliced

2 tablespoons chopped chives fresh or frozen (optional)

Lorenzo Dressing

Crisp greens, tear into bite-size pieces and place in salad bowl. Separate crabmeat, removing any bones and cartilage; mound in center, over greens. Arrange rows of tomato wedges, egg slices and avocado around crabmeat. Sprinkle with chives and dress with ½ cup Lorenzo Dressing. Serve extra dressing separately for those who wish it. Serves 6.

If sliced in advance, dip avocado in lemon juice to prevent discoloration.

Lorenzo Dressing

1 cup French Dressing, prepared
  or your own recipe
¼ cup chili sauce

½ cup finely chopped watercress
  or parsley
1 tablespoon lemon juice

Combine all ingredients and blend well. Makes 2 cups.

For dessert, prepare a no-bake cheese cake.

CHEF'S SALAD

Bounty in a salad bowl, amenable to change, substitution, or seasonal supply. We will start with a basic recipe.

6 cups salad greens
1 cup diced celery
1 cup thinly sliced cooked ham
1 cup thinly sliced cooked
  chicken
1 cup sliced Swiss cheese in ¼-
  inch strips

2 tomatoes, cut in wedges
2 hard-cooked eggs, sliced or
  quartered
⅔ cup dressing (French, Roquefort or Thousand Island)

Combine greens and celery in large salad bowl; arrange mounds of ham, chicken and cheese in spokelike fashion. Border with tomato wedges and sliced eggs. Chill. To serve pour dressing of your choice over all and toss lightly and thoroughly. Serves 4 to 6.

Serve with popovers and jelly.

OTHER WAYS

The Chef's Salad has great advantages:
1. Leftover vegetables such as beans, peas or carrots may be tossed with the greens.

2. Other leftover meats, veal or pork, may be the topping. For more flavor, marinate the meat in advance.

3. Another topping is crumbled bacon.

4. Add orange or grapefruit sections when tossing greens.

5. Use a prepared dressing or make your selection from the index.

NIÇOISE SALAD PLATTER

This luncheon salad is a thing of beauty and a palate's delight.

2 heads Boston lettuce	1 1-pound can sliced cooked pota-
1 7½-ounce can tuna, drained	toes, drained
3 tomatoes, cut in sixths	1 2-ounce can anchovy fillets
3 hard-cooked quartered eggs	1 6-ounce can pitted black olives
1 1-pound can whole green	1 2-ounce jar pimiento, cut in
beans, drained and chilled	strips (optional)

½ cup Oil and Vinegar Dressing

Remove core of lettuce; allow water to run through. Drain well and crisp in plastic bag in refrigerator. To arrange platter, tear lettuce into large pieces and line platter abundantly. Flake tuna and place down the center. Border each side with tomatoes alternated with eggs. At one end, pile the beans in a mound and do the same with potatoes at other end. Crisscross the anchovy strips around the tuna; scatter olives and pimiento attractively over other ingredients. Refrigerate and pour dressing over just before serving. Though the classic salad is tossed, I prefer serving it for the guests' individual selection, to toss or not, as they wish. Serves 6 to 8.

Chocolate Filled Crescents (page 370) would be a fine dessert.

OTHER WAYS

1. Garlic croutons may be an added ingredient; the original salad adds garlic to the dressing.

2. When a less hearty salad is desired, omit beans and/or potatoes. It is a salad with many opportunities for self-expression; great for those leftover vegetables.

OIL AND VINEGAR DRESSING
(French Dressing)

4 tablespoons salad oil	1 teaspoon salt
2 tablespoons tarragon vinegar	1 clove garlic, minced (optional)
⅛ teaspoon monosodium gluta-mate	dash freshly ground pepper

Mix all ingredients together in a bottle and shake very well. Makes about ⅔ cup.

ANOTHER WAY

To make Poppy Seed Dressing, which goes well with a simple fruit or tossed salad, add ½ teaspoon poppy seeds.

SUMMER PLATTER

Summer bounty is beautiful; the arrangements are endless, simple and inviting. This assortment is invariably popular.

1 head iceberg lettuce, shredded	2 Bermuda or Italian onions, sliced
6 individual assorted cans of sal-mon, tuna, or sardines (3½ ounces)	4 hard-cooked eggs, sliced
	12 cherry tomatoes
Farmer's Chop Suey	1 lemon, cut in wedges
	paprika

Spread shredded lettuce covering a large round platter or lazy Susan; remove tops of cans (salmon and/or other variety of fish); and place open cans at intervals, bordering platter. Center platter with bowl of Farmer's Chop Suey and encircle bowl with onion rings and cherry tomatoes. Place sliced eggs between cans. Garnish with lemon wedges dipped in paprika. If desired, add sliced cucumbers or seasonal vegetables of your choice, attractively arranged. Serves 4 to 6.

Serve with a coffee cake, specially selected from the bakery, or a frozen variety.

Farmer's Chop Suey

A wonderful old world dish; cool, yet hearty. An entrée in an ample serving; a salad serving with cold cuts; add shredded lettuce for a salad entrée in itself, and make it as large as your appetite indicates.

1 cup sliced radishes	½ teaspoon celery salt
2 cups cubed cucumbers	2 green onions, finely sliced
2 cups sour cream or sour half-and-half	lettuce cups
	paprika

Combine radishes, cucumbers, sour cream, celery salt and onions in a bowl. Toss lightly to blend well; refrigerate until chilled and flavors blend (15 minutes or more). Dust with paprika and serve in large bowls or in lettuce cups. Serves 4.

The recipe can be doubled if a larger amount is needed.

OTHER WAYS

1. Add 2 cups shredded lettuce and 1 cup sour cream, tossing lightly, just before serving.

2. Top with 1 cup cottage cheese.

3. Garnish with quartered tomatoes.

CHICKEN SALAD SUPERB

An elegant version of the tried and true chicken salad. Serve it on your prettiest plates for a glamorous luncheon.

1 head Boston lettuce, washed and crisped	¾ cup small green grapes, washed
3 cups cooked chicken, cut in large dice	¾ cup roasted, salted, pecan halves
1 4-ounce can water chestnuts, drained and sliced thin	1 cup mayonnaise
¾ cup diced celery	½ teaspoon salt
	½ teaspoon dry mustard

Accompaniments: paprika, watercress

Combine all ingredients except lettuce; mix thoroughly and chill. Place lettuce cups on individual plates and fill with the chicken salad mixture. Watercress and a dusting of paprika make an attractive garnish. Serves 8.

Serve Cherry Swirl (page 311) for dessert.

ANOTHER WAY

Use leftover turkey instead of chicken, or use canned chicken. A fine way to use frozen leftovers. Don't freeze the cut, cooked chicken longer than two weeks.

Soufflés and Such

Ending on a high note!

CHEESE PUDDING SOUFFLÉ   *Cooking time: 50 minutes*

This dish emerges a bubbling, golden puff; a joy for both experienced and novice cooks.

6 slices white bread, buttered	½ teaspoon salt
½ pound sharp Cheddar cheese, shredded	¼ teaspoon dry mustard
3 eggs, slightly beaten	1 teaspoon Worcestershire
1½ cups milk	¼ teaspoon monosodium gluta-mate

Cut bread into ½-inch cubes and layer one third of the bread cubes on bottom of greased 2-quart casserole; cover with one third of cheese and continue alternating layers with remainder of bread cubes and cheese. Combine eggs, milk, salt, mustard, Worcestershire and monosodium glutamate; pour over layered bread and cheese. Cover and refrigerate several hours or overnight. Bake in preheated 350° oven 50 minutes or until lightly browned. Serve at once to 6.

This is a wonderful recipe for a crowd and may be doubled to serve 12. Be sure to use 2 casseroles to insure even cooking.

OTHER WAYS

Add to the casserole:

1. Two cups cooked diced ham in layers.

2. Two cups cooked diced poultry.

3. One cup seafood or fish.

4. Omit white bread, substitute 6 slices caraway rye-bread — cut in 1-inch slices.

For dessert serve delicious Rosy Fruit Compote (page 84) and cookies.

QUICK CHEESY SOUFFLÉ   *Cooking time: 60 minutes*

Your guests will doff their hats to you when you appear with this "top hat."

1 cup cream of celery soup or Cheddar cheese soup
1 cup grated Cheddar cheese
dash cayenne
¼ teaspoon dry mustard
¼ teaspoon onion powder, optional
6 egg yolks, well beaten
6 egg whites

Heat soup and add cheese, stirring until melted; blend in cayenne, mustard and onion powder. Remove from heat and blend in egg yolks gradually. Beat egg whites until soft peaks form; they should not be dry. Fold into egg yolk mixture until well blended and no white appears. Turn into ungreased 6-cup casserole; make an indentation by running end of silver knife through soufflé 1 inch from rim. When baking a "top hat" will form. Bake in preheated 300° oven 1 hour to 1 hour and 15 minutes until set. Remove and serve at once. Serves 3 to 4.

Add a tossed green salad with Oil and Vinegar Dressing (page 409). For dessert, frozen strawberries, defrosted; top with sour cream and brown sugar.

ANOTHER WAY

Bake in 400° oven for 30 minutes. Serve immediately.

CRAB SOUFFLÉ   *Cooking time: 60 minutes*

This dish is unique; prepared in a double boiler, it puffs beautifully and will hold if dinner is delayed. Prepare the crabmeat mixture in advance and add eggs before cooking.

1 7-ounce can crabmeat	2 tablespoons flour
2 tablespoons butter or margarine	⅔ cup milk
¼ teaspoon onion powder or	1 tablespoon snipped parsley or
1 teaspoon grated onion	parsley flakes
¼ teaspoon curry powder	4 egg yolks, well beaten
½ teaspoon salt	4 egg whites, beaten stiff

¼ teaspoon cream of tartar

Drain crabmeat and remove all bony tissue. Heat butter in saucepan; stir in onion, curry powder and salt, then blend in flour, stirring until smooth and bubbly. Stir in milk and continue until sauce boils and cooks 1 minute; remove from heat. Stir in crabmeat and parsley. Set aside. Have eggs at room temperature. Beat yolks until thick and creamy; beat egg whites until frothy and add cream of tartar; beat until soft peaks form, but do not beat until dry. Blend crab mixture into egg yolks, then fold in egg whites carefully until no white appears. Turn into top of 8-cup double boiler and place over simmering water. Cover and cook over constant simmer for 1 hour or until set on top. Do not uncover before 1 hour. If dinner is not ready, keep soufflé covered and over simmering water. Serves 4.

Thickly sliced tomatoes with chopped chives go well with this soufflé. For dessert: instant strawberry-flavored gelatin.

SHRIMP SOUFFLÉ PIE   *Cooking time: 60 minutes*

Quickly put together in advance, this puffy pie may be refrigerated and ready for the oven when needed.

1 5-ounce can small shrimp	¼ teaspoon dry mustard
4 slices white bread, crusts removed	½ teaspoon salt
	1 cup milk
2 tablespoons chopped green pepper, fresh or frozen	¼ teaspoon freshly ground pepper
	¼ teaspoon curry powder (optional)
1 cup grated Cheddar cheese	
2 eggs, beaten	paprika

Drain shrimp and rinse with cold water; drain again; if large, cut in half. Line an 8-inch buttered pie pan with slices of buttered bread, cutting bread to fit snugly. Cover with shrimp, green pepper and half of cheese. Tear remaining bread into coarse crumbs and layer over mixture in pan, then sprinkle remaining cheese over all. Combine remaining ingredients, blending very well. Pour over "pie." Refrigerate several hours or until needed or bake at once in preheated 350° oven for 1 hour or until nicely browned. Bottom will be firm and pie may be removed to small platter. Serves 4.

Cucumbers in Dill Marinade (page 311) would be good. Have vanilla ice cream with crème de cacao for dessert.

ANOTHER WAY

For a fluffier texture, bake 45 minutes or until set in center.

BERRY OMELET

Cooking time: 20 minutes

An enticing omelet, which satisfies expectations.

6 egg whites	½ teaspoon vanilla
6 egg yolks	2 tablespoons butter or margarine
⅓ cup cream or milk	1 cup sour cream
½ teaspoon salt	Berry Sauce

Separate egg whites into large bowl and beat until soft peaks form when beaters are raised. Beat egg yolks until thick and lemon-colored; beat in cream, salt and vanilla. Fold into egg whites until well blended. Heat butter in large ovenware skillet, tilting so that bottom is well covered. Pour in omelet mixture and reduce heat to low; cook 10 minutes or until set on bottom. Remove to preheated 350° oven and bake 10 minutes until puffed and lightly browned; loosen around edge with spatula and lift gently to heated platter. Spread with sour cream and top with Berry Sauce. Serves 6.

Berry Sauce

Defrost your selection of one 10-ounce package frozen berries. To ¼ cup juice, add 1 tablespoon cornstarch and mix to a paste. Add to remaining berries and juice in saucepan and simmer 5 minutes until thickened and clear. Serve hot or cold. Makes a generous cup.

Serve with broiled grapefruit, each half sprinkled with 1 table-spoon brown sugar before broiling.

CHICKEN CRÊPES

Cooking time: crêpes 20 minutes
Baking time: 20 minutes

Fresh or from the freezer, these are a light delight.

Quick Crêpes

1 cup prepared biscuit mix	½ cup milk
2 eggs	½ teaspoon salad oil
½ cup water	⅛ teaspoon salt
	butter or salad oil for frying

Combine all crêpe ingredients in bowl of electric mixer, or in blender. Mix until batter is smooth and blended. If a blender is used, do not beat too long; batter should be consistency of heavy cream. (A rotary beater may be used.) Drop ¼ teaspoon butter in 5-inch skillet over medium high heat; when bubbly add 2 tablespoons batter, turning and tilting pan quickly to cover bottom completely. When golden and top is dry, turn pancake and brown reverse side. Remove to wax paper and stack until all are completed. Makes 20 to 24.

On each pancake, place 1 tablespoon filling and roll; place seam side down on buttered 9 x 13-inch pan. To heat, cover with Mushroom Sauce; place in 350° preheated oven and bake 20 minutes or until bubbly.

Filled crêpes freeze very well. To serve, thaw at room temperature for about 40 minutes. Place in baking pan, cover with Mushroom Sauce and bake in preheated 350° oven about 25 minutes or until very hot.

Chicken Filling

1½ cups finely diced, cooked, chicken	1 teaspoon dried minced green onion
2 tablespoons butter or margarine	1 bouillon cube
2 green onions, finely sliced, or	⅓ cup water
	¼ cup sherry or Madeira

Place chicken in bowl. Heat butter in skillet; add onions and sauté 2 or 3 minutes; stir in bouillon cube and water, mashing cube until dissolved. Combine with chicken and mix with sherry; check for salt. Makes 1 cup and will fill 1 dozen crêpes.

OTHER WAYS

1. Substitute for chicken, 1½ cups cooked shellfish, veal, or other poultry.

2. For a larger crêpe, use a 7-inch skillet, pour in scant ¼ cup batter for each pancake; fill each with 2 tablespoons Chicken Filling.

Mushroom Sauce

1 tablespoon butter or margarine	1 10-ounce can golden mushroom
2 tablespoons green minced on-	soup
ion, fresh, or 1 teaspoon dehy-	1 teaspoon Worcestershire
drated	½ cup half-and-half cream
1 2½-ounce can mushroom	2 tablespoons sherry (optional)
pieces, drained	

Heat butter in skillet; add onions and mushrooms; sauté about 5 minutes until onions are lightly browned. Add soup, Worcestershire and cream, then bring to boiling over moderate heat; stir in sherry. Makes about 1½ cups.

Just serve dessert, such as Raspberried Strawberries (page 320).

KULEBIAKA   *Cooking time: 35 minutes*
(Salmon Puff)

A Russian meat or fish pie, with innumerable spellings but basically the same fillings. A true party dish, simplified with the use of frozen pastry; a complete meal in a puff. It is easily prepared in advance. Just place the beauty in the oven to reheat before serving.

1 12-ounce package frozen puff pastry shells, defrosted	¼ teaspoon coarsely ground pepper
⅔ cup precooked rice	1 tablespoon onion flakes
⅔ cup boiling water	¼ cup melted butter or margarine
¼ teaspoon salt	1 tablespoon lemon juice
1 1-pound can salmon or 1 pound cooked salmon	1 4-ounce can sliced mushrooms, drained, or ¼ pound fresh mushrooms, sautéed
1 tablespoon snipped fresh parsley or parsley flakes	3 hard-cooked eggs, coarsely chopped
½ teaspoon salt	

Glaze: 2 tablespoons milk

The puff pastry shells will be sufficiently defrosted at room temperature in about 45 minutes. Roll out each shell on a lightly floured board to about 6 inches in diameter. Place them next to each other and roll into a rectangle about 13 x 16 inches; trim off outer edges, using pieces of dough to fill in openings.

Add rice to boiling water and salt, remove from heat, let stand 5 minutes. Spread one half of rice in 4-inch strip through center length of dough, leaving 1 inch at either end. Bone and flake salmon; combine with remaining ingredients, except mushrooms and eggs, blending well. Layer salmon over rice, next layer mushrooms over salmon, then a layer of the chopped eggs, pressing down firmly and top with a layer of remaining rice. Brush edges of dough with water, bring sides up and over layered mixture, sealing tightly; fold in ends, sealing tightly. Turn over carefully onto jelly roll pan, seam side down; brush top with milk and place puff in preheated 450° oven. Reduce heat immediately to 400° and bake 35 minutes or until golden brown. Serve hot, cut in 1-inch slices. Serves 8.

Kulebiaka may be prepared early in the day; in fact, it's sage advice to assemble pie in advance and leisurely serve it. Reheat in preheated 350° oven for 20 minutes until hot.

OTHER WAYS

1. Omit fish and substitute 2 cups julienne sliced cooked meat or poultry.

2. Serve with Caper Sauce or Mushroom Sauce (page 417).

Caper Sauce

1 1-ounce package white sauce mix	1 tablespoon drained capers
¼ cup parsley flakes or freshly snipped parsley	½ teaspoon salt
	½ teaspoon paprika

Prepare white sauce mix according to package directions, adding the increased amount of 1½ cups water. To serve, blend in remaining ingredients; heat and pour into serving bowl. Makes 1½ cups.

Cucumbers with French Blend Dressing (page 267) would complement the Salmon Puff. For dessert serve pears with Coffee Cream Topping.

Coffee Cream Topping

The topping is made by combining 1 cup frozen whipped topping, defrosted, with 2 teaspoons instant coffee, blending well.

ONION QUICHE   *Cooking time: 45 minutes*

The American adaptation of the French Quiche has had hearty acceptance. If you are an onion buff, this simple pie will be your "meat," if not try Quiche Lorraine which follows this recipe.

1 9-inch unbaked pie shell	4 eggs, slightly beaten
3 tablespoons butter	¼ teaspoon Tabasco
6 medium yellow onions, peeled and sliced thin	1 teaspoon salt
	¼ teaspoon seasoned or coarsely ground pepper
2 cups sour cream	½ teaspoon basil

Use a frozen prepared pie crust, one made with a pie crust mix, your favorite recipe, or Pie Pastry in the Pan (page 335). Chill the crust while preparing onions. Heat butter in skillet; add onions and sauté until soft and translucent but do not brown. Drain well and arrange in even layer in pie shell. Stir remaining ingredients together and pour over onions in shell. Place in preheated 375° oven, and bake 45 minutes or until custard is set. Serves 4 to 6.

A good accompaniment is a dessert salad. Serve 4 cups assorted sliced seasonal fruits, tossed with 2 tablespoons kirsch or brandy.

ANOTHER WAY

Quiche Lorraine

Omit onions and arrange ½ cup shredded Swiss cheese and ½ cup diced cooked ham or crumbled bacon in pastry shell, and proceed with rest of recipe.

QUICHE EILEEN
Cooking time: 45 minutes

Forget the calories — just indulge in the savory smoothness.

1 unbaked 10-inch pie shell
1 medium onion, thinly sliced
2 tablespoons butter
5 strips bacon, sautéed and crumbled
1 cup grated Swiss cheese

¼ cup grated Parmesan
1 cup whipping cream
½ cup half-and-half cream
3 eggs, beaten
½ teaspoon salt
⅛ teaspoon white pepper
⅛ teaspoon nutmeg

Bake crust partially until lightly browned, about 8 to 10 minutes in 450° oven. Sauté onion in butter until tender and lightly browned. Spread over partially baked crust, then sprinkle with bacon and cheeses. Combine remaining ingredients in pitcher or bowl with lip. Place prepared shell in 375° oven; pour egg mixture evenly into crust. Bake 45 minutes to one hour or until set. Slip a silver knife into custard; if knife is clear when removed, pie is done. Serves 8 to 10 as appetizer. Will serve 6 as entrée.

One must be a juggler to fill the pie shell and place it in the oven without spilling, so I put the shell in the oven first. Then fill with egg mixture to avoid annoyance.

FRIED RICE ELLIE
Cooking time: 15 minutes

When Mrs. Richard Himmel, wife of the well-known interior designer, "gifts" me with a recipe, I cook with anticipation of the gourmet touch she always adds. This is a simple version of the Chinese Fried Rice, a flavorsome luncheon dish.

2 cups cooked, fluffy rice
2 tablespoons salad or peanut oil
6 green onions, thinly sliced
3 eggs, well beaten

8 strips bacon, crisply cooked and crumbled
¼ cup soy sauce

Spread drained rice on paper toweling to dry thoroughly. Heat oil in large skillet and add rice, onions and bacon; heat quickly and well. Blend in soy sauce and push rice mixture to one side of skillet. Break eggs into cleared side; cook over medium heat until eggs are set and firm, stirring occasionally. Slice egg into ½-inch squares and toss with remaining ingredients in skillet. Serve piping hot. Serves 4 to 6.

Afterwards serve a compote of chilled Mandarin oranges and add Fortune cookies.

ANOTHER WAY

Add 1 cup diced, cooked shellfish, meat, or poultry to the fried rice mixture.

HAPPY ENDING CHOCOLATE SOUFFLÉ

The high-rise soufflé is a triumphant, though brief, finale for any meal. The true soufflé will inevitably fall — the hostess must not be dismayed! But it will usually soar for the few moments it takes to travel from oven to table and its entry will be rewarded with approval and enjoyment.

If, by chance, there is any remainder, the soufflé becomes a delicious cold pudding.

The bonanza in this recipe is the pudding mix, eliminating several ingredients in the traditional formula.

1 4-ounce package chocolate pudding and pie filling mix
1¾ cups milk
⅛ teaspoon salt
1 tablespoon sugar
1 1-ounce packet chocolate-flavored product or 2 tablespoons semi-sweet chocolate pieces

4 egg yolks, well beaten
1 teaspoon vanilla
1 tablespoon orange bits or grated orange peel
5 egg whites
1 cup whipping cream, whipped or 1 2⅛-ounce package whipped dessert topping mix

Prepare 6-cup soufflé dish: grease lightly and sprinkle with flour; rotate to cover well and shake out excess. Cut a strip of foil long enough to encircle rim of dish, about 8 inches wide. Double the foil and place it firmly around the dish; fasten with paper clips or by making a secure fold. Combine chocolate pudding, milk, salt and sugar in saucepan; cook, stirring constantly over moderate flame until mixture comes to bubbling boil. Add chocolate product or pieces; blend and set aside. Beat egg whites until soft peaks form when beaters are raised; they should be firm but not dry; set aside. Beat yolks until lemon-colored; add vanilla and orange bits. Add cooled chocolate mixture to yolks very gradually, beating continually; fold in beaten whites until blended. Pour into prepared soufflé dish or baking dish and place in preheated 400° oven; reduce to 350° immediately and bake 40 to 45 minutes until set. Remove foil collar before serving. Serve at once accompanied by a separate bowl of whipped cream. Serves 6.

Appendix
Index

Appendix

Helpful Appliances

HERE ARE a few indispensable appliances recommended for greater ease in cooking. Augment the list as you see fit.

electric mixer   electric portable beater
electric blender   rotary hand beater

A few smaller items which help to relieve anxiety:

meat thermometer   measuring cup with a lip
garlic press   spatula
food mill   assortment of sharp knives
assortment of measuring cups   hot pads and padded gloves
    and spoons   Teflon pans

Convenience Foods

Convenience foods make great contributions toward easy cooking and the imposing list of available products increases every day. The adventuresome will find each new preparation a tug on the imagination, offering opportunities to personalize the dish by adding an exotic flavor or seasoning. Many so-called convenience foods have been used with such frequency that one may term them staples. They have been used repeatedly in *The Countdown Cookbook* for time-saving results, with seasonings added to make each recipe distinctive.

The following list is comprised of various products included throughout the book:

FROZEN FOODS

Vegetables

Cleaned and ready for use

> chopped chives
> (use and measure as with fresh)
> chopped green pepper
> (½ cup equals 1 whole green pepper)
> chopped onions
> (½ cup equals 1 onion)
> whole mushrooms, ready for cooking

When a recipe calls for a fresh vegetable, many other similar frozen vegetables may be successfully substituted, including small whole potatoes which cook in 12 minutes. Assorted vegetables ready to heat in plastic bags can be served with no further preparation.

Fruits

A complete assortment of frozen fruits is available. All are exceptionally good. Strawberries and raspberries are especially recommended, for they are excellent in shortcakes, molds, sauces or combined with fresh seasonal fruits.

Frozen fruit juices and prepared mixes can be used in molds, sauces or in baking — wherever fresh juice is indicated.

Soups

Combinations of compatible soups with the addition of seasonings make unusual dishes. Some frozen soups also make a fine base for a sauce.

Miscellaneous

Frozen whipped topping mixes can be added to other ingredients wherever whipped cream is indicated.

Pie shells in pans come ready to bake and fill.

Puff pastry shells come ready to bake and fill for entrée or dessert. Slightly defrosted, the dough may be rolled out for large tarts or used as a crust for Beef Wellington or Ham en Croute. Salmon Puff (page 418) is a puff pastry roll using this pastry idea.

Frozen pastries are available in endless variety and completely prepared; defrost to serve.

REFRIGERATED BAKING ITEMS

Biscuits

These make delicious toppings for casseroles of meat, fish, vegetables or fruit.

Rolls

Serve with loads of butter as an accompaniment with the entrée. Or roll out triangles of dough and fill them with cheese, meat, fish or cocktail frankfurters to use as appetizers; seal and bake. For dessert, fill with fruit, chocolate pieces or cinnamon.

PACKAGED MIXES

soups	sauced noodles
sauces	sauced potatoes
gravies	seasoned rice mixes
salad dressings	puddings
mashed potatoes	seasoned chicken and beef bouillon

a great variety of dry packaged mixes for baking

TOPPINGS AND FROSTINGS

These preparations are fine when used according to package directions; many of them appear as basic ingredients in the recipes in this book.

Cake and frosting mixes may be transformed by combining flavors or by adding new flavors such as liqueurs, instant coffee powder, cocoa or grated citrus peel.

TINNED FOODS

Soups

Clear soups such as consommé, broth and bouillon are a base for gravies and sauces; they can be added to any recipe when stock is indicated. The already seasoned and thickened soups also make quick, good-tasting sauces. Those used principally for sauces in the text are Golden or Cream of Mushroom Soup, Tomato Soup, Cheese, Celery and Cream of Chicken.

Gravies

Both chicken and beef are good.

Both tomato sauce and stewed tomatoes are good in sauces needing a tomato base. Pizza sauce is exceptionally good.

Quick Italian sauce is heartily suggested for pasta, veal parmesan and, of course, for pizza.

Puddings

These are smooth and come in a variety of flavors. Though ready to serve as is, they may be accompanied with fruit or dressed with a sauce. In a recipe such as Cognac Cream (page 71) a prepared pudding becomes an exotic dessert.

Pie and pastry fillings

A variety of fruit, almond paste and poppy-seed preparations are available. The fruit fillings are particularly good pantry shelf items. As quick fillings or sauces with extra flavor added, they become delicious desserts. They are used in many recipes for quick and flavorful dinner desserts other than pies.

BREADS

Date and nut bread, sliced and topped with ice cream, is delicious. Brown bread, sliced and spread with cream cheese or marmalade, is a delightful salad accompaniment.

BOTTLED ITEMS

Condiments come in great variety and can be combined or added singly where zesty seasoning is needed. They are called for in many recipes.

Lemon juice and lime juice in this form are a great convenience when in a hurry.

Garlic juice and onion juice are both very satisfactory substitutes.

There are many fine salad preparations; for new flavors try combinations of dressings. They make excellent marinades for both meat and vegetables.

BASIC HERBS

Herbs are interesting and distinctive. If you have not used them, try a small amount as a sample and experiment until you find your favorite combination. The dry variety are fine to have on hand. The following are staple seasonings:

chopped green pepper	onion flakes
garlic flakes	parsley flakes
garlic powder	seasoned pepper
mixed Italian seasoning	seasoned salts

Many other herbs, too numerous to list, can be observed on the shelves at your market. Fines herbes, combining many flavors, is interesting and simpler than hastily making your own selection. But when time permits, experiment with your own combinations. You will find it a creative adventure.

Index